EASY

CASUAL

EVERYDAY

SPANISH

by Judy A. Nickell

Editor: Carmen Julia Holguín Chaparro

For more information and news about this book,
go to https://judyanickell.com
or email JudyNickell14@gmail.com

Library of Congress Cataloging-in-Publication Data

Names: Nickell, Judy, author. | Holguâin Chaparro, Carmen Julia, editor.
Title: Easy casual everyday Spanish / by Judy A. Nickell ; editor: Carmen
Julia Holguâin Chaparro.
Description: Los Ranchos, New Mexico : Nuevo Books, an imprint of the New
Mexico Book Co-op, [2018] | Includes bibliographical references and
indexes.
Identifiers: LCCN 2018005501 | ISBN 9781936745500 (pbk. : alk. paper)
Subjects: LCSH: Spanish language--Self-instruction.
Classification: LCC PC4112.5 .N53 2018 | DDC 468.2/421--dc23
LC record available at https://lccn.loc.gov/2018005501

Cover art by Lyndee Smith, © 2018

Table of Contents

INTRODUCTION

Don't expect this book to make you a conversationalist in Spanish.

The idea is to help you talk to your children, the plumber, the janitor, the yard man, the cleaning lady, the carpenter you hired.

Thus, this little book is designed to provide vocabulary and conversational helps for:

√ **people** who want to learn a little Spanish.

√ **adults** and high school and college students who need extra help in some aspect of the language that they either forgot or that was not well explained in the past.

√ **people** who grew up with Spanish spoken in the home but formal lessons were not part of the mix.

√ **home-schooling parents** who need a book that is not set in a brick-and-mortar school. (School texts usually have classroom settings. With this book the classroom is in the kitchen, the living room and even the garage.)

√ **people** who want to chat with in-laws who speak Spanish or who want to understand what co-workers are saying behind their backs.

√ **broadcasters** who want to make a good impression on their listeners or viewers by pronouncing Spanish as well as they do Arabic.

√ **people** who need to communicate with workers who have limited English.

√ **and principally** for people who are not traveling. (Books for travelers are easy to find. This one is for people who want to communicate at home and around town with family, friends, employees and customers.)

Maybe, as you continue with this book, you can watch some Spanish television, read some light fiction or read stories in Spanish to children or grandchildren.

The study of grammar – verbs, nouns and all that – can scare people. We'll go as easily on those as possible. However, some are necessary.

Verbs **are** essential. How can you **talk** without **using** verbs in **communicating** with friends?

Nouns and pronouns are important, too. How can **you** praise a **friend** about **her dinner** without referring to the **items** on the **table**?

Spanish has a huge list of verbs, more than English. They are more colorful than English verbs and some can be much more specific in meaning than a similar word in English.

For instance, in English the verb TO PLAY can include sports, playing a musical instrument, playing a role in the theater or in a movie. In Spanish, **jugar** is used for sports and games; **tocar** for musical instruments, and **representar** or **hacer un papel** for a theatrical role.

Verb conjugation lists are long. Notice how simple the English verb TO PLAY is: I PLAY, YOU PLAY, HE PLAYS, WE PLAY, YOU (ALL) PLAY, THEY PLAY. There's only one change. The past is also simple, and the future is accomplished by adding WILL or SHALL.

In Spanish, the verb tense for each person (I, YOU, HE, SHE, WE, THEY) can be somewhat different from the next person. Also, past and future and other tenses are accomplished with special word endings. One advantage to all this is that the "person" is often understood, so you don't always need to specify I, YOU, THEY or the rest. Granted, Spanish verbs are not easy. If you find that you can't remember a verb tense and must tell someone to do something, revert to the infinity. Your hearer will understand and you can look it up when you get home.

In this book we will stick to a few essentials in verb tenses: infinitive, present, past and future. The rest will wait for more advanced study. Later.

There are books with nothing but lists of verb conjugations. Anyone studying Spanish should have one of these books. Two popular ones are *501 Spanish Verbs fully conjugated* and *2,000+ Essential Spanish Verbs*. We also assume you have (or will get) a modern English-Spanish/Spanish-English (E-S/S-E) dictionary. Older dictionaries are good for most words, but a modern one should include new words from our modern technological world. Also, to make life easier for the beginner, the new dictionaries drop the old **ch** and **ll** as separate letters and mix them with the **c's** and **l's**. In some books even the **ñ** is mixed in with the **n's**. The older dictionaries had **ch, ll** and **ñ** as separate word entries.

This book doesn't include a "vocabulary" section in the back because words are explained as they appear. In addition you will enjoy having a separate dictionary that includes more expanded definitions.

In this *Easy Spanish*, we start with parts of speech, then go into word uses, phrases and charts for every day use around the home and around town.

Names of foods can come in handy when dealing with a cook or caterer or just for fun. Names of cleaning products and tools can come in handy with a janitor or the cleaning crew. Learn these with useful phrases.

To use this book, go through it to see which sections suit your needs and work on those. Then go back or forward as needed.

Here are some other ideas for using this book.

Make notes on 3x5 or 4x6 cards on what you need to work on. For instance, pronunciation of the vowels or the difficult consonants. Later, do cards with the uses of such tricky verbs as **ser** and **estar**.

Make similar cards with instructions for a cleaning person, cook or gardener.

As a family project, write the names of appliances on sticky notes and attach them to the appropriate items. That way everyone in the family can see them.

Use sticky notes for vowel sounds and attach to the bathroom mirror. These can serve as double duty: Repeat the sounds until you hit the right amount of time for hand washing.

Not included to any extent are musical instruments and terms. Most of those are Italian in origin and move from Italian to other languages with little change.

The illustrations and sentences deal with topics of daily life at home and not necessarily for travelers, though travelers can find this approach useful, too. Illustrations are not to scale. Illustrations are used only to symbolize the phrase or word. They are not comprehensive or definitive. Use them only as place markers and to increase your vocabulary. They are not intended to be "politically correct" either.

 Train your TV set to help with your Spanish. Tune in to the daily news programs on your local Spanish TV channel. Start by watching the news, as you already know what's happening. To watch a "telenovela," start at the beginning, as tuning in after the story has started could be confusing. These run three to six months and are not scheduled by season as with English series programs. Telenovelas are novels on TV. They are not soap operas. Each has a beginning, a middle and an end. Then, another novel starts, totally new.

Comedies can be difficult to follow because the punch lines tend to come fast.

Since chapters in this book are not formal lessons (except those dealing with parts of speech) use them as needed. The phrases and words are offered in specialized groups (food, gadgets, flowers, pets and the like). Some topics will be of more interest to you than others. Find those you like or need and start there. The final two chapters are topical lists to make finding a word quickly without having to thumb through a heavy dictionary.

Finally, you will find "**dichos**" scattered about and at the end. **Dichos** are sayings, many similar to ours. Among these are "Birds of a feather flock together," "He who has much wants much" and the like. Enjoy them.

About the pictures

There were some options for illustrating this book. One would have involved hiring an artist to create colored pictures, which would have added hugely to the cost (and weight) of this book. Another option was hiring a cartoonist to do original black-and-white sketches to illustrate the point.

The third option was to go back in history for some appropriate sketches that illustrate the lessons here. Dover Publications has a huge library of copyright-free art from past centuries, from old woodcuts to advertising illustrations from the 20th Century to current art work on specific topics, such as seasons, jobs and food.

Some of the collections from the past featured advertising art, characters from old comic strips, political cartoons or sketches of people from show business.

The sketches selected also show a great deal of talent in depicting emotions, problems, humor and other activities – putting on makeup, washing the ears, leaving the iron on, and more. Recent artists in these collections have done an equally wonderful job showing food, flowers, family life, jobs and seasonal activities.

The pictures were selected because they fit so well with the words and phrases used in this book. Learning a new (or reviewing a known) language can be fairly dull. These illustrations not only make the presentation more appealing but the humor also lends to quicker learning.

In addition we have used art work from Graphic Source, North Light, Pinnacle Publications, Sun Country Publications and Proof Positive.

Our thanks to all the artists and editors of the past and present who contributed to this great wealth of art work.

We hope you enjoy their use as much as the authors did in taking advantage of them. For a complete list, see the Bibliography.

Judy Nickell and *Carmen Julia Holguín Chaparro, 2018*

Art work

Here is a complete list of the books that furnished the drawings used in this book. Publishers include:

Dover, which has collected into books many public domain drawings from past centuries; advertising drawings from the early 20th Century, and a good many humorous daily life cartoons. These added humor to the lessons.

Graphic Source, which has books of clip art on many subjects.

North Light, Art of the State, Pinnacle Publications, Sun Country and Bonanza.
A more detailed list:

From Dover

3,800 Early Advertising Cuts 1991
864 Humorous Cuts from the 20s & 30s 1995
2001 Decorative Cuts & Ornaments 1988
Advertising Spot Illustrations of the 20s and 30s 1989
Big Book of Old-Time Spot Illustrations 2001
Cartoon Advertising Cuts of the Thirties 1996
Children: A Pictorial Archive 2002
Fashions of the Thirties 1993
Handbook of Pictorial Symbols 1976
Holiday and Special Occasions Illustrations 1983
House & Real Estate Illustrations 1988
Humorous Advertising Cuts of the 1940s 1998
Humorous Family Life Illustrations 1993
Humorous Four Seasons Illustrations 1991
Humorous Illustrations of Trades and Services 1993
Illustrations of Cars, Trucks, Trains, Ships & Planes 1988
Illustrations of Women at Work 1996
Montgomery Ward & Co. 1895 Catalogue No.57 1969
Old-Fashioned Illustrations of Books, Reading & Writing 1992
Old-Fashioned Sports Illustrations 1988
Old-Fashioned Transportation Cuts 1987
Popular Advertising Cuts of the 20s & 30s 1996
Spot Illustrations of the 20s and 30s 1992
Street Art 2011
Victorian Goods and Merchandise 1997
Vintage Illustrations of Children from the Teens & 20s 1990
Women: Advertising Cuts of the 20s and 30s 2006
Gourmet Food Illustrations, 1991
Wining and Dining Illustrations, 1090
Food and Drink (19th Century), 197
Food and Drink Spot Illustrations, 1982
Illustrations of Pets, 1994
Animal Illustrations, 1993
Flower Illustrations, 1996
Floral Illustrations, 1989
Illustrations of Plants, Shrubs and Trees, 1978

From Graphic Source, Wheeling, Ill.
Food Art 1,
Graphic Symbols, 1986
Great Outdoors, 1991
Health Care, 1991
Occupations and Trades, 1995
Potpourri, 1986

Seasons, 1991
Food & Drink, North Light, Peoria, Ill., 1992
Western Foods, Pinnacle Publications, Phoenix, 1995
Mexican Foods, Pinnacle Publications, Phoenix, 1995
Western Women , Sun Country, Phoenix, 1996
Art of the State, Proof Positive, Albuquerque, NM 1987

Thanks to these companies for art work in Chapter 12:
Corona Clipper Co.
Davids & Royston Bulb Co.
Monrovia Nurseries
Nretherland Flower Bulb Co.
True Temper Hardware
and U.S. Department of Agriculture publications

1
SAY IT IN SPANISH
Dígalo en español

Spanish is an easier language to learn to pronounce than English. For one thing, there are set rules on pronouncing words. If you can pronounce six English words and if you can growl like a dog, you can pronounce Spanish words. The words are FATHER, MET, SEE, PORTION, MOON, and CANYON.

Not to promote sloppiness, but beginners will be known by their pronunciation. To misuse or mispronounce a few words won't result in a sentence to the firing squad. The main thing is to communicate. Perfection comes with use, just as it did in learning to type or learning music.

Finally, the secret to learning a language is to THINK in that language. You've made it when you dream in it!

*A word on style: The **Spanish** is in **boldface**, the *pronunciation* in *italic* and the ENGLISH translation in THIS TYPE (SOMETIMES IN PARENTHESIS).

The Alphabet
The vowels

If you can say five English words you can pronounce Spanish vowels. These words are fAther, mEt, sEE, pOrtion and mOOn.

These correspond to the Spanish **a, e, i, o** and **u**. They are always pronounced the same, no matter where they appear in a word.

The verse to remember these is:
a, e, i, o, u más sabe el burro que tú.
A, E, I, O, U THE DONKEY KNOWS MORE THAN YOU.

There are some exceptions.

Mixed vowel/dipthongss

When an **a**, an **e** or an **o** are in the same syllable with an **i** or a **u**, they are run together. Examples are **diente** *DIEN-teh* (TOOTH); **pendiente** *pen-DIEN-teh* (PENDING); **hueso** *WEH-so* (BONE). In these combinations, the **i** and the **u** are the weaker vowels and are overshadowed by the stronger **a, e** and **o.** Notice that the **u** and **e**, pronounced quickly, come out *weh* and not *oo-eh*.

1

Sometimes an **i** or a **u** are stressed and are pronounced separately from the **a, e** or **o**. In those combinations they have an accent mark on the stressed letter. Examples are **día** *DEE-ah* (DAY), **río** *REE-oh* (RIVER) and **sabía** *sah-BEE-ah* (I KNEW).

If an **a**, an **e** or an **o** are found together, they are pronounced separately. Examples are: **feo** *FE-oh* (UGLY MALE), **fea** *FE-ah* (UGLY FEMALE), **creo** *CRE-oh* (I BELIEVE) and others that you will meet later.

The u

The **u** is generally pronounced as the **oo** in MOON. However, after **q** the **u** is silent: **que** *keh*, (WHAT).

The **u** hardens the **g** before **e** and **i**, making it a hard **g** as in GET or GO. Examples are **guepardo** *geh-PAR-doh* (CHEETAH), **guitarra** *gee-TAH-rra* (GUITAR) and that **u** is silent.

If the **u** is to be pronounced, an umlaut **ü** is necessary, as in **vergüenza** *vehr-GWEN-sah* (SHAME) and **pingüino** *pin-GWI-noh* (PENGUIN) and again the **g** is as in GET, or GO.

The consonants
The Ñ ñ

The sixth English word you already know is caNYon. This corresponds to the Spanish **ñ** as in **muñeca** *moo-NYEh-cah* (DOLL), **mañana** *mah-NYA-nah* (TOMORROW) or **piñon** *pin-YON* (PIÑON, a small pine tree). Say it fast so it comes out right.

Don't confuse the **ñ** with an ordinary **n**.

The ll and y

The **ll** and **y** should not be a problem, either. It is interesting that the farther south you go, the harsher the sound. In middle America, from Mexico south, the **ll** and **y** (inside or at the start of a word) is a **zsh**, while in Argentina it is almost an English **j**. Conversely, the farther north you go, the softer the sound, so that it can be a simple **y** as in English. In some areas the **y** or **ll** are swallowed so as to hardly exist. Take your pick. Listeners can tell where you are from by the way you say it.

Examples of the more standard pronunciation are **caballo** *cah-BAH-zsho* (HORSE), **relleno** *re-ZSHEH-no* (STUFFED FULL) and **yo** *zsho* (I). The more northern pronuciation, and one found in many texts, is *cah-BAH-yo, re-YEH-no* and *yo*.

The y at the end

The **y** at the end of a word is an **i** as in **voy** *voi* (I COME, I'M COMING). **Y** is AND and is pronounced *ee* as in EEK!

The c and s

The **c** and **s** are the same as in English. The **c** is soft **s** before **e** and **i**, and is hard **k** before **a, o** and **u**. In Spain and Cuba the **z** and **c** before **e** and **i** are lisped.

The **ch** is as the **ch** in CHURCH, neither a **k** nor an **sh**.

Don't confuse Spanish with Italian. The Spanish **c** is never a **ch**. In Italian we have *"la dolce vita,"* with the **ch** sound for the **c**. But in Spanish **dulce de leche** is pronounced *DOOL-seh deh LEH-cheh*, a sweet milk dessert.

The d

Some books will draw a fine line between an English and Spanish **d**. However, it takes a trained ear to tell the difference. Examples are **diga** (SAY) and **todo** (ALL). For now, stick to the English **d** until you want perfection. Communication is what counts.

The g

The **g** is hard (as in GO) before **a, o** or **u** as in **gastar** *gah-STAR* (TO SPEND); **gozar** *go-ZAR* (TO ENJOY), **gusto** *GOOS-toh* (ENJOYMENT).

The **g** is an English **h** before **e** and **i** as in **gente** *HEN-teh* (PEOPLE) and **gimnasio** *heem-NAH-see-oh* (GYMNASIUM).

The h

The **h** is silent. Some ordinary names, such as Herrera, Holguín and others are pronounced as if starting with E, O, etc. Sometimes the **h** appears in the middle of a word. It still remains silent. For instance **ahorro** *ah-OH-rro* (SAVINGS) has the **h** in the middle and is silent, but it helps separate the two strong vowels, **a** and **o**.

The j

The **j** corresponds to an English **h** as in **jugar** *hoo-GAR* (TO PLAY).

The r and rr

The seventh unfamiliar sound to pronounce is the **rr**.

The single **r** is trilled once, but works as in English until you have mastered the **rr**. It's the **rr** that can cause problems. It is double-trilled. If you can growl like a dog or make car sounds like little boys playing, you can do the Spanish **rr**. Examples are **guerra** (WAR) and **perro** (DOG). The **r** at the start of a word is also double trilled. Examples are **redondo** (ROUND) and **Roberto** (ROBERT). It may take a little practice, but it can be done. Try it in the shower.

Winding up

There is little concern with the **x**. It can be an English **x, s** or an **h** depending on placement. Other than words starting with **ex**, the **x** is rarely used. Examples are **explicar** *es-plee-CAHR* (TO EXPLAIN) and **extranjero** *es-trahn-HEH-ro* (STRANGER, FOREIGNER).

The **k** and **w** appear in foreign words that have been imported into Spanish. All

other consonants, **b, f, l, m, n, p, q, t** and **v** match their English equivalents. The **z** in Latin America is closer to an ordinary English **s**. Again, don't worry about this. If you pronounce the Spanish **z** like the English **z**, no one will complain.

There is very little difference between the **b** and the **v** in Spanish. So, when spelling a word with one of those letters, people say **"be de burro"** or **"ve de vaca,"** similar to our "B AS IN BOY" or "V AS IN VICTORY."

Putting it together
The accents

Spanish uses accent marks to show where to stress a word.

If no accent mark appears and the word ends in a consonant other than **n** or **s**, the word is stressed on the last syllable, as in **soledad** *so-leh-DAD* (LONELINESS). If the word ends in **n, s** or a vowel, the word is stressed on the next-to-last syllable: **casa** *CA-sa* (HOUSE), **abanico** *ah-bah-NEE-coh* (FAN) without the need for an accent mark. If a word is stressed on the next-to-last syllable and ends in a consonant other than **n** or **s**, it will have an accent mark. An example is **césped** *SEHS-ped* LAWN, GRASS).

Among last names we have the interesting case of the **Chávez** and **Chaves** families. The stress on both is on the next-to-last syllable. The **z** ending requires a written accent on the **a**, but the **s** ending does not.

Generally speaking, words ending –**ón** as in **avión, millón, sillón, callejón** (AIR-PLANE, MILLION, BIG CHAIR, ALLEY) carry an accent on the **o**.

If the word is stressed in the third-from-last (or earlier) syllable, the accent is written as in **periódico** *pe-ri-OH-dee-co* (NEWSPAPER).

Certain words take an accent in a question but not in the answer. This is not a problem in conversation but it would apply to written texts.

¿<u>Qué</u> es eso?
WHAT IS THAT?
Es la ventana <u>que</u> se quebró.
IT IS THE WINDOW THAT BROKE.

¿<u>Cuándo</u> viene? *(CWAN-doh veeEH-neh)*
WHEN DOES HE COME (ARRIVE)?
Vendrá <u>cuando</u> salga el sol.
HE WILL COME WHEN THE SUN RISES (COMES OUT).

¿De <u>quién</u> es esto?
WHOSE IS THIS?
Es de <u>quien</u> lo quiera.
IT BELONGS TO WHOEVER WANTS IT.

¿Cuánto cuesta?
HOW MUCH DOES IT COST?

Cuesta <u>cuanto</u> el vendedor quiera.
IT COSTS WHAT THE SELLER WANTS.

Most of the time the answer won't use the same word. Here are more common examples from the above questions:

¿<u>Qué</u> es eso? Es un lápiz.
WHAT IS THAT? IT'S A PENCIL.

¿<u>Cuándo</u> viene? Viene a las tres.
WHEN DOES HE ARRIVE (COME)? HE ARRIVES (COMES) AT 3.

¿De <u>quién</u> es esto? Es de Juan.
WHOSE IS THIS? IT'S JOHN'S.

¿<u>Cuánto</u> cuesta? Cuesta cinco dólares y diez centavos.
HOW MUCH DOES IT COST? IT COSTS FIVE DOLLARS AND TEN CENTS.

Those imports

Before we go into imports, notice that many Spanish words resemble English words. The reason for this is that both languages owe much to the Latin and Greek words that they have in common. However, not all similar words have similar meanings. For instance, **colorado** may sound like COLORED, but in reality it means RED. Another, **actual** in Spanish means AT THE PRESENT TIME.

As in other languages, technical and other words have come into Spanish. Some come "as is" and others need adjustments.

Technical words are adapted from the language of origin. Thus we have **automóvil, ciclón, computadora, electricidad, eléctrico, micrófono, microondas, radiador, telescopio, televisión** (the transmission system), **televisor** (the receiver) and **teléfono.** These translate to AUTOMOBILE, CYCLONE, COMPUTER, ELECTRICITY, ELECTRIC, MICROPHONE, MICROWAVE, RADIATOR, TELESCOPE, TELEVISION transmitter or company, TELEVISION set and TELEPHONE.

Those that have come in "as is" include **radio** and **radar.**
Spanish does not tolerate an **s+consonant**, so an **e** is placed in front of the **s.** Thus we have **espagueti** (Italian), **esqueleto** (Greek) and **esquí** (Norwegian), with the **e** in front so they can fit with Spanish. Also, the **k** of SKI and SKELETON are changed to **qu** to accommodate the lack of a **k** in the Spanish alphabet.

Some spellings change to keep the pronunciation. In sports we have **beisbol, fútbol,** and don't forget **gol,** often pronounced **g-o-o-o-ol!** on sportscasts. Among desserts we have **pay** so it is pronounced as the English PIE. It could not come into Spanish "as is" because **pie** is FOOT.

Another source of "imports" is Arabic. Because of the long Moorish occupation of Spain, the language has many words of Arabic origin. Among them: **alcohol, álgebra, alcalde, alfalfa, alpaca, almohada** and many more. Many words starting with **al** tend to be of Arabic origin. Even **alpaca** is a Spanish-Arabic version of the native word for that animal.

Don't add extra letters

Careful not to add extra letters where they don't belong. There is a tendency to do this to words or names similar to those of English.

For instance, **Vicente** is mispronounced VINCENTE; **Federico** is mispronounced FREDERICO, and **demostrar** can become DEMONSTRAR even when the person sees the word written in plain sight!

People unfamiliar with the difference between **n** and **ñ** tend to either mix them or misuse them. **Pena** is PITY. **Pino** is PINE TREE. **Piña** is PINEAPPLE. **Puño** is FIST. **Peña** is a big rock and a family name, as is also **Pino.** There is no piño.

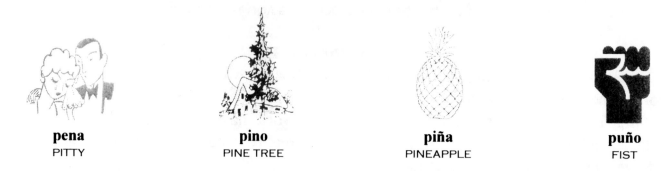

pena
PITTY

pino
PINE TREE

piña
PINEAPPLE

puño
FIST

Another set of words that confuse people are **campana** (BELL) and **campaña** (CAMPAIGN).

During a newsworthy scandal some time back, newscasters (and maybe even the Secret Service) messed up the Colombian city of **Cartagena**, *changing it to* **Cartageña**! *Confused? Don't be. Just get a good laugh at newscasters who mess these up.*

6

Patience with sounds

Don't be intimidated. All a beginner needs is patience. The solution: Start by pronouncing each letter or syllable slowly until it comes out right. If necessary, try it in the shower, or say it slowly as you write it out on a piece of scrap paper.

In summary:	Examples	Meaning
a = **aaah** as in fAther	**papá mamá**	DAD, MOM
b = as in English	**bebé, bobo**	BABY, SILLY ONE
c = **ka, ko, ku**	**cabeza, cucaracha**	HEAD, ROACH
c = **se, si**	**cerro, cinco**	HILL, FIVE
ch = as in English **CH**urch	**muchacho, chuleta**	BOY, PORKCHOP
d = as in English	**dar, dedo, duda**	TO GIVE, FINGER, DOUBT
e = **eh** as in mEt	**jefe, entre**	CHIEF, BETWEEN
f = as in English	**fácil, fósforo**	EASY, MATCH
g = **ga, go, gu** (hard g)	**galán, gozar**	LEADING MAN, TO ENJOY
g = **heh, hEE**	**gente, girasol**	PEOPLE, SUNFLOWER
gu = **gue, gui** (hard g, silent u)	**guerra, guisante**	WAR, PEA
gü = **gwe, gwi**	**vergüenza, pingüino**	SHAME, PENGUIN
h = silent; has special uses	**hoy, ahora**	TODAY, NOW
i = **eee** as in sEE	**sinfín, pila**	MANY, BATTERY
j = English h	**jamón, jirafa, joven**	HAM, GIRAFFE, YOUTH
k = English k	**kilo, kiosko**	KILO, KIOSK
l = as in English	**largo, listo, pantalones**	LONG, READY, PANTS
ll = **zh** or mi**LL**ion	**llanura, rellenar**	FLATLAND, TO REFILL
m = as in English	**madre, comprar**	MOTHER, TO BUY
n = as in English	**nada, ventana**	NOTHING, WINDOW
ñ = can**YO**n	**cañón, niña, otoño**	CANYON, GIRL, AUTUMN
o = **oh** as in pOrtion	**ocho, poco**	EIGHT, FEW
p = as in English	**papas, pepino**	POTATOES, CUCUMBER
q = **k** (always with a u)	**que, quitar**	WHAT, TO REMOVE
r = single trill	**pero, por, para**	BUT, FOR, FOR
rr = double trilled, dog bark	**perro, carro, río**	DOG, EXPENSIVE, RIVER
s = as in English	**sano, sin, sonido**	HEALTHY, WITHOUT, SOUND
t = as in English	**techo, también**	ROOF, ALSO
u = **OOO**ps	**luna, última**	MOON, LAST
v = as in English	**verdad, vidrio**	TRUTH, GLASS
x = x, with **e**	**exhibir, examen**	TO SHOW, TEST
x = s or j as per word	**México**	(the English h sound)
y = inside a word as the ll	**joya**	JEWEL
y = end of word as in sEE	**voy, soy**	I COME, I AM
z = closer to an **s**	**zanahoria, zapato**	CARROT, SHOE

7

2
A LITTLE BIT OF GRAMMAR
Un poco de gramática

Here we go with those bothersome parts of speech. The time has come to deal with some of these, unpleasant as it is.

Parts of speech
Nouns

In Spanish, as in English, nouns are persons, places or things. In Spanish they are either male or female, as there is no neutrality here.

It's easy enough with people and animals, but inanimate objects are also masculine or feminine. In English a TV set, a book and a pencil are neutral and use IT as a pronoun. In Spanish they are male. In English a table, a spoon and a chair are neutral. In Spanish they are female.

The best way to learn nouns is with their articles, since articles are also female or male and are used with nouns even more than we do in English.

Articles

In English THE can be male, female or neither. It has no gender.

In Spanish, gender is important. The male article THE is **el***. The plural is **los**. When sexes are mixed or undetermined, they take the masculine article. **Los hijos, los niños** can be all male or mixed male and female. They translate as THE SONS, THE BOYS or THE CHILDREN. Similar rules apply to animals.

*This **el** does not have an accent, distinguishing it from the pronoun **él**. More on that later.

The feminine THE is **la** and the plural is **las.** These are used with females only, animate or inanimate.

Here are some uses:

el hombre, la mujer*, los hombres, las mujeres
THE MAN, THE WOMAN, THE MEN, THE WOMEN
***mujer** can also mean "wife," depending on context.

8

el niño, la niña, los niños, las niñas

THE BOY, THE GIRL, THE CHILDREN (all boys or mixed), THE GIRLS (all girls)

el hijo, la hija, los hijos (all boys or mixed), **las hijas** (all daughters)

THE SON, THE DAUGHTER, THE SONS (can mean CHILDREN when including girls), THE DAUGH-TERS

el perro, la perra, los perros, las perras

THE DOG, THE BITCH*, THE DOGS (all male or mixed), THE BITCHES
```
*Don't be shocked. In show dog terminology, the correct term for a fe-
male dog is "bitch." It is not a derogatory term.
```

Watch out for **el** or **la** when using them in English texts that include Spanish names. There is a tendency to put a THE in front, as in *The La Niña* or *The El Niño*, the weather events. These come out as THE THE BOY or THE THE GIRL.

Boys or Girls?

Here are some general notes on inanimate objects and their articles. Not all can be included here, but these are some of the items you may encounter around the house or on the job.

MALE: Words ending in **o** are usually masculine. For instance: **el viento, los carros** (THE WIND, THE CARS). Days of the week are male: **el domingo, el lunes** (See Chapter 18 for a list of days of the week and months of the year.) Groups of people or animals of both sexes are male, as noted above.

FEMALE: Words ending in **a** are usually female. For instance **la cara, las mesas** (THE FACE, THE TABLES).

With people or animals, male and female are by actual sex:

el hermano, la hermana; el papá, la mamá; el gato, la gata.

THE BROTHER, THE SISTER; THE DAD, THE MOM; THE TOM CAT, THE FEMALE CAT.

Words ending in –**ista** are male or female, depending on the person's sex: **el artista, la artista, el periodista, la periodista** (THE ARTIST, THE NEWSPAPER REPORTER).

La moto and **la foto** (THE MOTORCYCLE, THE PHOTOGRAPH) keep the feminine article because they are shortened versions of **la motocicleta** and **la fotografía**.

Then we have feminine words that start with **a**. To avoid a run of two **a** sounds together, words such as **agua, hacha** or **arpa** take **el** as the article in the singular: **el agua** (THE WATER), **el hacha** (THE HATCHET), **un arpa** (A HARP). But in the plural, the article is feminine: **las aguas, las hachas, unas arpas**. And when WATER IS COLD, it's **el agua está fría**.

There are instances in which **el** or **la** change the meaning of a word. Some of these are illustrated in Chapters 17 and 18.

Agreement

When articles are used with nouns, they must agree in gender and number, as noted above.

The indefinite articles are **un, una, unos, unas**. They are used when in English you'd use ONE, AN or SOME:

un plato, unos pájaros, una mesa, unas bandejas
A PLATE, SOME BIRDS, A TABLE, SOME TRAYS

Un can also mean one, as in **un sofá**, ONE SOFA. The content would clarify. Again, these must agree in gender and number.

More on these later.

How Many?

Plurals are made pretty much as in English. In Spanish it is done by adding an **s** to words ending in a vowel or **es** to words ending in a consonant:

el caballo, los caballos (THE HORSE, THE HORSES); **la mesa, las mesas** (THE TABLE, THE TABLES); **el jardín, los jardines** (THE GARDEN, THE GARDENS), **el televisor, los televisores** (THE TV SET, THE TV SETS). A special note: **jardines** loses the accent mark in the plural because the **i** now falls in the next-to-last sylable.

Pronouns

General use pronouns are:

singular	*plural*
yo (I)	**nosotros**
tú (YOU, familiar), **usted** (YOU, formal)	**ustedes, (vosotros)**
él (HE)	**ellos**
ella (SHE)	**ellas**

Usted is a general use word for YOU; **tú** is also YOU, but is familiar and used with close friends, younger family members, children and pets. **Vosotros** is the plural form of **tú**. It is used in Spain and in prayers. It is seldom used in Latin America. **Usted** and **ustedes** will do for most uses. Your boss may not like being addressed as **tú** so sticking to **usted** avoids problems.

Here are other pronouns you may need.
mí is like ME in English.
El regalo es para mí. THE GIFT IS FOR ME.

mío, mía are equivalent to MINE.
La caja es mía. THE BOX IS MINE.
El conejo es mío. THE RABBIT IS MINE.
suyo is YOURS. The familiar is **tuyo**.
El cuchillo sucio es suyo. THE DIRTY KNIFE IS YOURS. (using the formal form)
El juguete es tuyo. THE TOY IS YOURS. (speaking to a child)

10

él with an accent is a pronoun, as it indicates a specific person, similar to HE in English.

Él es ingeniero HE IS AN ENGINEER.

El televisor es de él, THE TV SET IS HIS (BELONGS TO HIM).

Where are they?

Remember demonstrative pronouns and demonstrative adjectives from elementary school? Spanish has them, too. The rules have changed in recent years; now none use accents unless they are used to clear confusion. Now that you know all that, put it in the back of your mind and don't worry about it.

male	female		male pl	fem pl
este	**esta**		**estos**	**estas**
THIS			THESE	
ese	**esa**		**esos**	**esas**
THAT (NEAR US)			THOSE (NEAR US)	
aquel	**aquella**		**aquellos**	**aquellas**
THAT (YONDER)			THOSE (YONDER)	

Here are some contrasting uses. It's best to use the noun before using its pronoun. How you use these in daily conversations depends on the circumstances. The item may be near either the speaker or hearer, in which case merely pointing helps. The item could be elsewhere, in which case it may be necessary to name it. Notice that gender and number agree with the noun referenced.

No quiero que use <u>estos</u> huevos; quiero que use <u>esos</u>.

I DON'T WANT YOU TO USE <u>THESE</u> EGGS; I WANT YOU TO USE <u>THOSE.</u> (pointing).

Hay que* limpiar <u>esta</u> silla y también <u>esa</u>.

IT IS NECESSARY TO CLEAN <u>THIS</u> CHAIR, AND ALSO <u>THAT</u> ONE.

*"Hay que" is a common expression to indicate that something needs to be done.

Hay que planchar <u>estos</u> pantalones y también <u>aquellos</u> en el clóset.

IT IS NECESSARY TO IRON <u>THESE</u> PANTS AND ALSO <u>THOSE</u> IN THE CLOSET.

Prepositions

The most used prepositions are:

de	OF
del	OF THE
a	TO
al	TO THE
en	IN
con	WITH

por*	FOR, BY, THROUGH, etc.	
para*	FOR	

*more on these later

Spanish has two mandated contractions: **al,** a contraction for **a + el**; and **del,** a contraction for **de + el.**

Because Spanish doesn't have an apostrophe to show possessive, it is expressed with "of the owner." *Examples:*

de OF

El lápiz <u>del</u> abuelo es amarillo. THE GRANDFATHER'S PENCIL IS YELLOW. Literally: "THE PENCIL OF THE GRANDFATHER IS YELLOW".

de la OF

Las plumas <u>de la</u> abuela son rojas. THE GRANDMOTHER'S PENS ARE RED.

Note that **de el** contracts to **del** with the masculine, but it is **de la** with the feminine. In the first example, **amarillo** (the color) is singular masculine because the pencil is singular and masculine. In the second example, because **plumas** are feminine and plural, **son rojas** (the color) are feminine and plural.

More examples of prepositions:

a	TO	**Voy <u>a</u> Santa Fe.** I GO <u>TO</u> SANTA FE.
en	IN	**Estoy <u>en</u> la cama.** I AM <u>IN</u> BED.
por	FOR	**Me preocupo <u>por</u> el árbol.** I WORRY ABOUT THE TREE. The literal translation is WORRIED <u>FOR</u> THE TREE.)
para	FOR	**Estoy preparado <u>para</u> el trabajo.** I AM PREPARED <u>FOR</u> THE JOB.
con	WITH	**Estoy <u>con</u> el perro.** I AM <u>WITH</u> THE DOG.

You're not getting off easily yet. There are more:

desde	AFTER, SINCE
durante	DURING
entre	BETWEEN, AMONG
hacia	TOWARD, AROUND
hasta	AS FAR AS, UP TO
sin	WITHOUT
sobre	ABOVE, ON TOP OF

¿<u>Desde</u> cuándo?
<u>SINCE</u> WHEN?

Me gustaba el café <u>desde</u> que era niña.
I LIKED COFFEE <u>SINCE</u> I WAS A CHILD.

Nosotros vivimos en Santa Fe <u>durante</u> el incendio en Los Alamos.
WE LIVED IN SANTA FE <u>DURING</u> THE FIRE IN LOS ALAMOS.

El perro durmió <u>durante</u> la tormenta.
THE DOG SLEPT DURING THE STORM.

La película se llama "<u>Entre</u> la vida y la muerte".*
THE NAME OF THE MOVIE IS (Lit: THE MOVIE IS NAMED) "<u>BETWEEN</u> LIFE AND DEATH."

 *In Spanish, only the first word and proper names in a book or movie title are capitalized.

En el divorcio, mi amiga se encontró <u>entre</u> el marido y la mujer.
IN THE DIVORCE, MY FRIEND FOUND HERSELF <u>BETWEEN</u> THE HUSBAND AND THE WIFE.

No te encuentro <u>entre</u> tanta gente.
I CAN'T FIND YOU <u>AMONG</u> ALL THESE PEOPLE.

Salieron <u>hacia</u> las tres de la tarde.
THEY LEFT <u>AROUND</u> THREE IN THE AFTERNOON.

Caminaba <u>hacia</u> el baño cuando se cayó.
HE WAS WALKING <u>TOWARD</u> THE BATHROOM WHEN HE FELL.

¡<u>Hasta</u> mañana! ¡<u>Hasta</u> luego!
<u>UNTIL</u> TOMORROW! SO LONG!

<u>Hasta</u> aquí y no más.
<u>TO</u> HERE AND NO MORE.

<u>Hasta</u> los cocineros tienen que comer.
<u>EVEN</u> COOKS HAVE TO EAT.

Las papas <u>sin</u> sal no saben a nada.
POTATOES <u>WITHOUT</u> SALT DON'T TASTE LIKE ANYTHING (HAVE NO FLAVOR AT ALL)

El gato no debe caminar <u>sobre</u> la mesa.
THE CAT SHOULD NOT WALK <u>ON</u> THE TABLE.

Some take **de** to make them work:

antes de	BEFORE
cerca de	NEAR
debajo de	UNDER
delante de	IN FRONT OF
después de	AFTER
detrás de	BEHIND
encima de	ON TOP OF
en vez de	INSTEAD OF

Here are some sentences. Try mixing and matching, remembering to keep number and gender in agreement.

Antes de salir, tengo que ponerme los zapatos.
BEFORE LEAVING (I LEAVE), I MUST PUT ON MY SHOES.

La licuadora está cerca del reloj. `(this j is silent)`
THE BLENDER IS NEAR THE CLOCK.

El delantal se llama así porque se usa delante del vestido. THE APRON IS
NAMED THUS BECAUSE IT IS WORN IN FRONT OF THE RESS.
*Right, it doesn't make sense in English because in English apron has nothing
to do with its placement!*

Después de cortar la grama (el césped, el zacate), hay qué regar. AFTER MOWING THE
LAWN, IT IS NECESSARY TO WATER.

Las galletas están detrás del pan.
THE CRACKERS ARE BEHIND THE BREAD.

El gato está debajo de la mesa.
THE CAT IS UNDER THE TABLE.

No pongas el papel higiénico encima de las toallas.
DON'T PUT THE TOILET PAPER ON TOP OF THE TOWELS.

Usemos los tomates frescos en vez de los de lata.
WE'LL USE THE FRESH TOMATOES INSTEAD OF THE CANNED ONES.

Adjectives

Adjectives tell something of a noun or pronoun: its color, size, condition, etc. As a
general rule, the noun comes before the modifier. The adjective agrees with the noun in
gender and number.

la casa blanca	THE WHITE HOUSE (THE HOUSE WHITE)
la silla sucia	THE DIRTY CHAIR (THE CHAIR DIRTY)
el piso limpio	THE CLEAN FLOOR
los jarros quebrados	THE BROKEN JARS
un traje grande	A LARGE SUIT (OF CLOTHING)

However –

To tell what something is made of, the item is described with **de**. In English we use
two nouns to express the idea: THE LINOLEUM FLOOR, THE METAL TABLE, THE LEATHER SHOE.
In Spanish it's THE ITEM (MADE) OF (SOMETHING) Thus, **el piso de linóleo** (THE LINOLEUM
FLOOR), **la mesa de metal** (THE METAL TABLE), **el zapato de cuero** (THE LEATHER SHOE). This
is a common construction for many household and personal goods.

Colors

Some colors are male or female and have the male **o** or female **a** endings. Others are not as specific and may be regarded as neutral. All agree in gender and number with item described. Add an **s** for plural on those ending in a vowel or **es** for those ending in a consonant.

negro, negra BLACK

anaranjado, anaranjada ORANGE

rosado, rosada PINK, ROSY

morado, morada PURPLE (the color dark mulberry **mora** berries)

rojo, roja, colorado, colorada RED;

blanco, blanca WHITE

amarillo, amarilla YELLOW

Among the "neutral" colors we find:

azul BLUE; **gris** GRAY; **verde** GREEN; **rosa** PINK

Some examples:

la bicicleta negra THE BLACK BICYCLE

los carros negros THE BLACK CARS

una camisa amarilla A YELLOW SHIRT

varios lápices amarillos VARIOUS YELLOW PENCILS

mi perro blanco MY WHITE DOG

sus gatos blancos YOUR WHITE CATS

el sofá morado THE PURPLE SOFA

esos vestidos morados THOSE PURPLE DRESSES

The "neutral" colors take on the gender of the subject but must agree in number. Add **es** to make the item plural on words ending in a consonant.

el cielo azul THE BLUE SKY

las camisas azules THE BLUE SHIRTS

un traje gris A GRAY SUIT

las cajas grises THE GRAY BOXES

el libro verde THE GREEN BOOK

las hojas verdes THE GREEN LEAVES

Some fruits provide color names:

amarillo limón LEMON YELLOW

verde olivo OLIVE GREEN

color naranja ORANGE

Size and Number

Size and numbers also agree with their nouns. For plurals, add **s** or **es.**
These by gender:

poco, poca, pocos, pocas FEW IN NUMBER

mucho, mucha, muchos, muchas MANY IN NUMBER

pequeño, pequeña, pequeños, pequeñas SMALL IN SIZE

chico, chica, chicos, chicas SMALL IN SIZE

> (**chico** and **chica** also mean BOY or GIRL)

chiquito, chiquita, chiquitos, chiquitas SMALLER THAN CHICO

These go unchanged on either sex but must agree in number:

diferente, diferentes DIFFERENT

dulce, dulces SWEET

fuerte, fuertes STRONG

grande. grandes LARGE, BIG

pobre, pobres POOR

General looks, condition and character

These by gender:

simpático, simpática CHARMING, OF GOOD CHARACTER

limpio, limpia CLEAN

sucio, sucia DIRTY

hermoso, hermosa HANDSOME, GOOD LOOKING

guapo, guapa HANDSOME, GOOD LOOKING

bonito, bonita PRETTY, CUTE

feo, fea UGLY

sano, sana HEALTHY

enfermo, enferma ILL, SICK,

Legal standing

vivo, viva ALIVE

muerto, muerta DEAD

divorciado, divorciada DIVORCED

casado, casada MARRIED

soltero, soltera SINGLE, UNMARRIED

Smaller and bigger

Diminutives are made by adding **-ito** or **-ita** to adjective endings and making a few minor vowel changes. You just noticed **chico** and **chiquita**. Others include **niñita, conejito, gatito, perrito** LITTLE GIRL, LITTLE RABBIT, LITTLE CAT, LITTLE DOG. There's practically no end to the possibilities.

To show that something is even smaller add **-itito: chiquititito.**

To show a greater degree, add **-isimo: riquísimo** VERY RICH from simply **rico** RICH (note the **c** changes to **qu** to keep the **k** sound).

-**ote**, -**ota** or -**ón** makes it bigger: **grande** to **grandote** BIG to VERY BIG; double it and you get **grandotote** EVEN BIGGER. **Silla** CHAIR becomes **sillón** BIG CHAIR; **caja** BOX becomes **cajota** BIG BOX and **cuchara** SPOON becomes **cucharota** BIG SPOON.

Más and **menos** do the same as MORE and LESS: **más dulce** MORE SWEET (SWEETER); **menos pobre** LESS POOR.

Ifs, ands & buts

Here are some common Spanish conjunctions:

y AND
o OR
pero BUT
sino BUT rather (contrasting)
ni . . . ni NEITHER . . . NOR

y is AND
Tengo un hijo y una hija.
I HAVE A SON AND A DAUGHTER.

o is OR
Quiero comprar manzanas o naranjas.
I WANT TO BUY APPLES OR ORANGES.

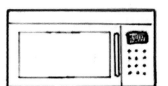

pero is BUT
No tengo estufa, pero sí tengo microondas.
I DON'T HAVE A STOVE BUT I DO HAVE A MICROWAVE.
Quiero ese carro nuevo, pero no tengo dinero para comprarlo.
I WANT THAT NEW CAR, BUT I DON'T HAVE MONEY TO BUY IT.

sino shows contrast
No es el jardinero sino el cocinero.
HE ISN'T THE GARDENER BUT (HE IS) THE COOK.

ni . . . ni is used the way we use NEITHER . . . NOR in English.
Él no es ni ingeniero ni abogado.
HE IS NEITHER AN ENGINEER NOR A LAWYER.

Spanish does not like to have an end vowel and a start vowel of the same sound, as noted with **agua**. When **y** or **o** bump into a matching vowel sound, the **y** is changed to **e** and the **o** is changed to **u** just that once:

Es médico e ingeniero. HE IS A DOCTOR AND AN ENGINEER.
This avoides **y ingeniero**, which runs two eee-eee sounds together.
Un caballo, una vaca u otro animal. A HORSE, A COW OR OTHER ANIMAL. This keeps **o otro** from grating the ears.

17

You'll find **u otro(s)** often in lists and literature, just as we find OR OTHER(S) quite often in English.

Yes, no & more

sí with an accent is YES and **no** is NO. At last an easy one!

Spanish allows for the use of double negatives. In English a second negative cancels the first, as in "I didn't go nowhere." In Spanish the double negative reinforces the negativity.

No necesito nada may appear to be "I don't need nothing," but in Spanish it really is I DON'T NEED ANYTHING AT ALL.

An old saying is

El que come granada no come nada.

HE WHO EATS POMEGRANATE EATS NOTHING.

Sí (with accent) is YES, as noted above

Sí, voy al banco hoy.

YES, I'M GOING TO THE BANK TODAY.

Sí, señor, estoy listo.

YES, SIR, I'M READY.

Si (no accent) is IF

Si se quema la carne, no la como.

IF THE MEAT BURNS, I WON'T EAT IT.

Si Dios quiere.

IF GOD WILLS IT. This is a common expression, especially when refering to an activity planned for the future.

más (with an accent) is MORE

Ella tiene más dinero que su esposo.

SHE HAS MORE MONEY THAN HER HUSBAND.

¡No más!

NO MORE! ENOUGH!

mas (no accent) is but. This **mas** is found in ancient writings, poetry and other languages, such as Portuguese. **Pero** is the most common but.

Tampoco adds negativity in a sequence. Here is an illustration from a roadstand fruit stand.

¿Vende pollo? DO YOU SELL CHICKEN?

No, señora. NO MA'AM.

¿Tocino? BACON?

Tampoco. NO, NOT THAT, EITHER.

¿Lomo? SIRLOIN?

Tampoco. NO (more emphatic)

¿Salchica? SAUSAGE?

Tampoco. NO. (He may be getting impatient by now)

¿Pavo? TURKEY?

Señora, aquí solo vendemos frutas y verduras.
MA'AM, HERE WE SELL ONLY FRUITS AND VEGETABLES.

Adverbs

Adverbs describe verbs. Some are formed by adding **-mente** behind an adjective. This is equivalent to adding **-ly** in English. Thus **lento(a)** SLOW becomes **lentamente** SLOWLY.

Camina rápidamente. HE (SHE) WALKS RAPIDLY.

Baila lentamente. SHE (HE) DANCES SLOWLY.

Sometimes the **-mente** ending is awkward. Another way to make adverbs is to use **con** WITH.

con calma CALMLY (lit. WITH CALM); **con prisa** HURIDLY.

Here, there and everywhere

In English we have HERE and THERE. Spanish refines these words of location a bit more.

acá HERE, near me

aquí HERE, near me, near us

ahí THERE, more or less precise placement; closer to you than me

allí THERE, more precise placement; similar to ahí

allá THERE farther away from both of us

más allá OVER THERE, even farther away.

por aquí AROUND HERE

La silla de madera está aquí.
THE WOODEN CHAIR IS HERE.

Busca el perro por allá, cerca del árbol.
LOOK FOR THE DOG OVER THERE, NEAR THE TREE.

Tira la pelota acá. THROW THE BALL HERE (TO ME).

Prefexes and such

Spanish uses prefixes much as we do in English,. Here a few with their meanings. There are others that you will find as you read books in Spanish, whether fiction, nonfiction or even grammar books.

Em- and **en-** relate to something combined with something else:

enchilada means it has chile

empanada means it's BREAD (**pan**) surrounding some other ingredient

empolvar means TO DUST (**polvo**)

empedrada means PAVED WITH STONES (**piedras**)

encarrilar means TO SET ON TRACKS (**carriles***)

enlatado means CANNED (**lata**) as in commercial or home canned foods

endemoniado means HAVING A DEMON (**demonio**)

***carriles** can also relate to highway lanes

Des- cancels the action of the verb:

> **desenchufar** TO UNPLUG cancels **enchufar** TO PLUG IN
>
> **desordenado** SLOPPY, DISORGANIZED cancels **ordenado** ORDERLY from **ordenar** TO PUT IN ORDER
>
> **desvestir** TO UNDRESS cancels **vestir** TO DRESS

In- creates an opposite action, so that **incumplido** is a person who does not follow through, from **cumplir**, TO DO ONE'S DUTY, TO FOLLOW THROUGH.

Re- does much the same as in English: **reusar** is TO REUSE; **reforestar** is TO RE-PLANT, as in planting where trees had been removed; **reconquistar** is TO RECONQUER; **redescubrir** is to DISCOVER AGAIN. You can put **re-** on almost any verb to repeat an action.

Ex- appears in in words such as **exclamar** to EXCLAIM, **exponer** TO EXPLAIN and **excavación** a HOLE from **excavar** TO DIG.

As you can see, the use of **ex-** is similar to its use in English.

Caveat: Not all similar syllables are prefexes. Many words contain these syllables in the ordinary fashion.

Capitalization and punctuation

Spanish capitailizes the first word and proper names in titles (books, music, etc) but not the rest of the title. We have followed this in this book as away of illustrating the difference.

Periods, commas, colons and semicolons are pretty much the same as in English.

In addition to the standard exclamation mark ! and question mark ? Spanish uses the upside down exclamation mark ¡ and upside down question mark ¿ ahead of the expression. This handy device warns the reader to put the right tone to the sentence. How many times have we had to re-read a sentence to get the right inflection because the question mark or exclamation mark caught us off guard on the next page?

Quotation marks also tend to go inside commas and periods. There are some exceptions, which we'll skip for now.

Another difference is that in Spanish the comma is the English decimal point in numbers, and the period is equivalent to the comma. Thus **$200.987,32** is equivalent to $200,987.32 in English.

3
FACING THOSE VERBS
Fíjandonos en los verbos

Verbs are probably the most complicated challenge for learning Spanish. However, they can be learned. Learning verbs by the installment plan is probably the best way for beginners (or even those of you who once learned them years ago and forgot 'em all).

In English we put "TO" in front of a word of action and that becomes the verb in its infinitive form: TO TALK, TO BREAK, TO ADD.

The infinitives of Spanish verbs, and thus the verbs themselves, are known by their endings.

There are verbs that end in –**ar**, –**er** and –**ir**.

Then there are regular verbs and irregular verbs and a whole bunch of tenses, multiple sets of persons and more.

Some verbs pick up minor changes in pronunciation or spelling as they move across the tenses and persons.

For beginners, it's probably best to stick to the infinitive, present, past and future tenses. To complicate matters, there are two past tenses. We give both here, but beginners may prefer to stick to one at first, then learn the other later.

For giving orders to friends or family members, Spanish offers commands. We include those here.

Further complications are reflexives – verbs that point back to the speaker or other person. This means the subject (I, YOU, HE, etc) and object (MYSELF, YOURSELF, HIMSELF, etc) are the same person. Some of these will be touched on in other chapters.

Who and how many are we?
Pronouns that go with verbs

Before tackling verbs, it is necessary to learn the "persons" first, since the verbs hang on those. The persons are pretty much the same as in English.

yo I
tú YOU (familiar, used with family members and close friends)
usted YOU (general, formal, used with the boss, the professor, etc)
él, ella HE, SHE
nosotros WE
ustedes YOU (plural)
ellos, ellas THEY (male and/or female)

21

The familiar **tú** is popularly used, especially among friends and co-workers. However a boss, college professor, teacher or school principal would resent being addressed the way you address your best friend or little brother. With those "authority figures" use the **usted** form and be safe.

In Spain the plural of **tú** is **vosotros**. It is used also in prayers and you'll find it in literature. In Latin America, **ustedes** is the commonly used word for YOU (plural), or as they say in the South, "YOU ALL."

Usted is abbreviated **Ud.** and **ustedes** is abbreviated **Uds.** In the conjugations below, we use **Ud.** or **Uds.** when space is limited. Also, we may use **él** or **ella** sporadically. You already know that both are included.

Tenses
When it happened

For now, we will stick to the present, the past (complete), the past (continuous), and the future.

The future can sometimes be expressed with the present, thus making the future a little less important than it is in English. For instance: **Le hablo mañana** uses the present **hablo** but refers to an act you plan for tomorrow. You could also say: **Le hablaré mañana**, which is also I WILL TALK TO YOU TOMORROW. You will find similar uses in many books, including this one, using the present as a future tense.

The two past tenses differentiate between a completed action in the past and a past action that continued.

An example of a completed past is:
Yo hablé con mi amigo la semana pasada.
I SPOKE WITH MY FRIEND LAST WEEK. The action had an end.

An example of a continuing past action is:
Ella hablaba por teléfono todos los días.
SHE TALKED ON THE TELEPHONE EVERY DAY. The action continued.
An equivalent in English would be: SHE USED TO TALK ON THE PHONE EVERY DAY.

Don't worry if you mix these up. Eventually you'll learn them. If you prefer, chose one for starters and learn the other later. Grammar books refer to these past tenses as *preterit* and *imperfect*. Now that you know those words, forget them for a while.

Regular verbs

Here are conjugations of these three regular verbs.
Notice the endings that are put at the end of the "stems". These appear on regu-

lar verbs, which is why those verbs are called "regular." If you are ambitious and like to memorize things, you could try memorizing those endings. However, most people won't be doing that. Just be aware of them and at least notice the pattern.

Doing it now – the present tense

Hablar translates TO TALK, TO SPEAK.

yo hablo	I TALK
tú hablas (familiar)	YOU TALK
usted habla (formal)	YOU TALK
él, ella habla	HE, SHE TALKS
nosotros hablamos	WE TALK
ustedes hablan	YOU (PLURAL) TALK
ellos, ellas hablan	THEY (MALE, FEMALE) TALK

In some cases the words indicate who is talking, so that in those cases the pronoun isn't always needed. If you say **hablamos** there is no doubt that WE TALK is meant. Also notice that the endings for **usted, él** and **ella** are the same, as are the endings for **ustedes, ellos** and **ellas**. They are separated here for clarity.

Although the "person" is not always needed, it may be necessary, on occasion, to say **"usted habla"** to make it clear that you mean YOU and not HE or SHE.

Romper translates TO TEAR, as in tearing fabric, paper or something semi-hard, as opposed to hard, like glass. It is also used in breaking an engagement.

yo rompo	I TEAR
tú rompes (familiar)	YOU TEAR
usted rompe (formal)	YOU TEAR
él, ella rompe	HE, SHE TEARS
nosotros rompemos	WE TEAR
ustedes rompen	YOU (PL) TEAR
ellos, ellas rompen	THEY (M,F) TEAR

Añadir translates TO ADD, a word frequently found in recipes.

yo añado	I ADD
tú añades	YOU ADD
usted añade	YOU ADD
él, ella añade	HE, SHE ADDS
nosotros añadimos	WE ADD
ustedes añaden	YOU ADD
ellos, ellas añaden	THEY ADD

Did it once – the completed past

yo habl<u>é</u>	I TALKED
tú habl<u>aste</u>	YOU TALKED
usted habl<u>ó</u>	YOU TALKED
él, ella habl<u>ó</u>	HE, SHE TALKED
nosotros habl<u>amos</u>	WE TALKED
ustedes habl<u>aron</u>	YOU TALKED
ellos, ellas habl<u>aron</u>	THEY TALKED

yo romp<u>í</u>	I TORE
tú romp<u>iste</u>	YOU TORE
usted romp<u>ió</u>	YOU TORE
él, ella romp<u>ió</u>	HE, SHE TORE
nosotros romp<u>imos</u>	WE TORE
ustedes romp<u>ieron</u>	YOU TORE
ellos, ellas romp<u>ieron</u>	THEY TORE

yo añad<u>í</u>	I ADDED
tú añad<u>iste</u>	YOU ADED
usted añad<u>ió</u>	YOU ADDED
él, ella añad<u>ió</u>	HE, SHE ADED
nosotros añad<u>imos</u>	WE ADDED
ustedes añad<u>ieron</u>	YOU ADDED
ellos añad<u>ieron</u>	THEY ADDED

Kept on doing it – the on-going past

yo habl<u>aba</u>	I USED TO TALK
tú habl<u>abas</u>	YOU USED TO TALK
Ud. habl<u>aba</u>	YOU USED TO TALK
él habl<u>aba</u>	HE USED TO TALK
nosotros habl<u>ábamos</u>	WE USED TO TALK
ustedes habl<u>an</u>	THEY USED TO TALK
ellas habl<u>aban</u>	THEY USED TO TALK

yo romp<u>ía</u>	I USED TO TEAR
tú romp<u>ías</u>	YOU USED TO TEAR
Ud. romp<u>ía</u>	YOU USED TO TEAR
ella romp<u>ía</u>	SHE USED TO TEAR
nosotros romp<u>íamos</u>	WE USED TO TEAR
ustedes romp<u>ían</u>	YOU USED TO TEAR
ellos romp<u>ían</u>	THEY USED TO TEAR

yo añad**ía**	I USED TO ADD
tú añad**ías**	YOU USED TO ADD
Ud. añad**ía**	YOU USED TO ADD
él añad**ía**	HE USED TO ADD
nosotros añad**íamos**	WE USED TO ADD
ustedes añad**ían**	YOU USED TO ADD
ellos añad**ían**	THEY USED TO ADD

Do it later – the future tense

yo habl**aré**	I WILL TALK
tú habl**arás**	YOU WILL TALK
usted habl**ará**	YOU'LLTALK
ella habl**ará**	SHE'LL TALK
nosotros habl**aremos**	WE WILL TALK
ustedes habl**arán**	YOU WILL TALK
ellas habl**arán**	THEY'LL TALK

yo romp**eré**	I WILL TEAR
tú romp**erás**	YOU WILL TEAR
Ud. romp**erá**	YOU'LL TEAR
ella romp**erá**	SHE W ILL TEAR
nosotros romp**eremos**	WE WILL TEAR
ustedes romp**erán**	THEY WILL TEAR
ellos, ellas romp**erán**	THEY WILL TEAR

yo añad**iré**	I WILL ADD
tú añad**irás**	YOU WILL ADD
usted añad**irá**	YOU WILL ADD
ella, él añad**irá**	SHE, HE WILL ADD
nosotros añad**iremos**	WE WILL ADD
ustedes añad**irán**	YOU (PL) WILL ADD
ellos, ellas añad**irán**	THEY WILL ADD

Giving orders

The Spanish verbs of command can be useful when talking to an employee who knows little English. The commands for the verbs just listed are **usted hable, tú habla**; **usted rompa, tú rompe** and **usted añada, tú añade**. On occasion the negative command may differ from the positive command. We show them as needed without any more explanation. A good idea for other verbs is to check your reference books.

Here are some sample sentences using the command:

No hable así por teléfono.
DON'T TALK THAT WAY ON THE PHONE.

Rompe este trapo para tener dos trapos para limpiar.
TEAR THIS RAG SO YOU (WE) HAVE TWO RAGS FOR CLEANING.

Por favor, añada esta lata de chile a la sopa.
PLEASE, ADD THIS CAN OF CHILE TO THE SOUP.

Like it?

Gustar TO ENJOY is an easy verb. It has fewer conjugation forms: **gusta, gustan; gustó, gustaron; gustaba, gustaban;** and **gustará, gustarán,** in the same order of tenses as above. A few other verbs fit this category. Among them are **encantar** TO LIKE, **fascinar** TO INTRIGUE and **importar** TO STRESS.

Weather forecast

Some verbs relating to weather are conjugated in their own way. These include **llover, nevar** and **helar** TO RAIN, TO SNOW, TO FREEZE. These are expressed (two presents, past on-going, past complete, future) as **llueve (está lloviendo), llovía, llovió, lloverá; nieva (está nevando), nevaba, nevó, nevará; hiela (está helando), helaba, heló, helará.** These and similar impersonal verbs exist, some more useful than others. They can be found in any of the books on conjugating Spanish verbs.

Irregular verbs

Some of the most important verbs are irregular. They may be –**ar**, –**er** or –**ir** verbs, but conjugations develop quite differently as they progress through tenses and persons.

To be and to be too

The verb "TO BE" is an example. To complicate matters, there are two TO BE verbs in Spanish. These are **ser** and **estar**.

Ser describes a permanent or almost permanent state of being.

Estar describes a temporary state of being [See the special section on **ser and estar** in Chapter 4].

Here are the conjugations. Notice that the irregular verbs are well-named. They don't use the "stems" you saw with the regular verbs.

SER present

yo soy	I AM
tú eres	YOU ARE
usted es	YOU ARE
él, ella es	HE, SHE IS

nosotros somos	WE ARE
ustedes son	YOU (PL) ARE
ellos, ellas son	THEY ARE

SER past completed

yo fui	I WAS
tú fuiste	YOU WERE
usted fue	YOU WERE
él, ella fue	HE, SHE WAS
nosotros fuimos	WE WERE
ustedes fueron	YOU (PL) WERE
ellos, ellas fueron	THEY WERE

SER past on-going

yo era	I USED TO BE
tú eras	YOU USED TO BE
usted era	YOU USED BE
él, ella era	HE, SHE USED TO BE
nosotros éramos	WE USED TO BE
ustedes eran	YOU (PL) USED TO BE
ellos, ellas eran	THEY USED TO BE

SER future

yo seré	I WILL BE
tú serás	YOU WILL BE
usted será	YOU WILL BE
él, ella será	HE, SHE WILL BE
nosotros seremos	WE WILL BE
ustedes serán	YOU (PL) WILL BE
ellos, ellas serán	THEY WILL BE

ESTAR present

yo estoy	I AM
tú estás	YOU ARE
usted está	YOU ARE
él, ella está	HE, SHE IS
nosotros estamos	WE ARE
ustedes están	YOU (PL) ARE
ellos, ellas están	THEY ARE

ESTAR past completed

yo estuve	I WAS
tú estuviste	YOU WERE

usted estuvo	YOU WERE
él, ella estuvo	HE, SHE WAS
nosotros estuvimos	WE WERE
ustedes estuvieron	YOU (PL) WERE
ellos, ellas estuvieron	THEY WERE

ESTAR past ongoing

yo estaba	I WAS, I USED TO BE
tú estabas	YOU WERE, YOU USED TO BE
usted estaba	YOU WERE, YOU USED TO BE
él, ella estaba	HE, SHE USED TO BE
nosotros estábamos	WE WERE, WE USED TO BE
ustedes estaban	YOU (PL) WERE, YOU USED TO BE
ellos, ellas estaban	THEY WERE, THEY USED TO BE

ESTAR future

yo estaré	I WILL BE
tú estarás	YOU WILL BE
usted estará	YOU WILL BE
ella, él estarán	SHE, HE WILL BE
nosotros estaremos	WE WILL BE
ustedes estarán	YOU WILL BE
ellos, ellas estarán	THEY WILL BE

Here are some uses:

<u>**Soy**</u> **amiga de Sara.** I AM A FRIEND OF SARA.

Nosotros <u>**éramos**</u> **jóvenes.** WE WERE YOUNG.

Ella <u>**era**</u> **rubia.** SHE WAS BLONDE (BUT NO LONGER IS).

Lo que <u>**será**</u>**, será.**   WHAT WILL BE WILL BE*

* From a song. Doris Day made the Italian version of the song famous in the movie "The Man who Knew Too Much."

Yo <u>**estoy**</u> **en casa.**
I AM AT HOME (IN THE HOUSE FOR NOW.)

La niña <u>**está**</u> **enferma.**
THE GIRL IS ILL (BUT WILL RECOVER.)

Los platos <u>**estarán**</u> **sucios.**

THE PLATES WILL BE DIRTY.

Ellos <u>**estaban**</u> **en Santa Fe cuando...** THEY WERE IN SANTA FE WHEN...

This sentence could end with what happened then, such as **cuando llovió** WHEN IT RAINED.

This is just an introduction to these two verbs. More details in other sections.

Going places

Another important irregular verb is **ir**, TO GO.

IR present

yo voy	I GO
tú vas	YOU go
usted va	YOU GO
él, ella va	HE, SHE GOES
nosotros vamos	WE GO
ustedes van	YOU (PL) GO
ellos van	THEY GO

IR past complete

yo fui	I WENT
tú fuiste	YOU WENT
usted fue	YOU WENT
él, ella fue	HE, SHE WENT
nosotros fuimos	WE WENT
ustedes fueron	YOU (PL) WENT
ellos fueron	THEY WENT

IR past on-going

yo iba	I USED TO GO
tú ibas	YOU USED TO GO
usted iba	YOU USED TO GO
ella iba	SHE USED TO GO
nosotros íbamos	WE USED TO GO
ustedes iban	YOU USED TO GO
ellos iban	THEY USED TO GO

IR future

yo iré	I WILL GO
tú irás	YOU WILL GO
usted irá	YOU WILL GO
él irá	HE WILL GO
nosotros iremos	WE WILL GO
ustedes irán	YOU WILL GO
ellos irán	THEY WILL GO

Nosotros vamos a casa de la abuela cada Navidad (domingo).
WE GO TO GRANDMOTHER'S HOUSE (THE HOUSE OF GRANDMOTHER) EVERY CHRISTMAS (SUNDAY).

Voy a votar porque ir a las urnas es importante.
I GO TO VOTE BECAUSE GOING TO THE POLLS IS IMPORTANT.

Here, the present **voy** takes on a future act, even though the election may not be until next November. It could also mean "going to vote today."

The commands are **ve, vaya** and **vayan.**

Ve con tu abuela. GO WITH YOUR GRANDMOTHER.

Vaya con Dios. GO WITH GOD.

Vayan al baño a lavarse los dientes.
GO TO THE BATHROOM (IN ORDER) TO CLEAN YOUR TEETH.

Compound interest

The verb **haber** (TO HAVE, TO HAVE TO) is used with other verbs to form compound tenses to express certain thoughts. These will be illustrated later. Meanwhile, here are the conjugations, in the usual order.

yo he	I HAVE
tú has	YOU HAVE
usted ha	YOU HAVE
él, ella ha	HE, SHE HAS
nosotros hemos	WE HAVE
ustedes han	YOU ALL HAVE
ellos han	THEY HAVE
yo hube	I HAD
tú hubiste	YOU HAD
usted hubo	YOU HAD
ella, él hubo	SHE, HE HAD
nosotros hubimos	WE HAD
ustedes hubieron	YOU HAD
ellos hubieron	THEY HAD
yo había	I HAD, I USED TO HAVE
tú habías	YOU HAD, USED TO HAVE
usted había	YOU HAD, USED TO HAVE
él, ella había	HE, SHE HAD, USED TO HAVE
nosotros habíamos	WE HAD, WE USED TO HAVE
ustedes habían	YOU HAD, USED TO HAVE
ellos habían	THEY HAD, USED TO HAVE

yo habré	I WILL HAVE
tú habrás	YOU WILL HAVE
usted habrá	YOU WILL HAVE
él, ella habrá	HE, SHE WILL HAVE
nosotros hemos	WE WILL HAVE
ustedes habrán	YOU WILL HAVE
ellos habrán	THEY WILL HAVE

There are many uses for this verb in idioms and everyday expressions. **Haber** is used with **que** when it becomes a semi-order, a suggestion of something to be done.

Among them:

Hay que limpiar (regar las plantas, estudiar, dormir, etc.) WE (YOU) MUST (IT IS NECESSARY TO) CLEAN (TO WATER PLANTS, TO STUDY, TO SLEEP, ETC).

This use comes in handy when dealing with employees, whether in a store, an office or in a home setting. It can imply a "WE MUST" as well as a "YOU MUST," or "WE OUGHT" or "WE SHOULD".

Some other examples of the use of **haber** don't use **que** and are a general statement or question rather than an order.

Hay muchas manzanas en la cesta.
THERE ARE MANY APPLES IN THE BASKET.

Hay luna llena.
THERE'S A FULL MOON.

¿Hay gasolina en el tanque?
IS THERE GAS IN THE TANK?

A similar construction with employees or family would use the verb **tener.** In these cases it is used with **que,** as with **haber.**

These are the conjugations in the present, which is a way to give orders, even to ourselves:

tengo, tienes, tiene, tenemos, tienen, tienen

Boss to employee:
Usted tiene que archivar estos papeles antes de las cinco.
YOU MUST FILE THESE PAPERS BEFORE 5 O'CLOCK.

Mother to child
Tienes que limpiar tu cuarto.
YOU MUST CLEAN YOUR ROOM.

31

Housewife to cleaning lady:
Tenemos que cambiar las sábanas.
WE MUST CHANGE THE (BED) SHEETS.

Self to self:
Tengo que llenar el tanque de gasolina.
I MUST FILL MY GAS TANK.

A general wish:
El gobierno tiene que gastar menos.
THE GOVERNMENT MUST SPEND LESS.

Tener is also used without **que** in expressions relating to TO HAVE, TO OWN, TO POSSESS:

Tengo hambre I'M HUNGRY
Tengo un amigo en Atlanta. I HAVE A FRIEND IN ATLANTA.
¿Tiene un lápiz? DO YOU HAVE A PENCIL?

Other useful verbs

Usar TO USE is a useful verb, especially when dealing with family or hired help. It means TO USE, TO EMPLOY.

Here are the conjugations:
Present: **yo uso; tú usas; usted, él, ella usa; nosotros usamos; ustedes, ellos usan.**
Past (complete): **usé, usaste, usó, usamos, usaron.**
Past (on-going): **usaba, usabas, usaba, usábamos, usaban.**
Future: **usaré, usarás, usará, usaremos, usarán.**

In Spanish **se usa** means "IT IS USED THIS WAY" or "THIS IS HOW WE DO IT." It's related to **se habla español**, meaning SPANISH IS SPOKEN HERE.

Keeping that in mind, here are some uses of **usar.**

Usamos este cuchillo para rebanar el pan.
WE USE THIS KNIFE TO SLICE BREAD.

Mañana usaremos los platos de papel.
TOMORROW WE WILL USE THE PAPER PLATES.

Por favor, usa (familiar)/**use** (formal) **esta escoba para barrer el piso de la cocina.**
PLEASE, USE THIS BROOM TO SWEEP THE FLOOR OF THE KITCHEN.

El trapo azul se usa para limpiar el lavamanos.
THE BLUE RAG IS USED FOR CLEANING THE WASH BASIN.

Ayer, cuando usé la manguera, se rompió.
YESTERDAY, WHEN I USED THE HOSE, IT BROKE.

Aquí reusamos* las bolsas de plástico.
HERE WE RE-USE THE PLASTIC BAGS.
*In Spanish **re**- works as in English.

Advancing a little

To start, we suggested you take one or another of the past tenses and learn that one, then learn the other. This was suggested to simplify life. It's now time to see a little more about their distinctions. Some of these differences are rather subtle.

The on-going past *(imperfect)* does suggest something that was happening routinely, while the completed past *(preterit)* suggests the event was finished by the time the speaker was describing it.

The on-going past can also suggest that when one event was going on something else happened.

Ella hablaba por teléfono todos los días.
SHE TALKED ON THE PHONE EVERY DAY. It does sound complete, but could also be used to preface something else that happened:

Ella hablaba por teléfono todos los días porque estaba enferma.
SHE TALKED ON THE PHONE EVERY DAY BECAUSE SHE WAS ILL.

This tense is also used to describe a period of time when something else happened:

La familia estaba en casa anoche cuando cayó un rayo.
THE FAMILY WAS HOME LAST NIGHT WHEN LIGHTNING STRUCK.

Some verbs change meaning between these two past tenses. **Saber** is among those. **Saber** is treated in Chapter 4 but this is the general idea.

Lo sabía I KNEW IT can mean I knew it over time.

Lo supe is also I KNEW IT, but implies you heard about it at a specific time.

These may not be terribly important in general conversations, so don't worry about them too much.

Reflexive verbs

Reflexive verbs are those in which the action is done to the subject. They take **me, te** or **se** (referring to the person). For instance, **se baña** YOU BATHE YOURSELF, or **se aburre** HE BORES HIMSELF. Some of these may sound strange to our ears, and learning them can come later. Here are some examples, including some negative results. Others are listed in the Chapter 11 Clothing and grooming.

Verb	example of use	English
acostarse	me acuesto.	I LIE DOWN.
	no me acuesto.	I DON'T LIE DOWN.
caerse	se cayó.	HE FELL.
	no se cayó.	HE DIDN'T FALL.
levantarse	me levanto.	I GET UP.
	no quiero levantarme	I DON'T WANT TO GET UP.
quemarse	se quemó con la vela.	HE WAS BURNED BY THE CANDLE.

Maybe?

Spanish also has subjunctive verbs, possibility verbs and more in the *woulda, shouda, coulda, mighta, maybe* ilk. Those are too advanced for the scope of this book.

Books to own and use

There are several books of conjugated Spanish verbs. Among these are *501 Spanish Verbs Fully Conjugated* (Baron's) and *2,000+ Essential Spanish Verbs* (Random House).

If you don't have one, buy one. These show up at used book stores, college and university book stores and even general purpose book stores. Some stores will order for you. These books can be ordered on line. If you don't buy on line, get a friend who does to get one for you.

These books have the complete conjugations, even for verbs that you may never need. More importantly, they can guide you through some of the trickier words, such as those that change spellings (**c** to **qu** to keep the **k** sound, those that go from **o** to **ue** and such).

It is also a good idea to find a basic grammar book for future reference. Needless to say you should have an English-Spanish/Spanish-English dictionary, the bigger the better, but find at least one reasonably modern one to include new techy terms.

4
IMPORTANT PAIRS
Parejas importantes

Several pairs of words need some extra explanation. These are **por** and **para** (FOR), **ser** and **estar** (TO BE), and **conocer** and **saber** (TO KNOW).

These explanations and examples may seem too limiting and detailed at first. Don't let that scare you. Read them over, then just keep them in mind for when the need arises. People you talk to will be tolerant and understanding of your confusion. Accept the corrections of those who speak Spanish natively and remember that things learned by mistake can make a more lasting impression that stuff merely memorized.

Two times for

You met **por** and **para** briefly in Chapter 2. Both are FOR, but with slight differences. These items should help illustrate the differences and show the use of these two words.

These are the ideas to jot on sticky notes and stick around the house where you can review them as you pass by.

POR is used in these occasions or activities:
The reason for doing something;
The cause or justification;
Movement through or around an area;
Provides a time frame or deadline;
With communication and transportation;
A trade or exchange;
When someone acts on behalf of another person;
In percentages;
In the multiplication tables in arithmetic;
With units of measure;
In asking and setting a price;
In ordering or sending for something;
Takes in tasks still to be done;
Takes in possibility of doing something in the near future;
It shows authorship;
It is used in a passive voice sentence because of, caused or known for;

Is used as "by way of," as in giving directions.

Sometimes **por** translates BY, PER, THROUGH, BECAUSE OF, and similar words, and TIMES (MULTIPLIED BY) in arithmetic.

POR *(the reason for doing something, cause, justification)*
El perro no quiere salir <u>por</u> la nieve y el frío.
THE DOG DOESN'T WANT TO GO OUT <u>BECAUSE OF</u> THE SNOW AND COLD.

Nos encontramos <u>por</u> casualidad.
WE MET (RAN INTO EACH OTHER) <u>BY</u> CHANCE.

POR *(movement around an area)*
Vamos por esa calle a la derecha.
LET'S GO BY THE STREET TO THE RIGHT.

Los ladrones entraron <u>por</u> la ventana del segundo piso y salieron <u>por</u> la puerta de atrás.
THE THIEVES ENTERED <u>THROUGH</u> THE WINDOW OF THE SECOND STORY AND LEFT <u>BY</u> THE BACK DOOR.

POR *(provides a time frame)*
Voy a Chicago <u>por</u> tres días.
I'M GOING TO CHICAGO <u>FOR</u> THREE DAYS.

El café hirvió <u>por</u> una hora.
THE COFFE BOILED <u>FOR</u> ONE HOUR.

POR *(communication, transportation)*
Mandé la carta (el paquete) <u>por</u> correo.
I SENT THE LETTER (THE PACKAGE) <u>BY</u> MAIL.

Ella habló <u>por</u> teléfono media hora.
SHE TALKED <u>ON</u> THE TELEPHONE HALF AN HOUR.

POR *(trade, exchange)*
Ella (Él) cambió el mantel rojo <u>por</u> el verde.
SHE (HE) CHANGED THE RED TABLE CLOTH <u>FOR</u> THE GREEN ONE.

En el mercado cambiaron mis bolsas <u>por</u> las de otro cliente.
IN THE MARKET THEY CHANGED MY BAGS <u>FOR</u> THOSE OF ANOTHER CLIENT.

POR *(an act on behalf of another)*
Un substituto dará la clase <u>por</u> mí.
A SUBSTITUTE WILL GIVE THE CLASS <u>FOR</u> ME.

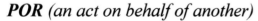

La cocinera hace comida por mi hermana.
THE COOK MAKES FOOD (AS A FAVOR) FOR MY SISTER.

POR (with percentages)
Cincuenta por ciento de los votantes son mujeres.
FIFTY PERCENT OF THE VOTERS ARE WOMEN.

El pago de esos impuestos es del 25 por ciento.
THE COST OF THOSE TAXES IS 25 PERCENT.

POR (in mathematics with multiplication)
Uno por uno es uno. (**uno** is singular and takes the singular verb)
ONE TIMES ONE IS ONE. (See Chapter 18 for more on math tables.)

Cinco por siete son treinta y cinco. (two or more are plural and take a plural verb form)
FIVE MULTIPLIED BY SEVEN IS 35. (In English we keep it

POR (with units of measure)
La carne se vende por libra.
MEAT IS SOLD BY THE POUND.

El límite de velocidad es de veinte millas por hora.
THE SPEED LIMIT IS 20 MILES PER HOUR.

POR (setting a price)
El carro se vende por dos mil dólares.
THE CAR SELLS FOR $2,000.

¿Cuánto pide por la computadora?
HOW MUCH ARE YOU ASKING FOR THE COMPUTER?

POR (sending for or ordering something)
Fueron por una pizza.
THEY WENT FOR A PIZZA.

Mandaron por la grúa.
THEY SENT FOR THE TOW TRUCK.

POR (tasks to be done at a future time)
Tengo algunas deudas por pagar.
I HAVE SOME DEBTS TO BE PAID.

Hay algunos planes por realizar.
THERE ARE SOME PLANS TO BE COMPLETED.

POR (possibility of doing something soon)

Estoy <u>por</u> salir al trabajo.
I AM <u>ABOUT TO</u> LEAVE FOR WORK

Estamos <u>por</u> casarnos.
WE ARE <u>ABOUT TO</u> BE MARRIED.

POR (shows authorship)

La primera novela moderna fue escrita <u>por</u> Cervantes.
THE FIRST NOVEL WAS WRITTEN <u>BY</u> CERVANTES.

POR (shows authorship)

Esa casa fue diseñada <u>por</u> Frank Lloyd Wright.
THAT HOUSE WAS DESIGNED <u>BY</u> FRANK LLOYD WRIGHT.

POR (because of, caused or known for)

Ese autor se conoce <u>por</u> escribir largas novelas.
THAT AUTHOR IS KNOWN <u>FOR</u> HIS LONG NOVELS.

Venezuela se conoce <u>por</u> tener la catarata más alta y el teleférico más largo del mundo.
VENEZUELA IS KNOWN <u>FOR</u> HAVING THE HIGHEST
WATERFALL AND THE LONGEST AERIAL TRAM IN THE WORLD.

PARA takes in destination, purpose, intent and use among others. Among these:
The recipient of something;
With a destination;
With words of action relating to purpose or use;
It shows a deadline or time element;
With verbs relating to work, the boss, a client;
Shows a comparison or contrast;
Shows something of oneself;
Shows advantage which **por** does, but in a different sense.
Sometimes **para** translates IN ORDER TO, CONSIDERING and similar words.

PARA (recipient)

La comida <u>para</u> el perro está en ese gabinete.
THE FOOD <u>FOR</u> THE DOG IS IN THAT CABINET.

El regalo es <u>para</u> usted.
THE GIFT IS <u>FOR</u> YOU.

PARA (destination)

Mi esposo salió <u>para</u> Santa Fe esta mañana.
MY HUSBAND LEFT <u>FOR</u> SANTA FE THIS MORNING.

Quiero que vengas <u>para</u> la cocina.
I WANT YOU TO COME <u>TO</u> THE KITCHEN.

PARA (purpose)
El microondas se usa <u>para</u> calentar la sopa.
THE MICROWAVE IS USED <u>FOR</u> HEATING THE SOUP.

Se usa* este jabón <u>para</u> lavar los platos y ese <u>para</u> la ropa.
WE USE THIS SOAP <u>FOR</u> DISHES AND THAT ONE <u>FOR</u> CLOTHES.

* remember that "**se usa**" is a somewhat impersonal, term for "WE USE" or "THIS IS USED FOR."

PARA (objective)
Estudia <u>para</u> ingeniero.
HE STUDIES (<u>IN ORDER TO</u>) BE AN ENGINEER.

Ella hace un pastel <u>para</u> celebrar el cumpleaños de su esposo.
SHE MAKES A CAKE (<u>IN ORDER) TO</u> CELEBRATE THE BIRTHDAY OF HER HUS-BAND.

Para (time element, deadline)
El pastel es <u>para</u> la próxima semana.
THE CAKE (PIE) IS <u>FOR</u> NEXT WEEK.

<u>Para</u> las ocho ya habremos senado.
<u>BY</u> EIGHT WE WILL HAVE HAD SUPPER.

PARA (relating to work)
Escribo <u>para</u> el periódico.
I WRITE <u>FOR</u> THE NEWSPAPER.

Mi hermano trabaja <u>para</u> el Sr. Fulano.
MY BROTHER WORKS <u>FOR</u> MR. DOE.

PARA (shows comparison or contrast)
<u>Para</u> ser un niño, escribe bien.
<u>CONSIDERING</u> HE'S A CHILD, HE WRITES WELL.

PARA (shows comparison or contrast)
<u>Para</u> no haber estudiado tanto, canta perfectamente.
<u>IN SPITE OF</u> NOT HAVING STUDIED MUCH, HE SINGS PERFECTLY.

PARA (shows something of oneself)
<u>Para</u> mí, el guacamole es el mejor modo de comer aguacate.
<u>FOR</u> ME, GUACAMOLE IS THE BEST WAY TO EAT AVOCADO.

Para nosotros es importante leer.
FOR US, IT IS IMPORTANT TO READ.

PARA (shows an advantage or disadvantage)
El cigarillo es malo para la salud.
CIGARETTES ARE BAD FOR ONE'S HEALTH.

Jugar al ajedrez es bueno para el cerebro.
PLAYING CHESS IS GOOD FOR THE BRAIN.

Which for?
¿Por o para?

The next two items can illustrate a difference between **por** and **para**. Here, **por** indicates "FOR THE SAKE OF," while **para** indicates the action is a favor.

Lo hizo por su primo.   HE DID IT FOR THE SAKE OF HIS COUSIN.
Lo hizo para su primo.   HE DID IT AS A FAVOR TO HIS COUSIN.

Quickies with por and para

Here are some quickies with these words.

¿Por qué?	WHY?
porque sí	BECAUSE YES (similar to BECAUSE I SAID SO).
porque no	BECAUSE NO (IT'S FORBIDDEN)
¿Para qué?	WHAT FOR?
para ti (usted) item	FOR YOU (as in giving a gift or other
por ejemplo	FOR INSTANCE, FOR EXAMPLE
por si acaso	JUST IN CASE
No sirve para nada.	IT'S NOT WORTH ANYTHING. IT IS USELESS.

To be and to be two
Ser y estar

These sentences show the difference between **ser,** being a permanent condition, and **estar**, being temporary. **Estar** is also used for location.
For the conjugations, see Chapter 3 or your verb book.
Ser is used with permanent states of being.
Ser is used with size, character and description when these are permanent or close to permanent, such as stages of life.
Ser is used with the clock and the calendar (time, date, etc.)

Estar is used with temporary states.
Estar is used with location.

SER (with permanent states, with characteristics of inanimate objects)

La casa es grande. THE HOUSE IS BIG.
El vidrio es duro. GLASS IS HARD.
Esta estufa es de gas. Esa es eléctrica. THIS STOVE IS GAS. THAT ONE IS ELECTRIC.

SER (with stages of life)
Es joven. HE (SHE) IS YOUNG.
Es viejo(a). HE (SHE) IS OLD.
Es calvo. HE IS BALD.

SER (with time and day)
¿Qué hora es? WHAT TIME IS IT?
Son las cuatro de la mañana. IT IS FOUR IN THE MORNING.

¿Qué hora era? WHAT TIME WAS IT?
Era la una de la tarde. IT WAS ONE IN THE AFTERNOON.

¿Qué día es? WHAT DAY IS IT?
Hoy es cinco de mayo. TODAY IS MAY 5.

¿Qué día era? WHAT DAY WAS IT?
Era la Navidad del 2011. IT WAS CHRISTMAS OF 2011.

¿Cuántos días hay en una semana? ¿Cuántos en un mes?
HOW MANY DAYS ARE THERE IN A WEEK? HOW MANY IN A MONTH?

Notice the agreement in number and gender in these examples: **Día** and **hora** are masculine. In the above they are singular. **Día** can be plural as in **Pasamos ocho días en Miami.** WE SPENT EIGHT DAYS IN MIAMI. Same with hora: **Estuvimos dos horas esperando a mi amigo.** WE SPENT TWO HOUR WAITING FOR MY FRIEND.

ESTAR
Estar is used for temporary conditions.
Estar is used for condition and location.

ESTAR (shows it is temporary)
El piso está limpio. THE FLOOR IS CLEAN.

La computadora está de venta. THE COMPUTER IS FOR SALE.

41

La gata está afuera. THE CAT IS OUTSIDE.

ESTAR (location and condition)

La licuadora está cerca del microondas. THE BLENDER IS NEAR THE MICROWAVE.

La escoba está en el garaje. THE BROOM IS IN THE GARAGE.

El lavaplatos está lleno. THE DISHWASHER IS FULL.

La carne estaba lista. THE MEAT WAS READY.

¿Dónde está el perro? WHERE IS THE DOG?

Here are some contrasts with **ser** *and* **estar**.

Ella es bonita. SHE IS PRETTY.
Ella está bonita (hoy). SHE LOOKS GOOD (TODAY).

Mi perro es muy bueno.　　MY DOG IS VERY GOOD. (BEHAVES WELL)
Estoy bien.　　I AM WELL.

El muchacho es de Arizona. THE BOY IS FROM ARIZONA.
El muchacho está en Arizona.　　THE BOY IS IN ARIZONA (TEMPORARILY).

El niño es malo (malcriado). THE BOY IS BAD (NAUGHTY).
El niño está mal (enfermo). THE BOY IS ILL.
Es feliz. (HE, SHE) IS GENERALLY A HAPPY PERSON.
Está feliz. (HE, SHE) IS HAPPY NOW, TODAY.

Las enchiladas son buenas. ENCHILADAS ARE NUTRITIOUS.
Esta enchilada está buena. THIS ENCHILADA IS TASTY.

Es seguro. IT'S SAFE.
Estoy seguro. I AM SURE.

El señor Salas es el jefe, pero no está aquí ahora.
MR. SALAS IS THE BOSS, BUT HE IS NOT HERE RIGHT NOW.

El árbol es grande y está floreciendo.
THE TREE IS LARGE AND IT IS IN FLOWER.

La niña está gritando porque es malcriada.
THE GIRL IS SHOUTING BECAUSE SHE IS BRATTY.

El carro es nuevo, pero está descompuesto.
THE CAR IS NEW BUT IT IS INOPERATIVE.

La puerta es de madera. La puerta está abierta.
THE DOOR IS OF WOOD. THE DOOR IS OPEN.

Los platos son azules y están sucios.
THE PLATES ARE BLUE AND THEY ARE DIRTY.

Estamos aburridos porque el candidato es aburrido.
WE ARE BORED BECAUSE THE CANDIDATE IS BORING (A BORING PERSON).

El gato está durmiendo porque es perezoso.
THE CAT IS ASLEEP BECAUSE HE IS LAZY.

Quickies with ser and estar

¿Cómo estás?	HOW ARE YOU?
Estoy bien.	I AM WELL (I AM FINE)
¿Donde estás?	WHERE ARE YOU? (familiar)
¿Donde está?	WHERE ARE YOU? (formal)
Estoy en __ (specify location)	I AM __ (specify location)
¿Dónde está el (la) ___ (item)	WHERE IS ___ (item)
Está ____ (location)	IT IS ___ (location)
¿De quién es el (la) __?	WHOSE IS ___? (item)
Es de __ (owner)	IT BELONGS TO ___ (owner)

How two know it
Conocer y saber

These words mean "TO KNOW" but with slight differences. These are irregular verbs, so you may need to consult your verb book for conjugations.
Saber has to do with knowing facts or knowing how to do something.
Conocer has to do with knowing people or things.

SABER (having knowledge about something)
Sabía un poco de español, pero lo olvidé todo. I KNEW A LITTLE SPANISH BUT I FORGOT IT ALL.

El perro no sabe cuándo ha comido suficiente.
THE DOG DOESN'T KNOW WHEN HE HAS EATEN ENOUGH.

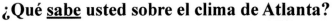

¿Qué <u>sabe</u> usted sobre el clima de Atlanta?
WHAT DO YOU <u>KNOW</u> ABOUT THE CLIMATE IN ATLANTA?

Más <u>sabe</u> el diablo por viejo que por diablo.
THE DEVIL <u>KNOWS</u> MORE BECAUSE OF HIS AGE THAN BECAUSE HE'S THE DEVIL.
This is an old "dicho" that one hears quoted often. A **"dicho"** is a "saying." Some of these parallel our English sayings, and others are original in Spanish.

CONOCER (related to knowing about certain things)

¿<u>Conoces</u> algo de la escritura de Cervantes?
DO YOU <u>KNOW</u> SOMETHING OF THE WRITINGS OF CERVANTES?

¿<u>Conoce</u> usted la música de Bizet?
DO YOU KNOW THE MUSIC OF BIZET?

CONOCER (related to knowing people)
This dialog demonstrates how it works:

¿<u>Conoce</u> usted al señor Martínez?
DO YOU <u>KNOW</u> MR. MARTINEZ?

There are three possible answers and the verb tense explains the anwer.

No lo <u>conozco</u>. (using the present tense)
I DON'T <u>KNOW</u> HIM . The answer implies that I never met him.

Lo <u>conocí</u> anoche. (using the completed past tense)
I <u>MET</u> HIM LAST NIGHT.
The implication is that you were introduced last night.

Lo <u>he conocido</u> por muchos años. (using the ongoing past tense)
I <u>HAVE KNOWN</u> HIM FOR MANY YEARS.
The present of **haber (he)** shows that the speaker has known the person for some time.

*Here some contrasts with **conocer** and **saber**:*

Él <u>sabe</u> todo lo que hay en el libro, pero no <u>conoce</u> ni películas ni canciones.
HE <u>KNOWS</u> EVERYTHING IN THE BOOK, BUT HE <u>KNOWS</u> NEITHER MOVIES NOR SONGS.

El perro siempre <u>conoce</u> a su amo, pero no <u>sabe</u> cuándo morder a un extraño.
THE DOG ALWAYS <u>KNOWS</u> HIS OWNER BUT HE DOESN'T <u>KNOW</u> WHEN TO BITE A STRANGER.

Ese cantante no <u>conoce</u> la música y por eso no <u>sabe</u> cantar.

THAT SINGER DOESN'T <u>KNOW</u> MUSIC AND FOR THAT REASON HE DOESN'T <u>KNOW</u> HOW TO SING .

Quickies with saber

Saber also appears in such idiomatic expressions as:

¿Quién sabe?	WHO KNOWS?
No sé.	I DON'T KNOW.
No lo sé.	I DON'T KNOW IT (IT, THE MATTER AT HAND).

5
LET'S TALK
Vamos a hablar

Now let's start with a few useful phrases. These will give you a start and we'll pick up more later.

Chatting at a lunch counter

Two people meet at a lunch counter and introduce themselves. Change the names as you wish. Later, after you've reviewed the food lists in other chapters, you can go back and change those, too.

`Susana speaks first:`
Buenos días. This is generally a way to start a conversation. It's about the same as "HELLO.")
GOOD MORNING. (**día** is DAY, but **buenos días** means "GOOD MORNING".)

Yo soy Susana. ¿Y tú?
I AM SUSANA. AND YOU?

> alternates are:
> **Yo me llamo* Susana.** I AM NAMED SUSANA.
> **Mi nombre es Susana.** MY NAME IS SUSANA.
> `*Other uses of` **llamar** `are treated later.`

`Sara answers:`
Yo soy Sara.
I AM SARA.

The waiter arrives.
¿Les puedo servir? `[servir]`
MAY I SERVE YOU?
*verbs in brackets will be explained later.

`Susana orders:`
Para mí, café con leche y un perro caliente**. De postre, quiero un helado.
FOR ME, COFFEE WITH CREAM (MILK)*** AND A HOT DOG. FOR DESSERT, I WANT A DISH OF ICE CREAM.
In many places, **hot dog is not translated because it is so universally known.
***leche is MILK, but **"café con leche"** is the English equivalent to "COFFEE AND CREAM."

Para postre, quiero una taza de   helado.
FOR DESSERT I WANT A DISH OF ICE CREAM

Sara places her order:
Yo quiero un refresco y una hamburguesa. *[querer]*
I WANT A SOFT DRINK AND A HAMBURGER.

The waiter leaves and the two resume their introductions, with Susana starting.

¿Dónde trabajas tú? *[trabajar]*
WHERE DO YOU WORK?

Trabajo en la oficina del señor Salas. ¿Y tú?
I WORK IN THE OFFICE OF MR. SALAS. AND YOU?

Soy cajera en un banco. Atiendo a los que vienen en automóvil.
[atender, venir]
I'M A TELLER IN A BANK. I SERVE THOSE WHO COME BY CAR.

The waiter brings the order and the two compare their lunches.

¿Cómo quieres tu hamburguesa? *[querer]*
HOW DO YOU LIKE YOUR HAMBURGER?

Me gusta caliente con tomate y lechuga.
I LIKE IT HOT WITH TOMATO AND LETTUCE.

Mi café está caliente y el perro caliente necesita mostaza. *[necesitar]*
MY COFFEE IS HOT AND THE HOT DOG NEEDS MUSTARD.

With lunch concluded, the women return to work.

How it works

Notice that the women say "**yo soy,**" using the verb **ser,** which is a permanent condition. With the food, the verb **estar** refers to a temporary condition. **Estar** would also be used if the hot foods were cold or if the soft drink had been warm.

Notice the drinks chosen by the women.

Refresco is a SOFT DRINK (SODA POP, COKE, PEPSI, 7-UP, ETC.).

Café is COFFEE. **Café con leche y azúcar** is COFFEE WITH CREAM AND SUGAR. **Leche** when combined with coffee is understood to be CREAM or even real MILK. Saccharine is **sacarina** or these could be named by trademark. POWDERED CREAM is labeled on packages as **crema no láctea para café**, which is rather long. A shorter term could be **crema en polvo** or **crema artificial** (POWDERED CREAM or ARTIFICIAL CREAM).

TEA is **té**. Iced, it's **té helado**.

JUICES are **jugos**. They are identified as **jugo de** (fruit name), thus **jugo de naranja** ORANGE JUICE, Lit: JUICE OF ORANGE; **jugo de manzana** APPLE JUICE, etc. But LEMONADE is **limonada**.

Hard drinks are **cerveza** BEER; **vino** WINE; **aguardiente** HARD LIQUOR; **whisky** WHISKEY etc. Some of these will merely change the spelling or pronunciation from the original language, such as **ron** for RUM.

Some foods don't translate or even transliterate into another language. For instance, there is no English word for **enchilada**, **taco** or **arepa**. Likewise, dishes such as CUP CAKES, GRITS, CORN PONE and CORN BREAD don't translate into Spanish.

Around town

Other social events are encounters in schools or work settings. When greeting a boss, professor or a person already known but is an "authority" type:

Buenos días, señor Fulano*. ¿Cómo está usted?
GOOD MORNING MR. DOE. HOW ARE YOU?

***Fulano** and **Fulano de tal** are equivalent to JOHN DOE.

You have a question for a boss or professor. Try something like this:

Tengo una pregunta. *[tener]*
I HAVE A QUESTION.

¿Me puede explicar esto? Por favor. *[explicar]*
CAN YOU EXPLAIN THIS, PLEASE?

¿Dónde dan las clases de matemáticas (biología, literatura)? *[dar]*
WHERE ARE THE CLASSES OF MATHEMATICS (BIOLOGY, LITERATURE)?

With close friends or children, the familiar **tú** is used:

Hola, amiga (amigo). ¿Cómo estás?
HELLO FRIEND. HOW ARE YOU?

Bien, gracias ¿y tú?
I'M FINE, THANK YOU, AND YOU?

Here are the other verbs in the above dialogs:

servir	TO SERVE **(le puedo servir)** commonly used in restaurants or stores
querer	TO WANT **(yo quiero)** can mean TO NEED as well as TO WANT
trabajar	TO WORK **(yo trabajo)** I WORK
venir	TO COME **(ellos vienen)** THEY COME
atender	TO SERVE, TO ATTEND TO **(yo atiendo)** I WAIT ON . . .
necesitar	TO NEED, TO LACK **(el perro caliente necesita)** THE (item) NEEDS
tener	TO HAVE **(yo tengo)** I HAVE
poder	TO BE ABLE TO **(me puede . . .)** a polite way to ask for or about
explicar	TO EXPLAIN **(me puede explicar)**
dar	TO GIVE **(dónde dan)** a way to say "WHERE ARE (CLASSES) HELD?"

These are very basic sentences. They deal with daily activities. More on these lines in the rest of the book. Use the space below to make notes of your own.

Calling, calling

Llamar has many applications. It can mean TO CALL, TO BE NAMED, TO TELEPHONE. And **llama** is also an animal in the camel family.

¿Cómo se llama usted? (formal)

¿Cómo te llamas? (familiar)

WHAT IS YOUR NAME?

¿Quién llama?

WHO'S CALLING?

Yo me llamo Fulano de tal

MY NAME IS JOHN DOE

I AM NAMED JOHN DOE

Llamar a gritos

CALLING BY SHOUTING

YELLING

Llamar por teléfono

CALLING BY TELEPHONE

El grosero llama al mesero

THE ILL-MANNERED MAN CALLS FOR THE WAITER.

Llamar al perro

TO CALL THE DOG

¿Por qué se llama la llama llama?

WHY IS THE LLAMA NAMED LLAMA?

an old play on words.

50

6
HOMES & FURNISHINGS
La casa y los muebles

Our houses
Nuestros hogares

These items can be found in an ordinary home, including the garage. Use sticky notes to label the various items to build up vocabulary.

Casa de dos pisos con garaje
TWO-STORY HOUSE WITH GARAGE

Casa estilo pueblo
PUEBLO STYLE HOUSE

Casa de dos pisos con balcón
TWO-STORY HOUSE WITH BALCONY

Casa de un piso con piscina
ONE-STORY HOUSE WITH SWIMMING POOL

In the house
En la casa

la **alfombra** THE RUG, THE CARPET

el **balcón** THE BALCONY

el **buzón** THE MAIL BOX

el **canalón** THE CANAL (to move water off a flat roof)

el **despacho, la oficina** THE HOME OFFICE

la **entrada** THE ENTRY

las **escaleras** THE STAIRS

la **esquina** THE CORNER (inside)

la **pared** THE WALL

el **pasillo** THE HALL

el **piso** THE FLOOR

la **puerta** THE DOOR

el **rincón** THE CORNER (outside)

la **salida** THE EXIT

el **sótano** THE BASEMENT

el **techo** THE ROOF

la **ventana** THE WINDOW

las **vigas** THE BEAMS

el **zaguán** THE ENTRY FROM STREET TO PATIO

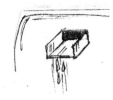

el canalón, el canal

THE CANAL

echa el agua del techo
MOVES WATER OFF A (FLAT)
ROOF

El niño ensucia el piso.
THE BOY SOILS THE FLOOR.

la puerta
THE DOOR

los buzones
THE MAILBOXES

la ventana con cortinas
THE WINDOW WITH CURTAINS

Mi casa tiene tres dormitorios.
MY HOUSE HAS THREE BEDROOMS.

Su casa tiene dos baños.
YOUR HOUSE HAS TWO BATHROOMS.

La casa de su hermano tiene garaje para dos carros.
YOUR BROTHER'S HOUSE HAS A GARAGE FOR TWO CARS.

Esa casa tiene un jardín con flores por todos lados.
THAT HOUSE HAS A FLOWER GARDEN ON ALL SIDES.

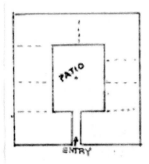

En las viejas casas de América Latina todos los cuartos daban al patio. La gente entraba de la calle por el zaguán.
IN OLD LATIN AMERICAN HOUSES ALL THE ROOMS FACED AN (OPEN) PATIO. PEOPLE ENTERED FROM THE STREET THROUGH A LONG HALL CALLED A **zaguán**.

53

La sala
The living room

La sala
el living *
THE PARLOR, THE LIVING ROOM
*Imported from English

el abanico eléctrico THE ELECTRIC FAN
la cama del perro THE DOG BED
la chimenea THE FIREPLACE
las cortinas THE CURTAINS, THE DRAPES
los cojines THE CUSHIONS
el cuadro en la pared THE PICTURE ON WALL
el estante para libros THE BOOK CASE
la mesa THE TABLE
el piano y el banco THE PIANO AND BENCH
la radio* THE RADIO
el reloj THE CLOCK
el sofá THE COUCH, SOFA
la silla THE CHAIR
la silla de cuero THE LEATHER CHAIR
la silla acolchonada THE UPHOLSTERED CHAIR
la silla de madera THE WOOD CHAIR
la silla moderna THE MODERN CHAIR
el televisor THE TV SET

el cuadro
THE PICTURE

*Sometimes one hears the radio reciever as **"el radio"** although technically it is feminine. The masculine **"el radio"** refers to the radius, as with a circle.

la silla moderna
THE MODERN CHAIR

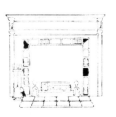

la chimenea
THE FIREPLACE

una silla de cuero
A LEATHER CHAIR

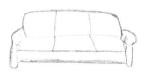

el sofá
THE SOFA

La sala (el living) es el cuarto más importante del hogar.
THE LIVING ROOM IS THE MOST IMPORTANT ROOM IN THE HOME.

El perro duerme en su cama mientras la familia mira el noticiero en la tele.
THE DOG SLEEPS ON HIS BED WHILE THE FAMILY WATCHES THE NEWS ON THE TV.

54

Las paredes de la sala son color marfil. La alfombra es persa.

THE WALLS OF THE PARLOR ARE IVORY (COLOR). THE RUG IS PERSIAN.

El sofá es rosado y los cojines son de distintos colores.

THE SOFA IS PINK AND THE CUSHIONS ARE OF DIFFERENT COLORS.

Las lámparas son modernas (antiguas).

THE LAMPS ARE MODERN (ANTIQUE).

La abuela teje en la sala cuando dan las noticias en la tele.

THE GRANDMOTHER KNITS WHILE THERE IS NEWS ON THE TV.

Caring for living room furniture
Cuidando los muebles de la sala

Usamos la aspiradora para limpiar la alfombra.

WE USE THE VACUUM CLEANER TO CLEAN THE CARPET (RUG).

Cada uno de nosotros tenemos nuestros productos favoritos para limpiar y pulir.

EACH ONE OF US HAS A FAVORITE PRODUCT FOR CLEANING AND POLISHING.

Se usan estos otros productos cuando limpiamos y pulimos en la sala:

WE USE THESE OTHER PRODUCTS WHEN CLEANING AND POLISHING IN THE LIVING ROOM:

Nombre de producto

PRODUCT NAME

_____	**cera para pulir madera**	WAX FOR WOOD
_____	**detergente para vidrio**	DETERGENT FOR GLASS
_____	**cepillo para la chimenea**	BRUSH FOR THE FIREPLACE
_____	_____	_____
_____	_____	_____
_____	_____	_____
_____	_____	_____
_____	_____	_____
_____	_____	_____

El comedor
The dining room

el florero con flores THE VASE WITH FLOWERS

un florero vacío AN EMPTY FLOWER VASE

el juego de café o té THE COFFEE OR TEA SERVICE

la mesa del comedor THE DINING TABLE

el mantel THE TABLE CLOTH

las servilletas THE NAPKINS

las servilletas de papel THE PAPER NAPKINS

las sillas del comedor THE DINING CHAIRS

la silla del bebé THE HIGH CHAIR

las ventanas con persianas THE WINDOWS WITH VENITIAN BLINDS

florero con flores
VASE WITH FLOWERS

la silla del bebé
BABY'S HIGH CHAIR

mesa de comedor
DINING TABLE

la silla de comedor
THE DINING ROOM CHAIR

las persianas
THE VENITIAN BLINDS

la cafetera con café
THE COFFEE SERVICE WITH COFFEE

La familia se reúne cada noche para comer y para convivir como familia.
THE FAMILY GETS TOGETHER EVERY NIGHT TO EAT AND FOR FELLOWSHIP AS A FAMILY.

Las cortinas se abren o se cierran con cuerdas.
THE CURTAINS ARE OPENED OR CLOSED WITH CORDS.

Caring for dining room furniture
Cuidando los muebles del comedor

Los muebles del comedor, porque son de madera fina, se limpian y se pulen con cera.

THE FURNISHINGS IN THE DINING ROOM, BECAUSE THEY ARE OF FINE WOOD, ARE POLISHED WITH WAX.

Se usan estos productos cuando limpiamos y pulimos en el comedor:

WE USE THESE PRODUCTS WHEN CLEANING AND POLISHING IN THE DINING ROOM:

Nombre de producto
PRODUCT NAME

_____ **crema para juegos de plata** SILVER POLISH

_____ **aromatizante para la alfombra** CARPET FRESHDNER

_____ **cera para las sillas de madera** POLISH OR WOOD FLOORS

_____ _____ _____

_____ _____ _____

_____ _____ _____

_____ _____ _____

_____ _____ _____

_____ _____ _____

_____ _____ _____

_____ _____ _____

The bedroom
El dormitorio

el dormitorio del matrimonio THE MASTER BEDROOM (COUPLE'S BEDROOM)

el dormitorio del niño, de la niña THE BEDROOM OF THE BOY, THE GIRL

el dormitorio del bebé THE BABY'S ROOM (THE NURSERY)

las almohadas THE PILLOWS

el buro THE NIGHT STAND

la cama THE BED (any size)

la cama de matrimonial THE BED OF THE COUPLE (a double, queen or king size bed)

la cama del gato THE CAT BED

la cobija THE BLANKET

el colchón THE MATTRESS

la cómoda THE CHEST OF DRAWERS

la lámpara THE LAMP

la radio, THE RADIO

el reloj despertador*THE ALARM CLOCK

*despertador from **despertar,** TO WAKE UP

las sábanas y las fundas de las almohadas THE SHEETS & PILLOW CASES

la silla THE CHAIR

la sobrecama THE BEDSPREAD

el teléfono THE TELEPHONE

el tocador THE DRESSING TABLE

_____ _____   _____

_____ _____   _____

la lámpara
THE LAMP

la (el) radio
THE RADIO

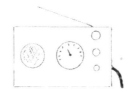
la cómoda
THE CHEST OF DRAWERS

la cama
THE BED

el tocador
THE DRESSING TABLE

The child's room
El cuarto del niño (de la niña)

la alfombra THE CARPET (RUG)
la cuna THE CRIB
el caballito THE ROCKING HORSE
el cuaderno THE NOTEBOOK
el escritorio THE DESK
los globos THE BALLOONS
los juguetes THE TOYS
los libros THE BOOKS
la mochila THE BACKPACK
las muñecas THE DOLLS
los pañales THE DIAPERS
los peluches THE STUFFED TOYS
la silla THE CHAIR
el tren THE TOY TRAIN

la cuna
THE CRIB

el peluche
THE STUFFED TOY

niños con juguetes
CHILDREN WITH TOYS

el caballito
THE ROCKING HORSE

la muñeca
THE DOLL

la mochila
THE BACKPACK

Cada niño tiene su propio escritorio en su cuarto.
EACH CHILD HAS HIS OWN DESK IN HIS ROOM.

Los niños leen y hacen la tarea de la escuela en su cuarto (en la sala).
THE CHILDREN READ AND DO THEIR HOMEWORK FROM SCHOOL IN THEIR ROOMS (IN THE LIVING ROOM).

Cuando yo era joven, mis padres nunca nos dejaron hacer la tarea de la escuela con la tele prendida.

WHEN I WAS YOUNG, MY PARENTS NEVER LET US DO OUR HOMEWORK FOR SCHOOL WITH THE TV ON.

El gato (perro) duerme sobre la cama del niño cuando él está en clase (la escuela).

THE CAT (DOG) SLEEPS ON THE BOY'S BED WHILE HE IS IN CLASS (IN SCHOOL).

Le echamos talco al bebé cuando cambiamos el pañal.

WE SPRINKLE TALCUM ON THE BABY WHEN WE CHANGE HIS DIAPER.

El bebé tiene por lo menos un peluche en su cuna.

THE BABY HAS AT LEAST ONE STUFFED TOY IN HIS CRIB.

Caring for baby
Cuidando el bebé

Se usan estos productos cuando cuidamos el bebé:

WE USE THESE PRODUCTS WHEN CARING FOR THE BABY:

Nombre de producto

PRODUCT NAME

_____	**crema para limpiar**	CLEANSING CREAM
_____	**pañales**	DIAPERS
_____	**jabón**	SOAP
_____	**talco**	TALCUM POWDER
_____	**aceite de bebé**	BABY OIL

The bathroom
El baño

la bañera, la tina THE TUB

el gabinete para medicina THE MEDICINE CABINET

los cepillos de dientes TOOTH BRUSHES

la cerámica, el mosaico THE TILE

la cortina de la bañera THE SHOWER CURTAIN

el drenaje THE DRAIN

la ducha THE SHOWER

el espejo THE MIRROR

el excusado, el inodoro THE TOILET

el lavamanos THE WASHBASIN

la llave, el grifo THE FAUCET

el papel higiénico TOILET PAPER

el taburete THE STOOL

las toallas THE TOWELS

*los productos para aseo propio PERSONAL HYGIENE PRODUCTS

*These are treated in more detail in **Chapter 11 Clothing and Care**

el gabinete
THE CABINET

**la llave,
el grifo**
THE FAUCET

las toallas
THE TOWELS

Esta casa tiene dos baños, uno para el matrimonio (marido y mujer) y otro para los hijos.
THIS HOUSE HAS TWO BATHROOMS, ONE FOR THE COUPLE (HUSBAND AND WIFE) AND ONE FOR THE CHILDREN.

En nuestra casa usamos un baño para las mujeres y otro para los hombres.
AT OUR HOUSE WE USE ONE BATHROOM FOR THE WOMEN AND ONE FOR THE MEN.

En las casas que tienen solo un baño cada persona tiene que tomar turno (hacer cola).
IN HOMES WITH ONLY ONE BATHROOM, EACH PERSON MUST TAKE TURNS (STAND IN LINE).

Los niños aprenden cuando pequeños que no deben meterse en el gabinete de las medicinas, en el baño.
CHILDREN LEARN WHILE THEY ARE LITTLE THAT THEY MUST NOT GET INTO THE MEDICINE CABINET IN THE BATHROOM.

Usamos productos distintos para limpiar la bañera y el lavamanos. Usamos un producto más fuerte para el excusado.
WE USE DIFFERENT PRODUCTS TO CLEAN THE TUB AND THE WASHBASIN. WE USE A VERY STRONG CLEANER FOR THE TOILET.

In the bathroom En el baño
Se usan estos productors para limpiar ___
WE USE THESE PRODUCTS FOR CLEANING ____

Nombre del producto
PRODUCT NAME

_____	**las ventanas**	THE WINDOWS
_____	**la bañera**	THE TUB
_____	**el excusado (inodoro)**	THE TOILET
_____	**el lavamanos**	THE WASH BASIN
_____	**las llaves (los grifos)**	THE FAUCETS
_____	**el piso**	THE FLOOR
_____	**la cortina de la ducha**	THE SHOWER CURTAIN
_____ _____	_____
_____ _____	_____
_____ _____	_____
_____ _____	_____
_____ _____	_____
_____ _____	_____
_____ _____	_____

La cocina
The kitchen
(Food and appliances covered in food chapters)

la basura THE GARBAGE

el bote de basura, el basurero THE GARBAGE CAN

el detergente para platos THE DETERGENT FOR DISHES

el drenaje THE DRAIN

los electrodomésticos THE ELECTRIC APPLIANCES*

la estufa, la cocina THE STOVE

la escoba THE BROOM

el gabinete THE CABINET

la gaveta, el cajón THE DRAWER

el lavaplatos THE DISH WASHER

la mesa de la cocina con sus sillas THE KITCHEN TABLE WITH ITS CHAIRS

el mostrador THE COUNTER TOP

la nevera, el refrigerador THE REFRIGERATOR

el reloj THE CLOCK

las toallas de papel THE PAPER TOWELS

los tubos del drenaje THE DRAINAGE PIPES

la vela THE CANDLE

* These are treated in Chapter 9

el lavaplatos
THE DISHWASHER

la nevera
el refrigerador
THE REFRIGERATOR

Muchas veces la cocina es el cuarto más usado de la casa.
MANY TIMES THE KITCHEN IS THE MOST USED ROOM IN A HOUSE.

Muchas familias comen casi todas las comidas en la cocina.
MANY FAMILIES EAT MOST MEALS IN THE KITCHEN.

El juego de mesa y sillas de la cocina es de metal y plástico y se cuidan fácilmente.
THE TABLE AND CHAIR SET IN THE KITCHEN ARE OF METAL AND PLASTIC AND ARE EASY TO CARE FOR.

Las luces en la cocina son LED y por eso los bombillos no se acaban en muchos años.
THE LIGHTS IN THE KITCHEN ARE LED, SO THE BULBS WON'T BURN OUT FOR MANY YEARS.

Nuestra ciudad tiene reciclaje para productos de papel, metal y plástico. Estos productos usados se botan en el contendor azul. La basura se bota en el basurero negro.
OUR CITY RECYCLES PRODUCTS MADE OF PAPER, METAL AND PLASTIC. THESE PRODUCTS WHEN USED ARE TOSSED IN THE BLUE BIN. GARBAGE PROPER IS TOSSED IN THE BLACK BIN.

In the kitchen En la cocina
Se usan estos productos para limpiar ____
WE USE THESE PRODUCTS FOR CLEANING ____

Nombre de producto
PRODUCT NAME

_____	**el fregador**	THE SINK
_____	**el mostrador**	THE COUNTER TOP
_____	**las llaves (los grifos)**	THE FAUCETS
_____	**el refrigerador**	THE REFRIGERATOR
_____	**la estufa (la cocina)**	THE STOVE
_____	**el lavaplatos**	THE DISHWASHER
_____	**el piso**	THE FLOOR
_____	**las ventanas**	THE WINDOWS
_____	**los electrodomésticos**	THE ELECTRIC APPLIANCES
_____	_____	_____
_____	_____	_____
_____	_____	_____
_____	_____	_____
_____	_____	_____
_____	_____	_____

The home office
La oficina, el despacho

el archivero THE FILE CABINET

el borrador THE ERASER

la carpeta THE FILE FOLDER

el clip THE PAPER CLIP

la computadora THE COMPUTER

el cuaderno THE NOTEBOOK

   el estante de libros THE BOOK CASE

   el escritorio THE DESK

   las gavetas THE DRAWERS

   la grapadora, el abrochador THE STAPLER

   la impresora THE PRINTER

   la lámpara THE LAMP

   el lápiz THE PENCIL

   los papeles THE PAPERS

   el pegamento, la goma, el pega-pega THE GLUE, PASTE

   la pluma THE PEN

la regla THE RULER

el sacapuntas THE PENCIL SHARPENER

la silla THE CHAIR

el teléfono celular THE CELL PHONE

la tinta   THE INK

la goma
THE GLUE

el calendario
THE CALENDAR

el teléfono
THE TELEPHONE

el escritorio
THE DESK

La mujer y el esposo tienen sus propias computadoras.
THE WIFE AND THE HUSBAND HAVE THEIR OWN COMPUTERS.

El señor usa su computadora para su negocio. La señora escribe novelas y usa la suya para escribir.
THE HUSBAND USES HIS COMPUTER FOR HIS BUSINESS. THE WIFE WRITES NOVELS AND USES HERS FOR WRITING.

El diccionario, un atlas del mundo, una enciclopedia y otros libros se encuentran en el despacho.   A DICTIONARY, A WORLD ATLAS, AN ENCYCLOPEDIA AND OTHER BOOKS ARE FOUND IN THE HOME OFFICE.

Notice the slight change of spelling for dictionary and encyclopeda from English to Spanish.

Nadie entra en el despacho cuando la puerta está cerrada porque el señor o la señora están trabajando y necesitan estar solos.
NO ONE ENTERS THE OFFICE WHEN THE DOOR IS CLOSED BECAUSE THE MAN OR THE WIFE ARE WORKING AND NEED TO BE ALONE.

No se usa la aspiradora cuando alguna persona está usando la computadora. La electricidad estática puede dañar la computadora.
THE VACUUM CLEANER IS NOT USED WHEN SOMEONE IS USING THE COMPUTER. THE STATIC ELECTRICITY COULD DAMAGE THE COMPUTER.

In the house
Adentro y por la casa

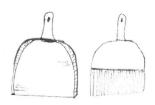

**el recojedor
y el cepillo**
THE DUSTPAN & BRUSH

**los fósforos,
los cerillos
las cerillas**
THE MATCHES

la bolsa de papel THE PAPER BAG

la bolsa de plástico THE PLASTIC BAG

el calefactor THE HEATER, HEATING SYSTEM

el calentador THE HEATER, WATER

la campana THE BELL

la cesta, la canasta THE BASKET

el cloro THE BLEACH

la extensión eléctrica THE EXTENSION CORD

los fósforos, los cerillos, las cerillas THE MATCHES

el globo THE BALLOON

la linterna THE FLASH LIGHT

el libro THE BOOK

la lupa THE MAGNIFYING GLASS

la pelota, la bola, el balón THE BALL

el recogedor THE DUST PAN

la revista THE MAGAZINE

las tachuelas THE THUMB TACKS (PUSH-PINS)

el teléfono celular, el celular THE CELL PHONE

el teléfono fijo THE FIXED (INSTALLED) PHONE

la linterna
THE FLASHLIGHT

**las tachuelas
y los clips**
TACKS AND THE CLIPS

la lupa
THE MAGNIFYING GLASS

La linterna se usa cuando hay un apagón.
THE FLASHLIGHT IS USED WHEN THERE IS A POWER FAILURE.

Se usa también la linterna cuando algo se busca detrás de un mueble o debajo de la cama.
THE FLASHLIGHT IS ALSO USED WHEN LOOKING FOR SOMETHING BEHIND A PIECE OF FURNITURE OR UNDER THE BED.

Los fósforos (los cerillos) se guardan en un gabinete alto dondo los niños no los alcancen.
MATCHES ARE KEPT IN A HIGH CABINET SO CHILDREN CAN'T REACH THEM.

Las tachuelas se usan para sujetar notas y agendas en el tablón donde la familia se comunica.
THUMB TACKS ARE USED TO FASTEN NOTES AND SCHEDULES ON THE BULLETIN BOARD THAT THE FAMILY USES FOR COMMUNICATION.

Around the house Por la casa

Se usan estos productos para limpiar ___
WE USE THESE PRODUCTS FOR CLEANING ___

Nombre de producto
PRODUCT NAME

_____	**las sillas acolchonadas**	UPHOLSTERED CHAIRS
_____	**las cortinas**	THE DRAPES
_____	**los muebles de madera**	THE WOOD FURNITURE
_____	**los productos de plástico**	THE PLASTIC ITEMS
_____	**los productos de vidrio**	THE GLASS ITEMS
_____	_____	_____

En el garaje
In the garage

el balde, el cubo THE BUCKET, THE PAIL

el basurero THE GARBAGE CAN

la bicicleta THE BICYCLE

las cajas THE BOXES

el carro THE CAR

la cuerda, el cordón THE STRING, THE ROPE

la escoba THE BROOM

las herramientas para el jardín THE GARDEN TOOLS

las herramientas para arreglos caseros HOUSEHOLD TOOLS
Casero is from **casa,** HOUSE. **Arreglos** is from **arreglar,** TO FIX.

el interruptor THE SWITCH

la lavadora THE CLOTHES WASHER

la secadora THE CLOTHES DRYER

El papá trabaja en madera en el garaje porque allí tiene un televisor para ver sus programas de deportes.
THE DAD WORKS WITH WOOD IN THE GARAGE BECAUSE THERE HE HAS A TV SET TO WATCH HIS SPORTS PROGRAMS.

Aquí él tiene sus herramientas para trabajar con madera.
HERE HE HAS HIS TOOLS FOR WORKING WITH WOOD.

El señor hace animalitos de madera con solo una navaja.
THE GENTLEMAN MAKES LITTLE ANIMALS OUT OF WOOD WITH ONLY A POCKET KNIFE.

La señora hace carteras de cuero y las vende a veinticinco dólares.
THE LADY MAKES PURSES FROM LEATHER AND SELLS THEM FOR $25.

Muchas familias guardan muchas cosas en el garaje.
MANY FAMILIES KEEP LOTS OF THINGS IN THE GARAGE.

A veces hay que botar o regalar las cosas que no se han usado en cinco años.
AT TIMES IT IS NECESSARY TO TO THROW OUT OR GIVE AWAY THOSE THINGS THAT HAVE NOT BEEN USED IN FIVE YEARS.

Algunos ponen arena sencilla (o arena para gato) en el piso del garaje debajo del carro para no manchar el suelo con el aceite que cae del vehículo.
SOME (PEOPLE) PUT PLAIN SAND (OR LITTERBOX SAND) ON THE FLOOR OF THE GARAGE UNDER THE CAR (SO AS) NOT TO STAIN THE FLOOR WITH OIL THAT FALLS FROM THE VEHICLE.

el balde
THE PAIL, BUCKET

la escoba
THE BROOM

el basurero
THE GARBAGE CAN

Here, there and everywhere

As in English, some Spanish words have multiple meanings. **Gancho** HOOK is one such word. **Ganchos**, like HOOKS, can be found in dozens of settings. These include, HOOKS on machinery of all sorts, HOOKS on horse gear, HOOKS in meat packing plants, HOOKS in various uses in architecture, construction and woodworking, HOOKS in restaurants for hanging coats or hats, HOOKS on firetrucks, hooks on musical instruments, and of course, HOOKS on the ends of fishing lines. Generally you will see these as **ganchos de** or **ganchos para**, with a description of use. HOOKS are also CLAWS on insects.

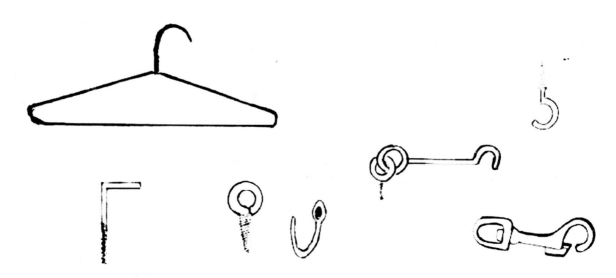

In the garage
En el garaje

Se usan estos productos para limpiar en el garaje
WE USE THESE PRODUCTS FOR CLEANING IN THE GARAGE

Nombre de producto
PRODUCT NAME

La escoba   **el piso**   THE FLOOR

_____   _____   _____

_____   _____   _____

_____   _____   _____

Cuando tenemos muchos objetos que no necesitamos, montamos una "venta de garaje."

WHEN WE HAVE TOO MANY OBJECTS THAT WE DON'T NEED, WE PUT ON A GARAGE SALE.

¿Qué hay de venta?

Veo un televisor, un mantel, unos libros, un gancho para abrigos, una mesita, un juego de golf, un espejo, unos jarros, dos lámparas y un sofá. ¿Qué ves tú?

WHAT IS FOR SALE?

I SEE A TV SET, A TABLECLOTH, SOME BOOKS, A COAT HANGER, A SMALL TABLE, A GOLF SET, A MIRROR, SOME JARS, TWO LAMPS AND A SOFA. WHAT DO YOU SEE?

7
IN THE KITCHEN
En la cocina

There are always chores in the kitchen or are otherwise related to food. In this and the next chapters we'll explore this favorite topic.

This list of kitchen items is for your use. Buy some sticky notes and use those to label items to use for reinforcing you vocabulary. Or use those notes to direct others in the family or to instruct the hired help.

The items are listed by general use rather than alphabetically. For instance instruments to grind are together, instruments for cutting are together and finally the handy-dandy electrical appliances are at the end. You have advanced enough in Spanish now that we are switching the English and Spanish subtitles, giving the Spanish first.

Utencilios
Utensils

Los platos, las tazas y lo demás para servir
THE PLATES, CUPS AND THE REST FOR FOOD service.

El juego de té o de café TEA OR COFFEE SERVICE SET
"**juego**" is used in the sense of "SET"

Los cuchillo, las cucharas, los tenedores
KNIVES, SPOONS, FORKS
El uso de las cucharas y los cuchillos es antiguos, pero el de los tenedores en la mesa no llegó hasta el siglo XVIII. SPOONS AND KNIVES ARE ANCIENT, BUT FORKS DID NOT COME TO USE AT THE TABLE UNTIL THE 18TH CENTURY.

El delantal THE APRON
Se usa delante del traje para no ensuciarlo.
IT IS USED IN FRONT OF THE CLOTHES SO AS NOT TO GET THE CLOTHES DIRTY.

Los libros de recetas COOKBOOKS
Empezaron a usarse alrededor de 1840.
USE STARTED IN THE 1840s

Ollas y cacerolas
Pots and pans

Las ollas y las cacerolas
POTS AND PANS
Cada tamaño tiene su propio uso.
EACH SIZE HAS ITS OWN USE.

El baño María
THE DOUBLE BOILER
Para cocinar en la olla de arriba con agua hirviendo en la de abajo.
FOR COOKING IN THE TOP PART WITH BOILING WATER IN THE LOWER PART.

La cacerola y la tapa
CASSEROLE AND LID
Se usa sin tapa o con tapa.
IT IS USED WITHOUT THE LID OR WITH THE LID.

El o la sartén
THE FRYING PAN
Utencilio sumamente antiguo. Los eléctricos son de la década de 1950.
A VERY ANCIENT DEVICE. ELECTRIC ONES FROM THE 1950S.
Dictionaries show both masculine and feminine for **sartén.**

La olla de presión
THE PRESSURE COOKER
Las caseras desde la década de los 1920s
HOME USE FROM THE 1920S

El wok
THE WOK
Olla de Asia para preparar platos típicos de la región
ASIAN DEVICE FOR PREPARING DISHES TYPICAL OF THE REGION

El molde para pan
THE BREAD MOLD
Para hornear pan
FOR BAKING BREAD

Los moldes redondos
ROUND MOLDS
Tienen muchos usos.
THEY HAVE MANY USES.

El balde
THE BUCKET, THE PAIL
Tiene muchos usos.
IT HAS MANY USES.

Para medir
For measuring

Las tazas de medir
MEASURING CUPS

Medir ingredientes empezó en 1896 con el libro de recetas llamado Boston Cook Book de Fanny Farmer.
MEASURING RECIPE INGREDIENTS DATES TO 1896 WITH FANNY FARMER'S BOSTON COOK BOOK.

Las cucharas de medir
MEASURING SPOONS

Para medir ingredientes
FOR MEASURING INGREDIENTS

El termómetro
THE THERMOMETER

Los primeros eran de Galileo (1593); Gabriel Fahrenheit hizo el primero usando mercurio.
THE FIRST ONES BY GALILIEO. FAHRENHEIT MADE THE FIRST ONES USING MERCURY

Preparando comida
Preparing food

El batidor, la batidora
EGG BEATER

En las cocinas desde la década de los 1870.
IN KITCHENS SINCE DECADE OF THE 1870S.

El machucador
THE (POTATO) MASHER

Para preparar más que papas
FOR PREPARING MORE THAN POTATOES

El palote, el rodillo
THE ROLLING PIN

Se usa para hacer galletas y panes
IT IS USED WHEN MAKING COOKIES AND SOME BREADS

El embudo
THE FUNNEL

Para mover líquidos o polvos de un utencilio a otro.
FOR MOVING LIQUIDS OR POWDERS FROM ONE UTENSIL TO ANOTHER.

El colador
THE STRAINER

Para separar granos pequeños
FOR SEPARATING SMALL GRAINS

El escurridor
THE COLANDER

Se usa cuando se lavan las verduras.
IT IS USED WHEN WASHING VEGETABLES.

El cedazo
THE SIFTER
Muchas recetas piden harina cedada.
MANY RECIPES CALL FOR SIFTED FLOUR.

La espátula y el cepillo
SPATULA & BRUSH
Tienen muchos usos.
THEY HAVE MANY USES.

Para cortar y batir
For cutting and beating

El rebanador de huevos
EGG SLICER
Para cortar huevos duros
FOR CUTTING HARD-BOILED EGGS

El rayador de queso
CHEESE SCRAPER
Se puede usar con zanahorias, ajos y otros ingredientes.
IT CAN BE USED WITH CARROTS, GARLIC AND OTHER INGREDIENTS.

El cortador de queso
CHEESE SLICER
Es de origen noruego.
IT IS ORIGINALLY FROM NORWAY.

El cascanueces
THE NUTCRACKER
Se usa para abrir nueces.
IT IS USED TO OPEN NUTS.

El molino de carne
THE MEAT GRINDER
Utencilio antiguo para moler carne
ANCIENT DEVICE FOR GRINDING MEAT

El molino de especies
THE SPICE GRINDER
Se usa para moler hierbas o especies.
IT IS USED FOR GRINDING HERBS OR SPICES.

El molino de café
THE COFFEE GRINDER
En uso desde 1820 cuando el café se vendía en forma de baya.
FROM 1820 WHEN COFFEE WAS SOLD IN BEAN FORM.

Las tijeras de cocina
KITCHEN SCISSORS

Son para cortar huesos, conchas, etc.
IT IS USED FOR CUTTING BONES, SHELLS, ETC.

Los cuchillos de cocina
KITCHEN KNIVES

Cada uno tiene su propia función.
EACH ONE HAS ITS OWN USE.

El pelapapas
POTATO PEELER

Es del siglo XIX.
IT IS FROM THE 19TH CENTURY.

Los afiladores
SHARPENERS

Hay manuales y hay eléctricos también.
SOME ARE MANUAL AND THERE ARE ELECTRIC ONES, ALSO.

Las latas
The cans

Las latas de comida
CANNED FOODS

La vida cotidiana cambió cuando se inventaron las latas de comida (siglo XIX). Con las latas es posible comprar carne y verduras todo el año.
DAILY LIFE CHANGED WHEN CANS FOR FOOD WERE INVENTED (19TH CENTURY). WITH CANS, IT WAS POSSIBLE TO BUY MEAT AND VEGETABLES ALL YEAR.

El abrelatas
CAN OPENER

Se usa desde 1858 para abrir las nuevas latas de comida; los eléctricos llagaron en la década de 1930.
FROM 1858 TO OPEN THE NEW CANS OF FOOD; ELECTRIC ONES FROM THE 1930s.

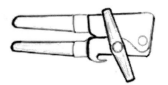

El abrebotellas
THE BOTTLE OPENER

Se usa desde 1838 cuando las tapas de botellas se hicieron más seguras.
IT HAS BEEN USED FROM 1838 WHEN MORE SECURE BOTTLE CAPS WERE BEING MADE.

Los electricodomésticos
The electric appliances

La batidora eléctrica
THE ELECTRIC MIXER

Se ha empleado en panaderías desde 1908; su uso casero es de 1919.
IT HAS BEEN USED IN BAKERIES FROM 1908; HOME USE FROM 1919.

La cafetera
THE COFFEE MAKER

Los modos de hacer café han cambiado poco desde que el café llegó a ser una de las bebidas más populares del mundo. Al principio, se hacía café echando agua hirviendo de la olla al café molido en la cafetera. Las cafeteras eléctricas que hacen el café automáticamente son del siglo XIX.
THE MEANS OF MAKING COFFEE HAS CHANGED LITTLE SINCE COFFEE BECAME ONE OF THE MOST POPULAR DRINKS IN THE WORLD. AT FIRST COFFEE WAS MADE BY POURING BOILING WATER ON THE GROUND BEANS. ELECTRIC COFFEEMAKERS, THAT MAKE COFFEE AUTOMATICALLY, ARE FROM THE 19TH CENTURY.

El tostador de pan
TOASTER

Los primeros son de 1909; los que se apagan automáticamente de 1926.
THE FIRST ONES ARE FROM 1909; POP-UPS FROM 1926

La licuadora
THE BLENDER

Las primeras eran para restaurantes; el uso casero empezó en la década de 1930
THE FIRST ONES WERE FOR RESTAURANTS; HOME USE FROM THE 1930S.

El tostador-horno, horno-tostador
TOASTER OVEN

Es del siglo XX; se usa como horno, para calentar comida o para tostar pan.
IT IS FROM THE 20TH CENTURY; USED AS AN OVEN, TO HEAT FOOD OR TO TOAST BREAD

El microondas
MICROWAVE OVEN

Los primeros aparecieron en 1954; los ejemplares caseros desde la década de 1970.
FIRST ONES APPEARED IN 1954; DEVICES FOR HOME USE FROM THE 1970S.

Otros utencilos de cocina
Other kitchen items

la balanza SCALE

la bandeja TRAY

la bolsa de papel BAG, PAPER

la bolsa de plástico BAG, PLASTIC

la botella BOTTLE

el calentador WATER HEATER

el cloro BLEACH

el corcho CORK

el detergente DETERGENT

la escoba BROOM

el horno OVEN

el jabón SOAP

la jarra PITCHER

el jarro JAR

el libro de recetas COOKBOOK

el mantel TABLE CLOTH

la pajilla, el popote STRAW

el papel de aluminio ALUMINUM FOIL

la pila BATTERY

el pimentero PEPPER SHAKER

el salero SALT SHAKER

la servilleta NAPKIN

las servilletas de papel PAPER NAPKINS

el tapa, el tapón LID

la toalla TOWEL

la toalla de papel PAPER TOWEL

la vasija, la bacía, el tazón BOWL

el vidrio GLASS

el vaso GLASS (DRINKING), TUMBLER

8
LET'S COOK
Vamos a cocinar

Here are cooking terms found in recipe books. Generally, they are written in a command form, as we do in English ("MIX THIS," "ADD THAT," etc.). Some may appear in the infinitive ("TO BEAT THE EGG" rather than "BEAT THE EGG.")

Herbs, spices and miscellaneous kitchen items are treated in earlier chapters.

Use these instructions when working with Spanish-speaking people, whether hired help or volunteers in a church kitchen. Or just try it on your own or your family to build up your skills in Spanish.

First, there is a list of words with their translations. Not every aspect of each word is included, only those that might be helpful when cooking. Also, what may appear as typographical or spelling errors are merely spelling changes in the conjugations of that particular verb. For instance, **cernir** is the infinitive, but **cierna** is the command form of the verb. There are several of these in the list. For a more complete list of the "odd" verbs, consult a Spanish conjugation book.

Palabras en recetas
Words in recipes

agregar, agregue, agregando means ADDING an ingredient to the mix. **agregado** means it has been mixed.

añadir, añada, añadiendo are similar.

amasar is to knead, as in making bread.

asar involves HEATING over a griddle; **asado** is the finished item.

batir, bata, batiendo is BEATING, or STIRRING BRISKLY, as with an eggbeater, fork or other device; **batido** is the beaten item.

blanda, blando is SOFTENED, as of meat or vegetables that have been cooked.

79

calentar, caliente, calentando tells you TO HEAT something; **caliente** also describes the heated item.

 cernir, cierna is SIFTING, as with the flour sifter, **(un cedazo);** or with a strainer, **(un colador)** See Chapter 9 for these devices.

cocinar, cocine is TO COOK; **cocinado** is cooked.

colar, cuele is FILTERING a liquid through a filter; **colado** describes the filtered product.

cortar, corte is TO CUT, usually with a knife.

cuajar is TO COAGULATE; **cuajado** is the coagulated item.

derretir tells you TO THAW a frozen item.

desleir, deslíe, diluir, diluya, DILUTING.

disolver, disuelva is DISSOLVING, as gelatin in water.

dorar, dore refers TO TURN GOLDEN by lightly frying in oil; **dorado** is the item turned golden. ("dorar" is related to El Dorado, the famed City of Gold of the days of exploration.)

echar, eche tells you TO ADD, TO PUT, TO TOSS IN, similar to **añadir** or **agregar.**

escaldar, escalde is related to the English TO SCALD, bathing in boiling water.

 **escalfar** is POACHING, as eggs.

escurrir, escurra is SQUEEZING water out of the item; **exprimir** and **exprima** are similar.

freír, fría is FRYING; **frito** is the fried item.

gratinar is BROWNING on top, as browning the tops of breads or cheeses.

guisar is a general term for COOKING; **guisado** is stew or a similar dish.

hervir, hirviendo, hierva refers to BOILING, as water or other liquid; **hervido** is the boiled item.

hornear is TO BAKE; **horneado** is the baked item.

lavar, lave tells you TO WASH the item.

licuar, licue tells you to LIQUIFY, as in a blender or juicing device; **licuado** is the resulting juice.

machacar, machaque is MASHING or POUNDING, as meat or potatoes.

mechar or **deshebrar** is SHREDDING, as in shredding meat; **mechada, deshebrada** is the shredded item.

menear, menee, meneando is STIRRING SOFTLY.

 **mezclar, mezcle, mezclando** is simply MIXING; **mezclado** is the mixed dish.

moler, muela involves MASHING herbs in a mortar. It can also involve passing meat through a meat grinder or coffee beans in a coffee grinder.

mondar is TO PEEL.

pelar, pele is PEELING; **pelado** is the peeled item.

picar, pique, picando involves CHOPPING FINELY, as with a knife; **picado** is the resulting little pieces.

poner, ponga, pon simply tells you TO PUT, TO ADD an ingredient to the mix.

rallar, ralle, rallando is SHREDDING on a shredder, as cheese or carrots; **rallado** takes in the shredded goods.

rellenar, rellene tells you TO FILL, TO STUFF, as with stuffed bell pepper or Thanksgiving turkey. **Relleno** describes the stuffed item.

revolver tells you TO STIR something.

rociar, rocíe involves COATING meat or other item with butter or whatever the recipe calls for.

sacar, saque, saca involves TAKING OUT, pulling out, removing.

sancochar, sancoche includes COOKING WITH A MEAT BASE; **sancochado** is the result.

sazonar, sazone is SEASONING as with herbs or salts.

servir, sirva is TO SERVE, once the dish is ready.

sofreír, sofría is FRYING LIGHTLY, SAUTEING.

triturar, triture is CHOPPING IN TINY PIECES, as in a blender; **triturado** is the result.

verter, vierta is POURING OUT or UN-MOLDING.

Recetas
Recipes

Here are samples from recipes from a South American cookbook. These are offered to get you started. More complete recipes later.

For this soup recipe, the ingredients include chicken or beef and a variety of vegetables, such as carrots, tomatoes, potatoes, celery and others.

Todos los ingredientes para el caldo se ponen en la olla y se dejan hervir hasta que la carne esté blanda.

ALL THE INGREDIENTS FOR THE BROTH ARE PUT IN A POT AND ARE BOILED UNTIL THE MEAT IS SOFT.

Luego se echan las verduras y se dejan hasta que estén blandas.

THEN ADD THE VEGETABLES AND LEAVE THEM UNTIL THEY ARE SOFT.

Se sirve caliente con galletas.

IT IS SERVED HOT WITH CRACKERS.

Some more sample lines from different dishes in the same book:

En su licuadora triture la cebolla, agregue el tomate pelado y sin semillas...

IN YOUR BLENDER, FINELY CHOP THE ONION, ADD THE TOMATO, PEELED AND WITHOUT SEEDS...

Sofría la cebolla en el aceite hasta que esté transparente.

SAUTÉ THE ONION IN THE OIL UNTIL IT IS TRANSPARENT.

Corte una corona a los pimientos y saque las semillas y el pellejo blanco. Rellene con granos de maíz...

CUT OUT A CIRCLE ON THE BELL PEPPER CROWNS AND TAKE OUT THE SEEDS AND THE WHITE MEMBRANES. FILL WITH WHOLE KERNEL CORN ...

>*<

Those above are just samples of what a Spanish cookbook may have.
Now here are some from an English language cook book:

Añada el queso, la harina y la paprika juntos. Mezcle la sopa y el agua en una olla. Caliente...
TOSS TOGETHER CHEESE, FLOUR AND PAPRIKA. COMBINE SOUP AND WATER IN A POT. HEAT ...

Mezcle media taza de agua, azúcar y canela. Hierva un minuto. Agregue el resto del agua. . .
COMBINE ½ CUP WATER, SUGAR AND CINNAMON. BOIL ONE MINUTE, ADD REMAINING WATER . . .

Lave y seque las naranjas. Quite la cáscara delicada con un cuchillo bien afilado. Corte la cáscara en pedazos delgados. . .
WASH AND DRY ORANGES. REMOVE THE THIN ORANGE RIND WITH A SHARP KNIFE. CUT RIND INTO VERY THIN SLIVERS. . .

>*<

Here's an easy recipe for juice.

Corte la pulpa de una sandía en pedazos y saque las semillas. Triture en la licuadora hasta que todo sea jugo. Agregue azúcar al gusto.
CUT WATERMELON PULP IN SMALL CHUNKS AND REMOVE SEEDS. PUT IN BLENDER AND RUN UNTIL ALL YOU HAVE IS JUICE. ADD SUGAR TO TASTE.

A regional word of caution when dealing with certain foods: **Salsa** in México is a sauce with chile. In other countries, **salsa** may or may not have chile. It could range from a spaghetti sauce with tomato to a white gravy for meat dishes.

>*<

Otras recetas
Other recipes
Here are a few complete recipes from a Latin American cookbook. Try these to add a bit of Spanish to your own cooking.

>*<

Mayonesa con aguacate
MAYONNAISE WITH AVOCADO.
Mezcle 2/3 de taza de aguacate machacado, ½ taza de mayonesa y 2 cucharaditas de jugo de limón. Esto es para servir imediatamente en la ensalada.
MIX 2/3 CUP AVOCADO MASHED, ½ CUP MAYONNAISE AND 2 TEASPOONS LEMON JUICE. THIS IS TO SERVE IMMEDIATELY IN A SALAD.

Salsa de tomate
TOMATO SAUCE

Se lavan 2 kilos de tomate.
WASH 2 KILOS OF TOMATO.

Se parten y se licuan, después se cuelan.
CUT AND BLEND THEM (IN A BLENDER), THEN FILTER THEM.

Se colocan en una caserola grande.
PLACE THEM IN A LARGE CASEROLE.

En 4 cucharadas de aceite se fríe 1 cebolla picada.
IN 4 TABLESPOONS OF OIL FRY 1 ONION CHOPPED.

Se agrega el tomate, 1 cucharada de azúcar, 1 rama de perejil y sal al gusto.
AND ADD THE TOMATO, 1 TABLESPOON SUGAR, 1 SPRIG PARSLEY, AND SALT TO TASTE.

Se pone todo al fuego, revolviendo con una cuchara de madera.
PLACE ALL OVER HEAT, STIRRING WITH A WOODEN SPOON.

Se disuelve 1 cucharada de harina en agua fría y se añade a esta mezcla ya retirada del fuego.
MIX 1 TABLESPOON FLOUR IN COLD WATER AND ADD TO THE MIX AND REMOVE FROM HEAT.

Se revuelve bien, se pone al fuego de nuevo unos minutos.
STIR WELL AND RETURN TO HEAT FOR A FEW MINUTES.

Se quita el perejil y se vuelva a colar.
REMOVE THE SPRIG OF PARSLEY AND FILTER AGAIN.

Una vez fría la salsa se envasa en frascos de cristal y se guarda en la nevera para usarla cuando se necesita.
ONCE COLD THE SAUSE IS PLACED IN GLASS JARS AND IS KEPT IN THE REFRIGERATOR FOR USE AS NEEDED.

>*<

Tortilla de jamón
HAM TORTILLA

Colocar en el recipiente de la licuadora:
PLACE IN THE CONTAINER OF A BLENDER:

5 huevos, 1 cebolla pequeña, 1 cucharada de perejil y sal y pimienta al gusto.
5 EGGS, 1 SMALL ONION, 1 TABLESPOON PARSLEY, AND SALT AND PEPPER TO TASTE.

Tapar y licuar a alta velocidad por 30 segundos, sin parar.
COVER AND BLEND AT HIGH SPEED FOR 30 SECONDS WITHOUT STOPPING.

Agregar ½ taza de jamón picado o cortado en trocitos.
ADD ½ CUP HAM, CHOPPED OR CUT IN SMALL PIECES.

Licuar hasta obtener una pasta muy tersa.
BLEND UNTIL IT RESULTS IN A SMOOTH PASTE.

Poner 2 cucharadas de manteca en una sartén.
PLACE 2 TABLESPOONS LARD IN A FRYING PAN.

Cuando esté bien caliente, agregar la mezcla de los huevos.
WHEN IT IS VRY HOT, ADD THE EGG MIX.

Cuando empiece a cuajar, doblar la tortilla y enrollar en la misma sartén.
WHEN IT STARTS TO GEL, FOLD IT OVER AND ROLL IT IN THE SAME FRYING PAN.

Debe quedar dorada por fuera y tierna por dentro.
IT SHOULD RESULT GOLDEN OUTSIDE AND SOFT INSIDE.

>*<

Budín de carne
MEAT LOAF

Poner 1 kilo de carne molida en un tazón.
PLACE 1 KILO OF GROUND MEAT IN A LARGE BOWL.

Poner en el recipiente de la licuadora estos ingredientes:
PUT IN THE CONTAINER OF A BLENDER THESE INGREDIENTS:

1½ taza de frijoles en lata, sin caldo; ½ taza del caldo de los frijoles; 1 rodajita de cebolla;
1 ½ CUP CANNED BEANS, DRAINED; ½ CUP LIQUID FROM THE BEANS; 1 SLICE ONION;

¼ taza de apio picado; 1/8 de cuchara de pimienta y 1 rebanada de pimiento verde.
¼ cup celery chopped; 1/8 tablespoon pepper, and 1 slice green bell pepper.

Mezclar a alta velocidad hasta que las legumbres estén parcialmente picadas.
BLEND AT HIGH SPEED UNTIL THE VEGETABLES ARE PARTLY CHOPPED.

Sacar la mezcla, usando la espátula si es necesario.
REMOVE THIS, USING A SPATULA IF NECESSARY.

Poner esta mezcla con la carne y revolver bien con una cuchara.
PLACE THIS MIX WITH THE MEAT AND STIR THOROUGHLY WITH A SPOON.

Poner en un molde para pan. Encima colocar 2 tiras de tocino.
PLACE IN A BREAD MOLD. TOP WITH 2 SLICES OF BACON.

Hornear 1 hora a 365ºF. BAKE 1 HOUR AT 365ºF.

>*<

Yuca frita
FRIED YUCA (one "c")

Hasta hace pocos años, la yuca no se conseguía en los supermercados de los EEUU. Actualmente se encuentra de vez en cuando.

UNTIL A FEW YEARS AGO, YUCA (CASSAVA) COULD NOT BE FOUND IN SUPERMARKETS IN THE U.S. IT NOW SHOWS UP OCCASIONALLY.

La yuca es muy dura. Primero se pela. Para pelarla se necesita un cuchillo bien afilado. Se quita toda la piel.

YUCA IS VERY HARD. FIRST IT IS PEELED. TO PEEL IT YOU NEED A VERY SHARP KNIFE. TAKE OFF ALL THE SKIN.

Se corta en pedazos del tamaño requerido para servir.

CUT THE YUCA IN PIECES THE SIZE NEEDED FOR SERVING.

Se ponen estos pedazos en bastante agua y se pone a hervir. Cuando está hirviendo rápdamente, se bota el agua y se le agrega agua nueva y se repite esto dos o tres veces.

PUT THESE PIECES IN PLENTY OF WATER AND PUT THEM TO BOIL. WHEN THEY ARE BOILING RAPIDLY, DUMP THE WATER AND ADD NEW WATER AND REPEAT THIS TWO OR THREE TIMES.

Cuando estos pedazos están blanditos, se sacan del agua. Se fríen en mantequilla (u otro producto para freír) con un poco de sal al gusto. Se fríen hasta que están dorados. Se sirven calientes.

WHEN THESE PIECES ARE SOFT, THEY ARE REMOVED FROM THE WATER. THEY ARE FRIED IN BUTTER (OR OTHER PRODUCT FOR FRYING) WITH A LITTLE SALT TO TASTE. THEY ARE FRIED UNTIL THEY ARE GOLDEN. SERVE HOT.

>*<

Masas
Doughs

La masa es una mezcla que se usa en muchas comidas antiguas y modernas.

MASA IS A MIX THAT IS USED IN MANY FOODS, ANCIENT AND MODERN.

La masa se hace mezclando harina con agua y revolviendo bien a mano, con una cuchara o con un electrodoméstico.

MASA IS MADE BY MIXING A FLOUR WITH WATER AND EITHER KNEADING IT OR MIXING IT THOROUGHLY BY HAND, SPOON OR ELECTRIC DEVICE.

En épocas antiguas se hacía masa con las semillas que se conocían, como el trigo, la cebada o el centeno.

IN ANCIENT TIMES MASA WAS MADE WITH THE SEEDS KNOWN THEN, SUCH AS WHEAT, BARLEY AND RYE.

Con el trigo se hace pan, tortillas y pasteles de muchas clases.

WITH WHEAT IS MADE BREAD, TORTILLAS AND PASTRIES OF MANY KINDS.

Los italianos usan masa de trigo para pizzas y raviolis.

THE ITALIANS USE MASA FROM WHEAT TO MAKE PIZZAS AND RAVIOLIS.

En el Continente Americano, se hace masa con maíz molido.

IN THE AMERICAN CONTINENT, MASA WAS MADE FROM GROUND CORN.

Este producto forma la base de muchos platos, como tamales y tortillas en México, arepas y hallacas en Venezuela y Colombia y pupusas en Guatemala y Costa Rica.

THIS PRODUCT FORMS THE BASE OF MANY DISHES TYPICAL OF THEIR OWN REGION, SUCH AS TAMALES AND TORTILLAS IN MEXICO, AREPAS AND THE HALLACAS IN VENEZUELA AND COLOMBIA AND PUPUSAS IN GUATEMALA AND COSTA RICA.

Se puede hacer masa con otros ingredientes, como coco o papas.

IT IS ALSO POSSIBLE TO MAKE MASA WITH OTHER INGREDIENTS, SUCH AS COCONUT OR POTATOES.

9
LET'S EAT
A COMER

Desde tiempos antiguos, los hombres han comido una variedad de carne, pan y productos lácteos. En siglos antiguos, la comida era lo que se conseguía cerca. En nuestra época, los viajes, la ciencia y los inventos nos han puesto todo tipo de comida al alcance.

SINCE ANCIENT TIMES, PEOPLE HAVE EATEN A VARIETY OF MEATS, BREADS AND DAIRY PRODUCTS. IN THOSE EARLY CENTURIES, FOODS DEPENDED ON WHAT WAS AVAILABLE LOCALLY. TRAVEL, SCIENCE AND INVENTION HAVE MADE ALL KNIDS OF FOODS AVAILABLE TO US.

Las carnes
The meats

Ovejas y chivos SHEEP AND GOATS

Las ovejas y los chivos fueron los primeros animales domesticados.
SHEEP AND GOATS WERE THE FIRST ANIMALS DOMESTICATED.

Los restaurantes griegos ofrecen platos de carnero.
GREEK RESTAURANTS OFFER DISHES OF MUTTON.

Otros productos OTHER PRODUCTS:
> **El carnero** LAMB, MUTTON
> **El chivo** THE GOAT
> **La costilla de carnero** MUTTON CHOP
> **La leche de chivo** GOAT MILK

El ganado   CATTLE

El ganado es una industria de los estados donde hay bastante pasto.
RANCHING IS AN INDUSTRY OF THE STATES WITH PLENTY OF FORAGE.

Carne de res BEEF

El bistec y el lomo son los platos preferidos de muchos.
BEEFSTEAK AND LOIN ARE FAVORITE DISHES.
Para muchos, la carne de res es el plato principal de la cena.
FOR MANY, BEEF IS THE MAIN DISH OF SUPPER,

Otros productos OTHER PRODUCTS:
> **Las albóndigas** MEAT BALLS
> **La carne a la parilla** BARBECUED MEAT

La carne mechada SHREDDED MEAT
La carne molida GROUND MEAT
El hígado LIVER
El pastel de carne, budín de carne MEAT LOAF
El perro caliente HOT DOG
El riñón KIDNEY

Puerco PORK, PIG,

Algunas religiones prohiben comer carne de puerco.
SOME RELIGIONS FORBID THE EATING OF PORK.

En el mercado compramos jamón rebanado para sandwiches.
IN THE MARKET WE BUY HAM SLICED FOR SANDWICHES.

Otros productos OTHER PRODUCTS:
La chuleta PORK CHOP
El jamón HAM
La manteca LARD
La salchicha SAUSAGE
El tocino BACON

Los peces FISH

Si hay un mar, un lago o un río cercano, podemos comer pescado fresco.
IF THERE IS A SEA, A LAKE OR A RIVER NEARBY, WE CAN EAT FRESH FISH.

Cuando no tenemos ríos o el mar cerca, podemos conseguir pescado congelado.
WHEN WE DON'T HAVE A RIVER OR AN OCEAN NEARBY, WE CAN FIND FROZEN FISH.
Otros productos OTHER PRODUCTS:
El atún TUNA
Los camarones SHRIMP
La langosta LOBSTER
El salmón SALMON
La sardina SARDINE
La trucha TROUT

Las aves FOWL

Hay muchas recetas para platos con pollo.
THERE ARE MANY RECIPES FOR DISHES WITH CHICKEN.

El pavo se prepara para el día de Acción de Gracias.
TURKEY IS PREPARED FOR THANKSGIVING DAY.

Otros productos OTHER PRODUCTS:
El caldo de pollo CHICKEN BROTH
El ganzo GOOSE
El pato DUCK
El pavo TURKEY
La pechuga de pollo CHICKEN BREAST
El pollo frito FRIED CHICKEN
El pollo horneado BAKED CHICKEN

Productos lácteos
Dairy products

El queso CHEESE
El queso es un producto muy antiguo.
CHEESE IS A VERY ANCIENT PRODUCT.

Hay quesos con nombres difíciles de pronunciar.
THERE ARE CHEESES WITH NAMES THAT ARE DIFFICULT TO PRONOUNCE.

Otros productos OTHER PRODUCTS:

El queso blanco WHITE CHEESE

El queso frito FRIED CHEESE

El queso mozzarella MOZZARELLA CHEESE

El queso parmesano PARMESAN CHEESE

El queso suizo SWISS CHEESE

El requesón COTTAGE CHEESE

El yogur YOGURT

La leche MILK
En el siglo XIX, Louis Pasteur, un científico francés, descubrió cómo pasterizar la leche y otras comidas.
IN THE 19TH CENTURY, LOUIS PASTEUR, A FRENCH SCIENTIST, DISCOVERED HOW TO PASTEURIZE MILK AND OTHER FOODS.

La leche se usa en muchas recetas de cocina, incluyendo dulces y bebidas.
MILK IS USED IN MANY FOOD RECIPES, INCLUDING CANDY AND DRINKS.

Para hacer dulces de chocolate, se necesita mezclar el chocolate con leche y azúcar.
TO MAKE CHOCOLATE CANDY, IT IS NECESSARY TO MIX THE CHOCOLATE WITH MILK AND SUGAR.

Otros productos OTHER PRODUCTS:

La crema CREAM

La crema en polvo POWDERED CREAM

La leche condensada azucarada SWEETENED CONDENSED MILK

La leche de almendra ALMOND MILK

La leche de chivo GOAT MILK

La leche de nogal MILK FROM PECAN OR WALNUT

La leche evaporada EVAPORATED MILK

La leche en polvo POWDERED MILK

La mantequilla BUTTER

El suero BUTTERMILK

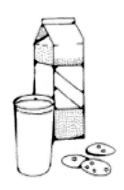

Los huevos
Eggs

Los huevos EGGS
Un huevo tiene tres partes: la clara, la yema y el casco.
AN EGG HAS THREE PARTS: THE WHITE, THE YOLK AND THE SHELL.

Los huevos se usan en recetas de pastas, de pan y de muchos otros platos.
EGGS ARE USED IN RECIPES FOR PASTA, BREAD AND MANY OTHER DISHES.

Otros productos OTHER PRODUCTS:

    Los huevos cocidos duros HARD-BOILED EGGS
    Los huevos escalfados POACHED EGGS
    Los huevos fritos FRIED EGGS
    Los huevos hervidos BOILED EGGS
    Los huevos pasados por agua SOFT-BOILED EGGS
    Los huevos revueltos SCRAMBLED EGGS

Los panes y las pastas
Breads and pastas

Desde los tiempos más antiguos, el hombre entendió cómo hacer harina con semillas.
SINCE ANCIENT TIMES, MANKIND LEARNED TO MAKE A FLOUR FROM SEEDS.

Las semillas que se usaban – y todavía se usan – son las del trigo, el centeno, la avena, la cebada, el arroz y el maíz. El arroz se usaba en el oriente y el maíz en América.
THE SEEDS THAT WERE USED THEN — AND ARE STILL USED TODAY — ARE WHEAT, RYE, OATS, BARLEY, RICE AND CORN. RICE WAS USED IN THE ORIENT AND CORN IN AMERICA.

Los panes BREADS
Todas las mujeres del mundo se alegraron cuando se empezó a vender pan rebanado.
EVERY WOMAN IN THE WORLD WAS HAPPY WHEN SLICED BREAD STARTED TO BE SOLD.

Pan hecho en casa es riquísimo, pero cuesta mucho trabajo.
BREAD MADE AT HOME IS DELICIOUS, BUT IT TAKES A LOT OF WORK.

La levadura es lo que hace que el pan se eponge.
YEAST IS WHAT CAUSES BREAD TO RISE.

Otros productos OTHER PRODUCTS:
    El bizcocho BISCUIT
    La galleta CRACKER, COOKIE
    El pan de ___ BREAD MADE OF ___
    El pan de arroz RICE BREAD
    El pan de maíz CORNBREAD
    El pan de papas POTATO BREAD
    El pan francés FRENCH BREAD
    El pan tostado TOAST
    Los panqueques PANCAKES

Las pastas PASTAS
Casi todas las pastas se hacen con harina de trigo.
NEARLY ALL PASTAS ARE MADE WITH WHEAT FLOUR.

Los italianos hacen muchos tipos de pasta.
ITALIANS MAKE MANY KINDS OF PASTAS.

Otros productos OTHER PRODUCTS:

> **El espagueti** SPAGHETTI
> **Los macarrones** MACARONI
> **La pizza** PIZZA
> **El ravioli** RAVIOLI
> **El tallarín** NOODLES

En la cocina
In the kitchen

También se usa en la cocina:
ALSO USED IN THE KITCHEN:

> **El aceite** OIL
> **El agua** WATER
> **El azúcar** SUGAR
> **El bicarbonato de sodio** BAKING SODA
> **Los champiñones** MUSHROOMS
> **La gelatina** GELATIN
> **El hielo** ICE
> **La jalea** JELLY, JAM
> **El jarabe** SYRUP
> **La maicena** CORN STARCH
> **La mantequilla de maní** PEANUT BUTTER
> **La margarina** MARGERINE, OLEO
> **La mayonesa** MAYONNAISE
> **La mermelada** MARMALADE
> **La miel** HONEY
> **Las pasas** RAISINS
> **El polvo de hornear** BAKING POWDER
> **La salsa de ___** SAUCE MADE OF ___
> **La salsa de carne, la salsa blanca** GRAVY
> **La salsa de chile** CHILE SAUCE
> **La salsa de tomate** TOMATO SAUCE
> **La salsa Tabasco** TABASCO SAUCE
> **El vinagre** VINEGAR

Otros platos
Other dishes

¿Buscas otros platos comunes? Aquí hay algunos.
ARE YOU LOOKING FOR OTHER COMMON DISHES? HERE ARE SOME.

La comida congelada FROZEN FOOD

La comida rápida FAST FOODS

Las empanadas de carne MEAT EMPANADAS

Las empanadas dulces SWEET EMPANADAS

La merienda SNACK, PICNIC

El helado ICE CREAM

Las natillas CUSTARD

La paleta POPSICLE OR SIMILAR TREAT

Las palomitas POPCORN

Las papas fritas FRIED POTATOES, POTATO CHIPS*

Las papas horneadas BAKED POTATOES

El ponche PUNCH

El postre DESSERT

El puré de papas MASHED POTATOES

Los totopos CORN CHIPS

* In general Spanish usage, potato chips and fried potatoes are **papas fritas**.

El desayuno
Breakfast

Here are some sentences with food terms. Use these as you go about cooking and serving the family.

El desayuno es importante.

BREAKFAST IS IMPORTANT.

Aquí nos gusta desayunar con avena caliente, pan tostado con mermelada, jugo de naranja y café con leche.

HERE WE LIKE BREAKFAST WITH HOT OATMEAL, TOAST WITH MARMALADE, ORANGE JUICE AND COFFEE WITH CREAM.

Remember that **leche** is MILK, but it generally means CREAM when coffee is involved.

Si estamos apurados, comemos un cereal frío con leche.

IF WE ARE IN A HURRY, WE EAT A COLD CEREAL WITH MILK.

Los domingos comemos panqueques o gofres* con jarabe.

ON SUNDAYS WE EAT PANCAKES OR WAFFLES WITH SYRUP.

*Many Spanish-speaking people give the English word WAFFLES a Spanish pronunciation, so it comes out *wah-flehs*

Estamos a dieta y usamos poco azúcar.

WE ARE ON A DIET AND WE USE LITTLE SUGAR.

Estamos a dieta. Usamos la sacarina de los sobres amarillos (rosados, azules, verdes).

WE ARE DIETING. WE USE SACCHARINE IN THE YELLOW (PINK, BLUE, GREEN) ENVELOPES.

Yo prefiero la crema en polvo porque no enfría el café, como lo hace la leche de vaca.

I PREFER POWDERED CREAM BECAUSE IT DOES NOT COOL THE COFFEE, THE WAY CREAM FROM COWS DOES.

Nos gusta la comida orgánica y usamos azúcar.

WE LIKE ORGANIC FOODS AND WE USE SUGAR.

El almuerzo
Lunch

Para el almuerzo me gusta:
FOR LUNCH I LIKE:

– un sándwich de queso con tocino o jamón, tomates rebanados y lechuga.
- A SANDWICH OF CHEESE WITH BACON OR HAM, SLICED TOMATOES AND LETTUCE.

– una hamburguesa de carne de res*, con tomates, lechuga y mayonesa.
- A BEEF HAMBURGER, WITH TOMATOES, LETTUCE AND MAYONNAISE.
*carne de res translates "meat from cattle"

– un perro caliente (un hotdog) con mostaza.
- A HOT DOG WITH MUSTARD.

A veces tomo sopa de tomate con galletas.
SOMETIMES I EAT TOMATO SOUP WITH CRACKERS.

Preferimos pan (tortillas) de trigo integral en vez de pan blanco.
WE PREFER WHOLE WHEAT BREAD (TORTILLAS) INSTEAD OF WHITE BREAD.

El señor de la casa (mi esposo) no puede comer trigo. Por eso usamos pan de arroz o de maíz.
THE MAN OF THE HOUSE (MY HUSBAND) CAN'T EAT WHEAT. FOR THIS REASON WE USE BREAD MADE OF RICE OR CORN.

En el verano, cuando hace calor, tomo té helado o café helado.
IN THE SUMMER, WHEN IT IS HOT, I DRINK ICED TEA OR ICED COFFEE.

A los jóvenes les gustan los refrescos o la limonada.
YOUNG PEOPLE LIKE SOFT DRINKS OR LEMONADE.

En el invierno tomamos café caliente todo el día.
IN WINTER WE DRINK HOT COFFEE ALL DAY.

A mi hija le gusta el chocolate caliente con crema batida.
MY DAUGHTER LIKES HOT CHOCOLATE WITH WHIPPED CREAM.

La cena
Supper

Esto es lo que comemos para la cena:
THIS IS WHAT WE EAT FOR SUPPER:

– una sopa rica hecha de caldo de res, con tomates, granos de elote (jojotos), apio rebanado, papas cortadas y pepinos.
- A RICH SOUP MADE WITH BEEF BROTH, TOMATOES, WHOLE KERNEL CORN, SLICED CELERY, SLICED POTATOES AND BELL PEPPERS.

– jamón con piña, verduras y una ensalada
- HAM WITH PINEAPPLE, GREENS AND A SALAD.

– rosbif con puré de papas y ejotes cortados al estilo francés. Tomamos té porque es demasiado tarde para café.
- ROAST BEEF WITH MASHED POTATOES AND FRENCH CUT GREEN BEANS. WE DRINK TEA BECAUSE IT IS TOO LATE FOR COFFEE.

– espagueti y albóndigas con salsa de tomate y una ensalada de fruta.
- SPAGHETTI AND MEATBALLS WITH TOMATO SAUCE AND A FRUIT SALAD.
"Salsa" in Mexico has chile; in other countries chile is not necessary.

Si estamos apurados comemos platos congelados.
IF WE ARE IN A HURRY WE EAT FROZEN DINNERS.

Cuando era niña, los platos congelados no tenían sabor.
WHEN I WAS A LITTLE GIRL, FROZEN DINNERS HAD NO FLAVOR.

Ahora los platos congelados son mejores y hay varios de verdad deliciosos.
NOW FROZEN DINERS ARE BETTER AND SOME ARE ACTUALLY DELICIOUS.

También se hacen platos congelados para personas a dieta.
ALSO THERE ARE FROZEN DISHES FOR PEOPLE ON A DIET.

10
FOOD from PLANTS
Plantas Que Dan Comida

Frutas, nueces, vegetales y especies
Fruits, nuts, vegetables and spices

This list of some of our basic vegetables and fruits should help in learning the names of many of the items we eat. The list is by category and includes the **Spanish common name**, ENGLISH COMMON NAME and *scientific name*. The latter is of interest when you notice that many Spanish names resemble the scientific name, more so than in English. Try to spot these as you go through the list. Start with **trigo** and its similarity to *triticum*.

Nuestras comidas
Our foods

Los comestibles que comemos vienen de todas partes del mundo. Algunos son muy viejos y algunos tienen usos nuevos.

THE FOODS WE EAT COME FROM ALL OVER THE WORLD. SOME ARE VERY OLD AND SOME HAVE NEW USES.

Semillas
Seeds

El trigo WHEAT *Triticum sativum*
El uso del trigo es tan antiguo que su origen no se conoce.
THE USE OF WHEAT IS SO OLD THAT ITS ORIGIN IS NOT KNOWN.

Otros granos importantes son:
OTHER IMPORTANT GRAINS ARE:

El centeno RYE *Secale cereale*;

La avena OATS *Avena sativa*;

La cebada BARLEY *Hordium vulgare;*

El arroz RICE *Oriza sativa.*

El maíz, CORN *Zea mays*
Oriundo de América desde México a Chile, se cultiva por todo el mundo. Se usa en comidas, es fuente de jarabe y hasta se agrega a la gasolina.
ORIGINALLY FROM AMERICA, FROM MEXICO TO CHILE, IT IS GROWN THROUGHOUT THE WORLD. IT IS USED IN FOODSTUFFS; AS A SOURCE OF SYRUP AND IT IS EVEN ADDED TO GASOLINE.

Las lentejas LENTILS *Lens esculenta*
Oriundas de Europa y las regiones del Mediterráneo. Las lentejas figuran en la historia de Esaú y Jacob en la Biblia.
ORIGINALLY FROM EUROPE AND THE MEDITERRANEAN REGIONS. LENTILS FIGURE IN THE STORY OF ESAU AND JACOB IN THE BIBLE.

Los frijoles, los guisantes, los ejotes, las caraotas
BEANS, PEAS *Pisum spp, Phaseolus spp*
De origen de América del Norte. Son muy nutritivos.
ORIGINALLY FROM NORTH AMERICA. THEY ARE VERY NUTRITIOUS.
(There are dozens of varieties of peas and beans, with many common names and lots of named hybrids. These are beyond the scope of this book.)

El maní, el cacahuate PEANUT *Arachis hypogaea*
Originario, se dice que es del Brasil. Se cultivaba en tiempos precolombianos. Las semillas producen aceites, mantequillas, margarinas y productos industriales.
ORIGINALLY, IT IS SAID, FROM BRAZIL. IT WAS CULTIVATED IN PRE-COLOMBIAN TIMES. THE SEEDS PRODUCE OILS, BUTTERS, MARGARINES AND INDUSTRIAL PRODUCTS.

Bajo tierra
Underground

Las batatas, el camote, el boniato
SWEET POTATOES *Ipomoea batatas*
Oriundos de América del sur.
ORIGINALLY FROM SOUTH AMERICA.

La cebolla ONION *Allium cepa*
Oriunda de África y Asia. Hay muchas variedades: rojas, blancas, amarillas y más.
ORIGINALLY FROM AFRICA AND ASIA. THERE ARE MANY VARIETIES: REDS, WHITES, YELLOWS AND MORE.

El nabo TURNIP *Brassica rapa*
De origen desconocido es uno de los productos comestibles más antiguos del mundo.
ORIGIN UNKNOWN, IT IS ONE OF THE WORLD'S OLDEST FOOD PRODUCTS.

La papa POTATOES *Solanum tuberosum*
Oriunda del Perú. Los incas sabían cómo congelarlas secas para usarlas más tarde. Cambió el modo de comer en Europa.
ORIGINALLY FROM PERU. THE INCAS KNEW HOW TO FREEZE-DRY THEM FOR FUTURE USE. POTATOES CHANGED THE WAY PEOPLE ATE IN EUROPE.

El puerro LEEK *Allium porrum*
Originario de Europa y África. Se conoce desde tiempos antiguos.
ORIGINALLY FROM EUROPE AND AFRICA. IT HAS BEEN KNOWN SINCE ANCIENT TIMES.

El rábano RADISH *Rhaphanus sativus*
Oriundo de Europa. Las raíces se comen en ensaladas.
ORIGINALLY FROM EUROPE. THE ROOTS ARE EATEN IN SALADS.

La remolacha BEET *Beta vulgaris*

Se conoce del norte de Europa. Se usa como comestible. Otras especies se usan como fuente de azúcar.

KNOWN FROM NORTHERN EUROPE. IT IS USED AS A FOOD. OTHER SPECIES ARE A SOURCE OF SUGAR.

El taro TARO *Colocasia esculenta*

Una de las plantas cultivadas más antiguas. Se ha usado en el Oriente por diez mil años o más.

ONE OF THE OLDEST PLANTS IN CULTIVATION, IT HAS BEEN USED IN THE ORIENT FOR 10,000 YEARS OR MORE.

La zanahoria CARROT *Daucus crrota*

Se ha conocido desde la época de los romanos. Se comen las raíces.

KNOWN FROM ROMAN TIMES. THE ROOTS ARE EATEN.

Hojas y tallos
Leaves and shoots

La alcachofa ARTICHOKE *Cynara scholymus*

Lo que se come son las brácteas de las flores.

WHAT IS EATEN ARE THE BRACTS OF THE FLOWERS.

El apio CELERY *Apium graveolens*

Se conoce desde los tiempos antiguos en Europa y Asia. Se comen los pecíolos y las hojas.

IT IS KNOWN FROM ANCIENT TIMES IN EUROPE AND ASIA. THE PETIOLES AND LEAVES ARE EATEN.

El brócoli BROCCOLI *Brassica oleracea capitata*

Lo que se come son las florecitas todavía verdes.

WHAT IS EATEN ARE THE SMALL FLOWERS, STILL GREEN.

El coliflor CAULIFLOWER *Brassica oleracea capitata*

Lo que se come son las flores blancas por ser tapadas por las hojas.

WHAT IS EATEN ARE THE FLOWERS THAT ARE WHITE BECAUSE THEY WERE COVERED BY LEAVES.

El col de Bruselas, los repollitos de Bruselas

BRUSSELS SPROUTS

Brassica oleracea gemmifera

Oriundo de Europa.

ORIGINALLY FROM EUROPE.

El espárrago ASPARAGUS *Asparagus officinalis*

Oriundo de Asia y Europa. Se comen los tallos jóvenes.

ORIGINALLY FROM ASIA AND EUROPE. YOUNG SHOOTS (STEMS) ARE EATEN.

La espinaca SPINACH *Spinacea oleracea*

Oriunda de Asia. Se come cruda en ensaladas o cocinada en platos calientes.

ORIGINALLY FROM ASIA. IT IS EATEN RAW IN SALADS OR COOKED IN HOT DISHES.

La lechuga LETTUCE *Lactuca sativa*

Conocida desde tiempos antiguos; una de las hierbas de la pascua de los hebreos cuando salieron del Egipto. KNOWN FROM ANCIENT TIMES; ONE OF THE HERBS OF THE PASSOVER WHEN THE HEBREWS LEFT EGYPT

Frutas y nueces
Fruits & nuts

El abelmosco OKRA *Abelmoschos esculentus*
Oriundo del continente Asiático. Se usa en comidas del estado de Louisiana.
ORIGINALLY FROM THE ASIAN CONTINENT. IT IS USED IN FOODS OF THE STATE OF LOUISIANA.

La aceituna OLIVE *Olea europea*
Se han cultivado desde tiempos antiguos por sus frutos y por el aceite que ellos dan. Las aceitunas que comemos enlatadas se cocechan antes de madurar y se someten a unos baños y procesos para darles el sabor y el color que conocemos. Para aceite se cosechan maduros. El árbol de olivo puede vivir hasta mil años o más.
IT HAS BEEN CULTIVATED SINCE ANCIENT TIMES FOR THE FRUITS AND THE OIL THAT THEY GIVE. THE OLIVES THAT WE EAT FROM CANS ARE HARVESTED BEFORE THEY RIPEN AND ARE SUBJECTED TO BATHS AND PROCESSES TO GIVE THEM THE FLAVOR AND COLOR THAT WE KNOW. FOR OIL THEY ARE HARVESTED RIPE. THE OLIVE TREE CAN LIVE UP TO 1,000 YEARS OR MORE.

El aguacate AVOCADO *Persea americana*
Oriundo de América Central. Se cultivaba desde la época precolombina desde México a Perú. Se come crudo en ensaladas, guacamole y hasta en helado.
ORIGINALLY FROM CENTRAL AMERICA. CULTIVATED IN PRE-COLOMBIAN TIMES FROM MEXICO TO PERU. IT IS EATEN RAW IN SALADS, GUACAMOLE AND EVEN IN ICE CREAM.

El albaricoque APRICOT *Prunus armeniaca*
Oriundo de Asia y las regiones del Medio Este. Se dice que es el árbol de Adán y Eva.
ORIGINALLY FROM ASIA AND REGIONS OF THE MIDDLE EAST. IT IS SAID TO BE THE TREE OF ADAM AND EVE.

La almendra ALMOND *Prunus dulcis*
Lo que se come es la semilla como si fuera una nuez dulce, y se usa en confitería, como marzipán.
THE SEED IS USED AS A SWEET NUT AND IS USED IN CONFECTIONS, SUCH AS MARZIPAN.

La berengena EGGPLANT *Solanum melongena*
Oriunda de Asia. Se come frita o en otros platos calientes.
ORIGINALLY FROM ASIA. THEY ARE EATEN FRIED OR IN OTHER HOT DISHES.

La calabaza, la auyama PUMPKIN *Cucurbita pepo*
De origen desconocido. Se cultiva por sus frutos grandes que se usan en comidas y como ornamentos.
UNKNOWN ORIGIN. IT IS CULTIVATED FOR ITS LARGE FRUITS THAT ARE USED AS FOOD AND AS ORNAMENTS.

Las calabazas GOURDS, SQUASHES *Cucurbita spp*
Hay muchas clases de calabazas, varias de origen americano.
THERE ARE MANY VARIETIES OF GOURDS AND SQUASHES, MANY OF AMERICAN ORIGIN.

El cambur, el banano BANANA *Musa sapientum*
Parece que es oriundo de África. Hay muchas variedades de cambur. Cuando la planta da frutos, se muere. Se propaga una nueva mata por las rizomas que salen al morir la planta madre.
IT MAY HAVE ORIGINATED IN AFRICA. THERE ARE MANY VARIETIES OF BANANA. WHEN THE PLANT SETS FRUITS, IT DIES. A NEW PLANT IS PROPAGATED FROM THE RHIZOMES THAT SPROUT WHEN THE MOTHER PLANT DIES.

La cereza CHERRY *Prunus serotina*
Algunos tipos requieren otro cerezo cercano para la polinización.
SOME VARIETIES REQUIRE ANOTHER CHERRY TREE NEARBY FOR POLLINIZATION.

El chile CHILE *Capsicum anuum*
Esta es otra clase del género *Capsicumm,* pero tiene su propio carácter. Se usa sobre todo en la comida mexicana.
THIS IS ANOTHER VARIETY OF THE GENUS CAPSICUM BUT IT HAS ITS OWN CHARACTER. IT IS USED PRIMARILY IN MEXICAN FOODS.

El arándano azul o el chivacú BLUEBERRY *Vaccinium spp*
Se cultiva en suelos ácidos. Se usa como fruta de mesa y en jaleas, helados y otros dulces.
IT IS USED AS A TABLE FRUIT AND IN JELLIES, ICE CREAMS AND OTHER SWEETS.

La ciruela europea PLUM *Prunus domestica*
Oriunda de Europa. Se come fresca o en jaleas.
ORIGINALLY FROM EUROPE. IT IS EATEN FRESH OR IN JELLIES.

El coco COCONUT *Cocos nucifera*
Es posible que sea de las islas del Pacífico. Se encuentra en todas las regiones tropicales del mundo.
IT IS POSSIBLE THAT IT IS FROM THE ISLANDS OF THE PACIFIC. IT IS FOUND IN ALL THE TROPICAL REGIONS OF THE WORLD.

El dátil DATE *Phoenix dactylifera*
Esta palma se ha cultivado por siglos en Egipto y en otras partes de África y el Mediterráneo. Se cultiva por sus frutos y por la 'miel' que da.
THIS PALM HAS BEEN CULTIVATED FOR CENTURIES IN AFRICA AND THE MEDITERRANEAN. IT IS CULTIVATED FOR ITS FRUITS AND A 'HONEY' THAT IT GIVES.

El durazno PEACH *Prunus persica*
Oriundo de China. Se cultiva por todo el mundo.
ORIGINALLY FROM CHINA. IT IS CULTIVATED THROUGHOUT THE WORLD.

La frambuesa, la zarzamora BLACKBERRY, RASPBERRY *Rubus spp*
Hay docenas de especies de *Rubus.* Se comen frescas o en jaleas y jugos.

THERE ARE DOZENS OF SPECIES OF RUBUS. THEY ARE EATEN FRESH OR IN JELLIES AND JUICES.

La fresa STRAWBERRY *Fragaria spp*
Se conoce en Europa desde la época de los romanos. Hay especies de América del norte y del sur.
IT HAS BEEN KNOWN SINCE ROMAN TIMES. THERE ARE SPECIES FROM NORTH AND SOUTH AMERICA.

La granada POMEGRANATE *Punica granatum*
Se conoce desde los tiempos antiguos. Tiene muchas semillas. Hay un refrán que dice "el que come granada no come nada".
KNOWN FROM ANCIENT TIMES. IT HAS MANY SEEDS. THERE IS A REFRAIN THAT SAYS "HE WHO EATS POMEGRANATE EATS NOTHING."

La guayaba GUAVA *Psidium guayaba*
Oriunda de América tropical, desde México hasta Brasil y Perú. Se cultiva por su fruto que se usa en jugos y jaleas.
ORIGINALLY FROM TROPICAL AMERICA, FROM MEXICO TO BRAZIL AND PERU. CULTIVATED FOR FRUITS THAT ARE USED IN JUICES AND JELLIES.

El higo FIG *Ficus carica*
El cultivo del higo es antiguo. El higo se menciona en casi cada libro de la Biblia. Se come crudo o enlatado.
THE GROWING OF FIGS IS VERY OLD. THE FIG IS MENTIONED IN NEARLY EVERY BOOK OF THE BIBLE. IT IS EATEN RAW OR CANNED.

El kiwi KIWI *Actinidia deliciosa, Actinidia chinensis*
De origen chino. Se cultiva en Nueva Zelanda, en el Japón y en el estado de California en los Estados Unidos.
ORIGINALLY FROM CHINA. IT IS CULTIVATED IN NEW ZEALAND, IN JAPAN AND IN CALIFORNIA IN THE UNITED STATES.

El kumquat KUMQUAT *Fortunella marginata*
La más pequeña del grupo de los citros, la fruta se come con la piel.
THE SMALLEST OF THE CITRUS GROUP, THIS FRUIT IS EATEN WITH THE SKIN.

La lechosa PAPAYA *Carica papaya*
Oriunda de América central, se conoce en todos los países tropicales. Se come cruda y también es fuente de productos para ablandar la carne.
OF CENTRAL AMERICAN ORIGIN, IT IS KNOWN IN ALL TROPICAL COUNTRIES. IT IS EATEN RAW AND IT IS ALSO A SOURCE OF PRODUCTS TO SOFTEN MEAT.

El limón LEMON *Citrus limon*
Como la naranja, es de origen chino. Se cultiva por el sabor de sus frutos.
LIKE THE ORANGE, IT IS OF CHINESE ORIGIN. IT IS CULTIVATED FOR THE FLAVOR OF THE FRUITS.

La mandarina, la tangerina MANDARIN, TANGERINE *Citrus reticulata*
Esta fruta pequeña tiene cáscara fácil de separar de la pulpa.
THIS SMALL FRUIT HAS SKIN THAT IS EASILY SEPARATED FROM THE PULP.

El mango MANGO *Mangifera indica*
Se conoce desde tiempos antiguos en la India. Se cultiva en lugares tropicales por todo el mundo por su fruto, del cual hay muchas variedades.
KNOWN FROM ANCIENT TIMES IN INDIA. CULTIVATED IN TROPICAL REGIONS AROUND THE WORLD FOR ITS FRUIT, OF WHICH THERE ARE MANY VARIETIES.

La manzana APPLE *Malus domestica, M. communis*
Oriunda, se cree, del Cáucaso. Muchas clases de manzana se cultivan por todo el mundo.
ORIGINALLY, IT IS BELIEVED, FROM THE CAUCASUS. MANY VARIETIES OF APPLE ARE CULTIVATED THROUGHOUT THE WORLD.

El melón CANTALOUPE *Cucumis melo*
Se conoce desde tiempos antiguos en Asia y África. Hay muchas variedades.
KNOWN FROM ANTIQUITY IN ASIA AND AFRICA. THERE ARE MANY VARIETIES.

El merrey CASHEW *Anacardium occidentale*

Originario de América tropical, de México a Brasil. La semilla crece afuera del fruto. Se cultiva por las nueces y por el jugo que se hace de la pulpa.
ORIGINALLY FROM TROPICAL AMERICA, FROM MEXICO TO BRAZIL. THE SEED GROWS OUTSIDE THE FRUIT. IT IS CULTIVATED FOR THE NUTS AND THE JUICE THAT IS MADE FROM THE PULP.

La naranja ORANGE *Citrus sinensis*
Se cultiva en regiones tropicales y subtropicales por todo el mundo. Oriunda de Asia.
CULTIVATED IN TROPICAL AND SUBTROPICAL AREAS AROUND THE WORLD. ORIGINALLY FROM ASIA.

El pepino* CUCUMBER *Cucumis sativus*
El pepino se come crudo o enlatado. Se ha cultivado desde épocas antiguas.
CUCUMBERS ARE EATEN RAW OR CANNED. THEY HAVE BEEN CULTIVATED SINCE ANCIENT TIMES.

La pera PEAR *Pyrus communis*
Se desconoce su origen, pues se ha cultivado desde la antigüedad.
OF UNKNOWN ORIGIN, IT HAS BEEN CULTIVATED SINCE ANCIENT TIMES.

El pimiento* BELL PEPPER *Capsicum anuum*
El pimiento es de origen americano. Hay muchas variedades y colores, de verde a rojo. Se comen verdes o maduros. THE BELL PEPPER IS OF AMERICAN ORIGIN. THERE ARE MANY VARIETIES AND COLORS, FROM GREEN TO RED. THEY ARE EATEN GREEN OR RIPE.

La piña PINEAPPLE *Ananas comusus*
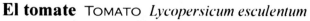
Oriunda de Mato Grosso, Brasil. Se cultiva en regiones tropicales a nivel mundial. Hay muchas variedades en el comercio.
ORIGINALLY FROM MATO GROSSO, BRAZIL. IT IS CULTIVATED IN TROPICAL REGIONS WORLDWIDE. THERE ARE MANY VARIETIES IN COMMERCE.

La sandía, la patilla WATERMELLON *Citrollus lanatus*
Oriunda de África tropical. Se ha cultivado por siglos. Se come rebanada. También se puede triturar para hacer jugo.
ORIGINALLY FROM TROPICAL AFRICA. IT HAS BEEN CULTIVATED FOR CENTURIES. IT IS EATEN SLICED. IT CAN ALSO BE BLENDED INTO A JUICE.

El tomate TOMATO *Lycopersicum esculentum*
Probablemente es oriundo del Perú. Desde América fue llevado a Europa y de Italia a los Estados Unidos. Es el fruto más cultivado en jardines caseros.
PROBABLY ORIGINALLY FROM PERU. FROM AMERICA IT WAS TAKEN TO EUROPE AND FROM ITALY IT CAME TO THE U.S. IT IS THE FRUIT MOST CULTIVATED IN HOME GARDENS.

La toronja, el pomelo GRAPEFRUIT *Citrus paradisi*
También es de origen asiático. Hay muchas variedades en el comercio. Algunas variedades no tienen semillas.
ALSO OF ASIAN ORIGIN. THERE ARE MANY VARIETIES. SOME DON'T HAVE SEEDS.

La uva GRAPE *Vitis vinifera*
El cultivo de la uva y la fabricación del vino son tan antiguos que no se conocen sus orígenes.
THE CULTIVATION OF GRAPES AND MANUFACTURE OF WINE ARE SO OLD THAT THEIR ORIGINS ARE NOT KNOWN.

Bebidas
Drinks

el café COFFEE *Coffea arabica*
Se originó en África o Arabia. El café se produce en muchos países tropicales. ORIGINALLY FROM AFRICA OR ARABIA. COFFEE IS PRODUCED IN MANY TROPICAL COUNTRIES.

El té TEA *Thea sinensis*
Bebida popular en China en siglos pasados. Llegó a Europa en el siglo XVII. Se toma caliente o helado. También se hacen tes de hojas, de flores, de frutas o de semillas de docenas de plantas. A POPULAR DRINK IN CHINA IN CENTURIES PAST. IT ARRIVED IN EUROPE IN THE 17TH CENTURY. IT IS CONSUMED HOT OR ICED. ALSO, TEAS ARE MADE FROM THE LEAVES, FLOWERS, FRUITS OR SEEDS OF DOZENS OF PLANTS.

El cacao, el chocolate COCOA, CHOCOLATE *Theobroma cacao*
Oriundo de América tropical. De las semillas se produce el chocolate de bebidas y dulces. La fruta que dan las semillas es grande y crece directamente del tronco del árbol. ORIGINALLY FROM TROPICAL AMERICA. FROM THE SEEDS ARE PRODUCED THE CHOCOLATE OF DRINKS AND CANDIES. THE FRUIT THAT PRODUCES THE SEEDS IS LARGE AND GROWS DIRECTLY FROM THE TRUNK OF THE TREE.

Los jugos JUICES
Los jugos vienen de frutas y llevan los nombres de las frutas, por ejemplo: jugo de manzana, jugo de patilla, jugo de naranja, jugo de limón o limonada. JUICES COME FROM FRUITS AND CARRY THE NAMES OF THE FRUITS, FOR INSTANCE: APPLE JUICE, WATERMELON JUICE, ORANGE JUICE, BUT JUICE OF LEMON IS LEMONADE.

Los refrescos SOFT DRINKS
Hay muchas marcas y muchos sabores, algunos con azúcar y otros marcados "lite" o "diet". THERE ARE MANY BRANDS AND MANY FLAVORS, SOME WITH SUGAR AND SOME LABELED "LITE" OR "DIET".

El chicle no es ni comida ni bebida, pero se mete en la boca. El chicle empezó con el uso de un producto del árbol *Achras zapota*, también conocido como chicozapote, en Guatemala, donde crece en la selva. La cocecha es cara, y ahora el chicle se hace con otros ingredientes. CHEWING GUM IS NEITHER FOOD NOR DRINK, BUT IT IS PUT IN THE MOUTH. CHEWING GUM STARTED WITH THE USE OF A PRODUCT FROM A TREE ACHRAS ZAPOTA, ALSO KNOWN AS CHICOZAPOTE IN GUATEMALA, WHERE IT GOWS IN THE JUNGLE. HARVESTING IS EXPENSIVE, SO CHEWING GUM IS NOW MADE WITH OTHER INGREDIENTS.

103

Hierbas y especies
Herbs and spices

In English there is a technical distinction between herbs and spices, herbs being annual or perennial plants of temperate or tropical origin. Spices are technically the seeds, bark or other parts of tropical trees or shrubs. There can be some shades of difference between these.

In this list, the spices and herbs are listed in alphabetical order in Spanish. An English cross reference is also included.

La ajedrea SAVORY *Satureja spp*
Se usa en recetas para rellenar el pollo o el pavo; también en platos con frijoles.
IT IS USED IN RECIPES FOR STUFFING CHICKEN OR TURKEY; ALSO IN DISHES WITH BEANS.

el ajo GARLIC *Allium sativum*
Se conoce desde tiempos antiguos en el Egipto. Hay referencias en la Biblia.
KNOWN FROM ANCIENT TIMES IN EGYPT. THERE ARE REFERENCES IN THE BIBLE.

La alacravea CARROWAY *Carum carvi*
Las semillas se usan en tortas y galletas dulces, en té y también se puede echar en sopas.
THE SEEDS ARE USED IN CAKES AND COOKIES, IN TEA TO DRINK AND THEY CAN BE PUT IN SOUPS.

La albahaca BASIL *Ocimium basilicum*
Las hojas se usan en platos italianos.
THE LEAVES ARE USED IN ITALIAN DISHES.

La alcaparra CAPER *Capparis licula*
Una planta de Asia tropical. Lo que comemos son las yemas de las flores del arbusto. A PLANT OF TROPICAL ASIA. WHAT WE EAT ARE THE BUDS OF THE FLOWERS OF THE SHRUB.

El anís ANISE *Pimppinella anisum*
Se usa en recetas de galletas, especialmente en los bizcochitos de Navidad.
IT IS USED IN COOKIE RECIPES, ESPECIALLY IN "BISCOCHITOS" FOR CHRISTMAS.

El azúcar SUGAR *Saccharum officinarum*
La planta es un tipo de grama, bastante grande. Se ha conocido por siglos, pero refinarlo como azúcar no se conoció hasta el siglo VII.
THE SUGAR PLANT IS A TYPE OF GRASS, QUITE LARGE. IT HAS BEEN KNOWN FOR CENTURIES BUT REFINED AS SUGAR WAS NOT KNOWN UNTIL THE SEVENTH CENTURY.

El berro WATERCRESS *Nasturtium officinale*
Crece en el agua. Las hojas se usan en ensaladas.
GROWS IN WATER. LEAVES ARE USED IN SALADS.

La canela CINNAMON *Cinnamomum camphora*
La canela viene de la corteza de un árbol de Asia y de las islas del Pacífico. Se usa en platos dulces.
CINNAMON COMES FROM THE BARK OF A TREE FROM ASIA AND THE PACIFIC ISLANDS. IT IS USED IN SWEET DISHES.

Los cebollines CHIVES *Allium schoenosprasum*
Oriundos de Asia. Se usan en ensaladas.
ORIGINALLY FROM ASIA. USED IN SALADS.

El cilantro, el coriandro   CILANTRO, CORIANDER *Coriandrum sativum*
Cuando se usan las hojas, el nombre es cilantro; cuando se usan las semillas, el nombre es coriandro. Es la misma planta.
WHEN THE LEAVES ARE USED, THE NAME IS CILANTRO; WHEN THE SEEDS ARE USED, THE NAME IS CORIANDER. IT IS THE SAME PLANT.

El clavo CLOVE *Syzygium aromaticum*
El clavo viene de un árbol de las islas del Pacífico.
CLOVE COMES FROM A TREE OF THE PACIFIC ISLANDS.

El comino CUMIN *Cuminum cyminum*
Se usa en enchiladas y otras recetas mexicanas.
IT IS USED IN ENCHILADAS AND OTHER MEXICAN DISHES.

El eneldo DILL *Anethum graveolens*
De Europa. Se usa preparando pepinos para enlatarlos.
FROM EUROPE. IT IS USED IN PREPARING CUCUMBERS FOR CANNING.

El estragón TARRAGON *Artemisia dracunculus*
Se usa en ensaladas, en sopas o con carne o pescado. Le da sabor a algunos vinagres.
IT IS USED IN SALADS, IN SOUPS OR WITH MEAT OR FISH. IT FLAVORS SOME VINEGARS.

El hinojo FENNEL *Foeniculum vulgare*
Se usa con pescado, con queso y con otros platos.
IT IS USED WITH FISH, WITH CHEESE AND IN OTHER DISHES.

El jengibre GINGER *Zingiber officinale*
El jengibre de la cocina viene de las raíces de una hierba tropical. Se usa en platos con pescado y en dulces.
THE GINGER OF THE KITCEN COMES FROM THE ROOTS OF A TROPICAL HERB. IT IS USED IN DISHES WITH FISH AND IN SWEETS.

El laurel BAY LEAF *Laurus nobilis*
Las hojas de este árbol se usan en sopas, salsas y con verduras. Tienen sabor fuerte.
THE LEAVES OF THIS TREE ARE USED IN SOUPS, SAUCES AND WITH VEGETABLES. THEY HAVE A STRONG FLAVOR.

La mejorana MARJORAM *Marjorana spp*

el orégano OREGANO *Origanum spp*

Estas dos yerbas se usan in platos de carne, pollo, queso y huevos.

THESE TWO HERBS ARE USED IN MEAT, CHICKEN, CHEESE AND EGG DISHES.

La menta, la hierbabuena MINT *Mentha* spp

Se usa para dar sabor al té helado y caliente. Hay muchas variedades de menta.

IT IS USED TO ADD FLAVOR TO TEA, ICED OR HOT. THERE ARE MANY VARIETIES OF MINT.

La mostaza MUSTARD *Brassica nigra*

Se vende en latas o en polvos. Se usa en hamburguesas, perros calientes y en varias recetas más.

IT IS SOLD IN JARS OR IN POWDER. IT IS USED IN HAMBURGERS, HOT DOGS AND VARIOUS RECIPES.

La nuez moscada NUTMEG *Myristica fragrans*

Oriunda de las islas Molucas. Es sólo el arilo rojo que cubre la semilla lo que se usa en comestibles y perfumes.

ORIGINALLY FROM THE MOLUCCAS ISLANDS. ONLY THE RED ARIL THAT COVERS THE SEED IS USED FOR FOOD AND PERFUMES.

El onoto ANNATTO *Bixa orellana*

Las semillas dan color rojo a la comida sin cambiar el sabor.

SEEDS GIVE RED COLORING TO FOODS WITHOUT CHANGING THE FLAVOR.

El perejil PARSLEY *Petroselium crispum*

Se usa en ensaladas. Es rico en Vitamina C. Cortado en pedacitos se usa en ensaladas, en sopas y en platos de huevo.

IT IS USED IN SALADS. IT IS HIGH IN VITAMIN C CUT IN LITTLE PIECES IT IS USED IN SALADS, IN SOUPS AND IN EGG DISHES.

El perifollo CHERVIL *Anthriscus cerefolium*

Las hojas son más finas que las del perejil. Se usa con pollo, en ensaladas y en otras recetas.

THE LEAVES ARE FINER THAN PARSLEY. IT IS USED WITH CHICKEN, IN SALADS AND IN OTHER RECIPES.

There are several spices with similar names:

El pimentón* ALLSPICE *Pimenta diocia*

Hay dos productos con nombres de pimentón. Este pimentón (ALLSPICE) **es un polvo que se usa en algunas recetas. Viene de la baya de un árbol de América tropical. Tiene sabor de canela, clavo y nuez moscada.**

THERE ARE TWO PRODUCTS NAMED **pimentón**. THIS ONE (ALLSPICE) IS A POWDER THAT IS USED IN SOME RECIPES. IT COMES FROM A BERRY. IT HAS THE FLAVOR OF CINNAMON, CLOVES AND NUTMEG.

La paprika, el pimentón*, PAPRIKA *Capsicum annuum*

Esta especie es el otro de los dos productos con nombres de pimentón, que también se conoce como paprika. Este se produce de una variedad del mismo género que el chile de la comida mexicana, Capsicum anuum. Se vende en polvo y es menos picante que el chile.

THIS IS THE OTHER OF THE PRODUCTS CALLED PIMENTÓN, WHICH IS ALSO KNOWN AS PAPRIKA. THIS ONE IS PRODUCED FROM A VARIETY OF THE SAME GENUS AS THE CHILE OF MEXICAN FOOD, CAPSICUM ANNUUM. IT IS SOLD IN POWDER AND IS LESS PUNGENT THAN CHILE.

La pimienta* PEPPER, BLACK PEPPER *Piper nigrum*

En los siglos pasados la pimienta llegaba de la India a Europa por mar, un viaje de casi un año. Esto es lo que empeñó a Cristóbal Colón a arriesgarse a buscar un viaje más corto a la India. Hay dos tipos de pimienta, la negra y la blanca. Para la negra los frutos se secan al sol. Para la blanca los frutos se cubren con agua y cuando se cae la piel, se secan.

IN PAST CENTURIES PEPPER CAME FROM INDIA TO EUROPE BY SEA, A VOYAGE OF ALMOST ONE YEAR. THIS IS WHAT PUSHED CRISTOBAL COLUMBUS TO RISK FINDING A SHORTER TRIP TO INDIA. THERE ARE TWO TYPES OF PEPPER, BLACK AND WHITE. FOR BLACK PEPPER THE FRUITS ARE DRIED IN THE SUN. FOR WHITE PEPPER THE FRUITS ARE SOAKED IN WATER AND WHEN THE SKINS FALL, THE FRUITS ARE DRIED.

!

Advertencia * warning

Con el pimentón hay que tener cuidado leyendo recetas. Uno se usa en postres o platos dulces, y el otro en platos un poco picantes, como sopa, carne o pollo.

With **pimentón** one must be careful reading recipes. One is used in desserts or sweet dishes, and the other in lightly pungent dishes such as soup, meat or chicken.

*

El romero ROSEMARY *Rosmarinus officinalis*

Oriundo de Europa y el Mediterráneo. Se usan las hojas en sopas, con carne y en perfumes.

ORIGINALLY FROM EUROPE AND THE MEDITERRANEAN. THE LEAVES ARE USED IN SOUPS, WITH MEATS AND IN PERFUMES.

La salvia SAGE *Salvia officinalis*

Se usan las hojas en comidas y se cultivan otras especies por sus flores.

THE LEAVES ARE USED IN FOODS AND OTHER SPECIES ARE CULTIVATED FOR THEIR FLOWERS.

El tomillo THYME *Thymus vulgaris & spp*

Hay muchas especies de esta planta. Se puede poner, bien picado, en sopas o sobre carne. THERE ARE MANY SPECIES OF THIS PLANT. IT CAN BE USED, FINELY CHOPPED, IN SOUPS OR OVER MEAT.

La vainilla VANILLA *Vanilla planifrons*

El sabor de la vainilla se originó de una orquídea mexicana. Muchos productos actuales en botella son artificiales.

THE FLAVOR OF VANILLA ORIGINATED FROM A MEXICAN ORCHID. MANY OF TODAY'S PRODUCTS IN BOTTLES ARE ARTIFICIAL.

La sal SALT

Aunque la sal no es un producto de una planta, cabe en esta lista porque se ha usado para mejorar el sabor de la comida y para preservar la carne. Se conoce desde los tiempos más antiguos. A veces también se ha usado como herbicida.

ALTHOUGH IT IS NOT A PLANT PRODUCT, SALT FITS IN THIS LIST BECAUSE IT HAS BEEN USED TO IMPROVE THE TASTE OF FOOD AND TO PRESERVE MEAT. IT HAS BEEN KNOWN SINCE THE MOST ANCIENT TIMES. AT TIMES IT HAS ALSO BEEN USED AS AN HERBICIDE.

* These products are very similar in name. This short list is here for reference:

pepino CUCUMBER *Cucumis sativus*

pimentón ALLSPICE *Pimenta diocia*

pimentón, paprika PAPRIKA *Capsicum annuum*

pimienta PEPPER, BLACK PEPPER *Piper nigrum*

pimiento BELL PEPPER *Capsicum anuum*

La lista en inglés
The list in English

English	Spanish	Scientific name
ALLSPICE	pimentón	*Pimntia diocia*
ANISE	anís	*Pimppinella anisum*
ANNATO (BIXA)	onoto	*Bixa orellana*
BASIL	albahaca	*Ocimium basilicum*
BAY LEAF	laurel	*Laurus nobilis*
CAPER	alcaparra	*Capparis licula*
CARAWAY	alacravea	*Carum carvi*
CHERVIL	perifollo	*Anthriscus cerefolium*
CHIVES	cebollines	*Allium schoenosprasum*
CILANTRO (THE LEAVES)	cilantro	*Coriandrum sativum*
CINNAMON	canela	*Cinnamomum camphora*
CLOVE	clavel	*Syzygium aromaticum*
CORIANDER (THE SEEDS)	coriandro	*Coreandrum sativum*
CUMIN	comino	*Cuminum cyminum*
DILL	eneldo	*Anethum graveolens*
FENNEL	hinojo	*Foeniculum vulgare*
GARLIC	ajo	*Allium sativum*
GINGER	jengibre	*Zingiber officinale*
MARJORAM	mejorana	*Marjorana spp*
MINT	menta, yerba buena	*Mentha spp*
MUSTARD	mostaza	*Brassica nigra*
NUTMEG	nuez moscada	*Myristica fragrans*
OREGANO	orégano	*Origanum spp*
PAPRIKA	pimentón	*Capsicum spp*
PARSLEY	perejil	*Petroselium crispum*
PEPPER, BLACK PEPPER	pimienta	*Piper nigrum*
ROSEMARY	romero	*Rosmarinus officinalis*
SAGE	salvia	*Salvia officinalis*
SAVORY	ajedrea	*Satureja spp*
SUGAR	azúcar	*Saccharum officinarum*
TARRAGON	estragón	*Artemiia dracuculus*
THYME	tomillo	*Thymus vulgaris & spp*
VANILLA	vainilla	*Vanilla planifrons*
WATERCRESS	berro	*Nasturium officinale*

11
CLOTHING
La ropa

This chapter goes into the closet, the dresser drawer and the jewelry box. Use this to communicate with family members. Don't confuse the word **ropa** CLOTHING for the English word ROPE. If you need a rope moved, don't ask your Spanish-speaking companion to **"quite la ropa"** or you might be surprised at the outcome!

Of interest is that in Spanish you "CARRY" rather than WEAR clothing. The usual term is **llevar**. **Yo llevo un chaleco nuevo.** I'M WEARING A NEW JACKET. Even so, **llevar** also includes our more literal TO CARRY, TO TOTE.

Later in the chapter we will deal with our personal hygiene, a topic that leads us to those reflexive verbs we skipped earlier.

Lo que llevamos
What we wear

el traje THE SUIT OF CLOTHING

la ropa CLOTHING IN GENERAL

el traje de baño THE BATHING SUIT

el abrigo, el saco THE COAT

el vestido THE DRESS

el abrigo de piel THE FUR PIECE

la chamarra, la chaqueta THE JACKET

los jeans THE JEANS (keeps English pronunciation)

la piyama THE PAJAMA

los pantalones THE PANTS, THE SLACKS

la bata THE ROBE

la camisa THE SHIRT

el suéter THE SWEATER (spelling keeps the original pronunciation)

la camiseta THE T-SHIRT

los interiores, la ropa interior UNDERWEAR

el chaleco THE VEST

Ropa de mujer
Women's clothing

la blusa, la prenda THE BLOUSE
la falda THE SKIRT
las pantaletas UNDERPANTS
el sostén THE BRA
el traje THE SUIT
el traje de gala THE BALL GOWN
el traje con pantalones THE PANTS SUIT
el vestido THE DRESS

Ropa de hombre
Men's clothing

la camisa THE SHIRT
la corbata THE TIE
los pantalones THE PANTS
los shorts THE SHORTS
el traje THE SUIT

Ropa de niños y jóvenes
Clothing for children and youth

la gorra CAP
la gorra de visera CAP WITH VISOR
los pantalones largos LONG PANTS
los pantalones cortos SHORT PANTS
los pañales DIAPERS
la ropa de bebé y de niño CHILDREN'S CLOTHING
los zapatitos de niño BABY SHOES

Muchos jóvenes prefieren llevar jeans y camiseta a la escuela y hasta a la iglesia los domingos.
MANY YOUNG PEOPLE PREFER WEARING JEANS AND T-SHIRTS TO SCHOOL AND EVEN TO CHURCH ON SUNDAYS.

Accesorios
Accessories

la billetera THE WALLET
la bufanda THE SCARF
la cartera THE PURSE
el cinturón THE BELT
los guantes THE GLOVES
el sombrero THE HAT

Some sentences with these words

Las mujeres pueden llevar sombrero adentro, pero los hombres se quitan el sombrero cuando entran a la casa.
WOMEN MAY WEAR HATS INDOORS BUT MEN TAKE OFF THEIR HATS WHEN THEY ENTER A HOUSE.

Las mujeres cargan muchas cosas dentro de sus carteras.
WOMEN CARRY MANY THINGS INSIDE THEIR PURSES.

Los jeans son muy cómodos.
JEANS ARE VERY COMFORTABLE.
`Jeans` keeps the English spelling and pronunciation.

Ese vestido le cae bien. THAT DRESS LOOKS GOOD ON HER.
(`le cae` is an idiomatic way to say 'it looks good on. . .')

Cuando era un joven estudiante, compraba mi ropa en tiendas de segunda mano. Ahora que tengo un buen trabajo puedo comprar mis trajes nuevos.
WHEN I WAS A YOUNG STUDENT, I BOUGHT MY CLOTHES IN SECOND-HAND STORES. NOW THAT I HAVE A GOOD JOB, I CAN BUY MY OUTFITS NEW.

Esa falda es demasiado corta para una mujer de su edad.
THAT SKIRT IS TOO SHORT FOR A WOMAN OF HER AGE.

Ese señor es demasiado viejo para llevar shorts fuera de casa.
THAT MAN IS TOO OLD TO WEAR SHORTS OUTSIDE THE HOME.

Siempre podemos bolitas para polilla cuando guardamos los trajes de lana.
WE ALWAYS TOSS IN MOTH BALLS WHEN WE STORE WOOL CLOTHING.

Las joyas
Jewelry

el anillo THE RING
el anillo de compromiso THE ENGAGEMENT RING
los aretes, los zarcillos, los pendientes THE EARRINGS
el collar THE NECKLACE
los lentes, los anteojos THE GLASSES
los lentes oscuros THE SUN GLASSES
la pulsera THE BRACELET
el reloj de pulsera THE WRIST WATCH

el diamante THE DIAMOND
la esmeralda THE EMERALD

las perlas THE PEARLS
el rubí THE RUBY

el oro GOLD
la plata SILVER
hecho de fondo de la botella   MADE FROM BOTTLE BOTTOMS (cheap glass jewelry)

Los diamantes son los mejores amigos de las mujeres.
DIAMODS ARE A WOMAN'S BEST FRIEND.

¿Por qué es eso?
WHY IS THAT?

Porque cuando el hombre la abandona, ella todavía tiene sus joyas.
BECAUSE WHEN THE MAN ABANDONS HER, SHE STILL HAS HER JEWELS.

Zapatos y calcetines
Shoes and socks

las botas THE BOOTS
los calcetines, las medias SOCKS
las medias largas, las medias de nilón STOCKINGS, NYLON HOSE

las pantuflas SLIPPERS
las sandalias SANDALS
los zapatos de mujer WOMEN'S SHOES
los zapatos THE SHOES (generic)
los zapatos de hombre MEN'S SHOES
los zapatos de niño CHILDREN'S SHOES
los zapatos de tacón alto HIGH-HEEL SHOES

Es difícil caminar en zapatos apretados.
IT IS DIFFICULT TO WALK IN TIGHT SHOES.

Si los zapatos aprietan, todo el cuerpo duele.
IF THE SHOES ARE TIGHT, THE WHOLE BODY HURTS.

Los jóvenes prefieren zapatos deportivos.
YOUNG PEOPLE PREFER SPORTS SHOES.

Las sandalias son cómodas para andar en la playa.
SANDALS ARE COMFORTABLE FOR TALKING ON THE BEACH.

Se necesitan botas de cuero para escalar las montañas.
LEATHER BOOTS ARE NEEDED FOR CLIMBING MOUNTAINS.

Costura, coser
Sewing, to sew

Fabrics
el acrílico ACRYLIC
el algodón COTTON
el cuero* LEATHER
el encaje LACE
el fieltro FELT
la franela FLANNEL
la lana* WOOL
el lino LINEN
el nilón, el nailon NYLON
la piel FUR
el poliéster POLYESTER

la plancha
THE IRON

*One way to remember these are from the song "Rancho Grande," where the girl sings about her sewing project for her man. **"Se los empiezo de lana y se los acabo de cuero".**
I START THEM WITH WOOL AND FINISH THEM WITH LEATHER.

Sewing needs
la aguja THE NEEDLE
el almidón STARCH
el dedal THE THIMBLE
el hilo THE THREAD
la máquina de coser THE SEWING MACHINE
la mesa de planchar THE IRONING BOARD
la plancha THE IRON
las tijeras THE SCISSORS

An easy way to identify clothing and jewelry is to use **"de"** to what the item is made of: **pulsera de oro** (GOLD BRACELET), **traje de lana** (WOOL SUIT). This construction is used with other household goods, such as **la mesa de metal** THE METAL TABLE.

With colors or condition, it's what you learned earlier with regard to adjectives: **la camisa azul** (THE BLUE SHIRT); **los pantalones negros** (THE BLACK PANTS); **una camisa vieja** (AN OLD SHIRT).

No es necesario planchar los trajes de acrílico.
IT IS NOT NECESSARY TO IRON CLOTHES MADE OF ACRYLIC.

No se debe lavar los trajes de lana en agua porque se encogen.
WOOL CLOTHES SHOULD NOT BE WASHED BECAUSE THEY SHRINK.

Los trajes de lana no se lavan, se llevan a la tintorería.

WOOL CLOTHES ARE NOT WASHED, THEY ARE TAKEN TO THE DRY CLEANER.

Here **se llevan** literally means to carry, to take.

Es más fácil hacer un vestido nuevo que arreglar uno viejo que necesita cambios de tamaño o de estilo.

IT IS EASIER TO MAKE A DRESS FROM THE START THAN TO ALTER AN OLD ONE THAT NEEDS CHANGES OF SIZE OR STYLE.

El aseo personal
Personal grooming

el aseo GROOMING
el cepillo THE HAIR BRUSH
el cepillo para dientes THE TOOTH BRUSH
la crema de afeitar THE SHAVING CREAM
el champú THE SHAMPOO
el desodorante THE DEODORANT
la ducha THE SHOWER
el espejo THE MIRROR
el jabón THE SOAP
el lápiz labial THE LIPSTICK
la máquina de afeitar THE ELECTRIC RAZOR
el maquillaje MAKEUP
la pasta dental THE TOOTH PASTE
el peine THE COMB
el perfume THE PERFUME

Se pone el maquillaje.

SHE PUTS ON MAKEUP.

Se pone el perfume.

SHE PUT ON PERFUME.

Se lava el cabello.

SHE WASHES HER HAIR.

Se limpia las orejas.

HE WASHES HIS EARS.

Se quita los calcetines.

HE TAKES OFF HIS SOCKS.

Se mira en el espejo.

SHE SEES HERSELF IN THE MIRROR.

115

Estamos limpios
We are clean

Several chapters back we made passing reference to **reflexive** verbs, those in which the action doubles back on the subject. This means that the person does the action to himself. The **se** at the end of the infinitive of the verb indicates this reflection. Many personal care verbs are reflexive. In conversation, the **se** or its other forms (**me, te**) fall before the verb.

In English you may say I TAKE A BATH. In Spanish the equivalent is **me baño,** literally I BATHE MYSELF.

Here are some reflexive personal care verbs.

bañarse TO BATHE

lavarse TO WASH

ducharse TO SHOWER

mojarse TO GET WET

secarse TO DRY ONESELF

ponerse el desodorante, el lápiz labial, etc. TO APPLY DEODORANT, LIPSTICK, ETC.

afeitarse TO SHAVE

peinarse TO COMB

cepillarse TO BRUSH

lavarse los dientes TO CLEAN TEETH (In Spanish you WASH your teeth rather than CLEAN or BRUSH them)

limpiarse TO CLEAN

cortarse las uñas (uñas de los pies) TO CUT FINGER(TOE)NAILS

pintarse las uñas TO PAINT ONES NAILS

vestirse TO DRESS

ponerse TO PUT ON (CLOTHES, SHOES, ETC.)

quitarse TO TAKE OFF

prepararse TO PREPARE

sentarse TO SIT

pararse TO STAND

Me afeito.
I SHAVE MYSELF.

Bañarse
TO BATHE YOURSELF

Se lava la cara.
HE WASHES HIS FACE

Examples of how these verbs are used

When referring to oneself, it's **me** plus the verb. When referring to another person, it's **se** or **te** plus the verb. When it's you and your friends, it's **nos** plus the verb. Past or future actions require the proper verb tense. The **me, te, se** and **nos** can come before the verb or be attached at the end.

Notice that some of these verbs change spelling and pronunciation from the infinitive. This is common, and about all we can recommend is to make mental note of them and if necessary check other parts of the word in your "Spanish Verbs Conjugated" book. **Probarse** and **sentarse** are among these. Note also the change of spelling for **secarse**, in which a **qu** substitutes for the **c** to keep the **k** sound in front of an **e**.

Use these examples to mix and match for your own family.

verb	*examples of use*
afeitarse	**Me afeito por la mañana.** I SHAVE IN THE MORNING.
ducharse	**¡Dúchate, hijo!** TAKE A SHOWER, SON!
lavarse	**Me lavo la cara.** I WASH MY FACE.
limpiarse	**Él se limpia las orejas.** HE CLEANS HIS EARS.
maquillarse	**Ella se maquilla. (Se pone maquillaje).** SHE PUTS ON MAKEUP.
mirarse	**Ellos se miran en el espejo.** THEY LOOK AT THEMSELVES IN THE MIRROR.
mojarse	**El niño se moja en la bañera.** THE BOY GETS WET IN THE BATHTUB.
pararse	**Se para frente al espejo.** (HE, SHE) STANDS IN FRONT OF THE MIRROR.
peinarse	**Me peino con este peine.** I COMB (MY HAIR) WITH THIS COMB.
pintarse	**Se pinta las uñas.** (SHE) PAINTS HER FINGERNAILS.
ponerse	**El niño se pone los zapatos.** THE BOY PUTS ON HIS SHOES.
preocuparse	**Ella se preocupa por su cutis.** SHE WORRIES ABOUT HER FACE.
prepararse	**Nos preparamos para la fiesta.** WE PREPARE FOR THE PARTY.
probarse	**Se prueba la blusa antes de comprarla.** (SHE) TRIES THE BLOUSE BEFORE BUYING IT.
quitarse	**Se quitó el sombrero.** (HE) TOOK OFF HIS HAT.

secarse	**Séquese con esta toalla.** DRY YOURSELF WITH THIS TOWEL.
sentarse	**Se sienta para maquillarse.** (SHE) SITS TO PUT ON MAKEUP.
vestirse	**Se viste después de la ducha.** (SHE) DRESSES AFTER HER SHOWER.

A mi esposo no le gusta afeitarse con las cremas en latas de aerosol. Le gustan que son cremas verdaderas.
MY HUSBAND DOES NOT LIKE TO SHAVE WITH CREAMS IN AEROSOL CANS. HE LIKES CREAMS THAT ARE REAL CREAMS.
`Aerosol` has come into Spanish "as is."

Mi esposo se afeita con una máquina eléctrica.
MY HUSBAND SHAVES WITH AN ELECTRIC RAZOR.

Pintarse las uñas de los pies es un lujo para muchas mujeres.
PAINTING ONE'S TOE NAILS IS A LUXURY FOR MANY WOMEN.

Muchas mujeres se pintan las uñas de los pies cuando llevan sandalias.
MANY WOMEN PAINT THEIR TOE NAILS WHEN THEY WEAR SANDALS.

Hay que lavarse las manos a menudo.
IT IS NECESSARY TO WASH ONE'S HANDS OFTEN.

Me lavo el cabello con champú marca Espuma.
I WASH MY HAIR IN SHAMPOO BRAND NAME SUDS.
`"Marca"` is BRAND, TRADE MARK or other similar designation. It can also mean MARK in the ordinary sense.

En una casa se encuentran muchos tipos de cepillos con muchos usos: para dientes, para el cabello, para afeitarse, para pintar una pared, para pintar un cuadro, para lavar platos o sartenes. ¿Conoces otros tipos de cepillos?
IN A HOUSE WE FIND MANY KINDS OF BRUSHES WITH MANY USES: FOR CLEANING TEETH, FOR HAIR, FOR SHAVING, FOR PAINTING A WALL, FOR PAINTING A PICTURE, FOR CLEANING DISHES OR FRYING PANS. DO YOU KNOW OTHER TYPES OF BRUSHES?

12
ENJOYING the GARDEN
Disfrutando el jardín

Growing pretty flowers or delicious vegetables is one the major hobbies of people all over the United States. This chapter takes us outdoors to work with our plants and to share the fun of gardening with our children and friends.

First a look at the kinds of plants we grow.

Types of garden plants:

anual

ANNUAL

plantas que brotan, florecen, dan semillas y mueren en una época de crecimiento.

PLANTS THAT SPROUT, BLOOM, SET SEED AND DIE IN ONE GROWING SEASON

bienal

BIENNIAL

plantas que brotan y les salen hojas en una estación; florecen, dan semillas y mueren en la segunda estación.

PLANTS THAT SPROUT AND SET OUT LEAVES IN ONE SEASON; FLOWER, SET SEED AND DIE THE SECOND SEASON.

perenne

PERENNIAL

plantas que florecen en primavera o en verano, pero sus raíces siguen funcionando en invierno. Estas duran muchos o pocos años, según la especie.

PLANTS THAT BLOOM IN SPRING OR SUMMER, BUT WHOSE ROOTS CONTINUE TO FUNCTION IN WINTER. THESE LAST MANY TO A FEW YEARS, ACCORDING TO SPECIES.

arbusto

SHRUB, BUSH

plantas con tallos leñosos; las hojas caen o se quedan durante invierno; salen hojas nuevas y flores cada época de crecimiento. Más pequeñas que un árbol.

PLANTS WITH WOODY STEMS; LEAVES DROP OR REMAIN DURING WINTER; THEY PUT OUT NEW LEAVES AND FLOWERS EACH GROWING SEASON. SMALLER THAN A TREE.

árbol

TREE

plantas leñosas, casi siempre con un solo tronco y muchas veces más grandes que un arbusto.

A WOODY PLANT, GENERALLY WITH A SINGLE TRUNK, AND USUALLY TALLER THAN A SHRUB.

hoja, hojas
LEAF, LEAVES
Lo verde de una planta donde está la clorofila.
THE GREEN PART OF THE PLANT THAT MAKES CHLOROPHYLL.

clorofila
CHLORPHYLL
El color verde de las hojas que fabrican la comida para la planta.
THE GREEN COLOR OF LEAVES THAT MANUFACTURE FOOD FOR THE PLANT.

tallo, tallos
STEM, STEMS
las partes blandas o leñosas que soportan las hojas y las flores.
SOFT OR WOODY PORTIONS OF THE PLANT THAT SUPPORT LEAVES AND FLOWERS.

flor, flores
FLOWER, FLOWERS
la parte de la planta que contiene los órganos reproductivos.
THE PART OF THE PLANT THAT CONTAINS THE REPRODUCTIVE ORGANS.

semilla, semillas
SEED, SEEDS
Los órganos reproductivos que están en la flor.
THE REPRODUCTIVE ORGAN IN THE FLOWER.

Flores y arbustos
Flowers & shrubs

Here is a list of some plants that may be grown in a home garden. Common names are given in ENGLISH and **Spanish.** *Scientific* names are listed only with *genus*. Because several species may exist in each genus, we omit those. Also different species of the same genus occur in different parts of the country. For most people the genus name will lead the gardener to further information.

Scientific names are necessary because common names (in either language) are not standard and can vary from one part of the country to another and from one country to another.

The generic word for GRASS is **grama**, and can include any species of grass used in lawns.

Plant names are either male or female: **la rosa, el lirio.** THE ROSE, THE LILY. The system is similar to that described in Chapter 2.

Here is a brief list of common garden plants:

Spanish	English	genus
agave	AGAVE	*Agave*
amapola	POPPY	*Papaver*
amaranto	AMARANTHUS	*Amaranthus*
azafrán	CROCUS	*Crocus*
begonia	BEGONIA	*Begonia*
bella a las once	MOSS ROSE	*Portulaca*
buenas tardes	PERIWINKLE	*Catharanthus*
caladio	CALADIUM	*Caladium*
capacho	CANA	*Cana*
cinia	ZINNIA	*Zinnia*
clavel	CARNATION	*Dianthus*
coqueta	IMPATIENS	*Impatiens*
cosmos	COSMOS	*Cosmos*
cresta de gallo	COCK'S COMB	*Celosia cristata*
crisantemo	CHRYSANTHEMUM	*Chrysanthemum*
dalia	DAHLIA	*Dahlia*
flor de lis	IRIS	*Iris*
girasol	SUNFLOWER	*Helianthus*
gladiolo	GLADIOLUS	*Gladiolus*
gomphrena	GOMPHRENA	*Gomphrena*
hortensia	HYDRANGEA	*Hydrangea*
lila	LILAC	*Syringa*
lirio amarillo, lirio anaranjado	DAYLILY	*Hemerocallis*
lirio	LILY	*Lilium*
madreselva	HONEYSUCKLE	*Lonicera*
maravilla, clavel de muerto	MARIGOLD	*tagetes hybrids*
margarita	DAISY	*Chrysanthemum hybrids*
narciso	DAFFODIL	*Narcissus*
ojo de pajarito	BLACK-EYED SUSAN	*Thunbergia alata*
rosa de berbería	OLEANDER	*Nerium oleander*
orquídea	ORCHID	too many to list
petunia	PETUNIA	*Petunia*
rompenieve	SNOWDROP	*Galanthus*
rosa	ROSE	*Rosa*
salvia	SALVIA	*Salvia*
tulipán	TULIP	*Tulipa*
tuna	PRICKLY PEAR	*Opuntia*
yuquillo-camburito	MILKWEED	*Asclepias*

Begonia
BEGONIA

Caladio
CALADIUM

Dalia
DAHLIA

Clavel
CARNATION

Rompenieve
SNOWDROP

Flor de lis
IRIS

Narciso
DAFFODIL

Amapola
POPPY

Tulipán
TULIP

Tropical plants generally grown as houseplants in temperate areas.

ave de paraíso	BIRD OF PARADISE	*Strelitzia reginae*
trinitaria	BOUGAINVILLEA	*Bougainvillea spp*
caña muda	DUMBCANE	*Dieffenbachia*
caucho	RUBBER PLANT	*Ficus elastica*
cayena	HIBISCUS	*Hibiscus rosa-sinensis*
flor de cera	HOYA	*Hoya*
flor de pascua	POINSETTIA	*Euphorbia pulcherrima*
geranio	GERANIUM	*Pelargonium*
lirio amarilis	AMARYLLIS	*Hippeastrum*

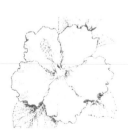

Cayena
HIBISCUS

Trinitaria
BOUGAINVILLEA

Ave de paraíso
BIRD OF PARADISE

Flor de pascua
POINSETTIA

Lirio amarilis
AMARYLLIS

Caucho
RUBBER PLANT

Trees

<u>Spanish</u>	<u>English</u>	<u>genus</u>
aguacate	AVOCADO	*Persea americana*
álamo	COTTONWOOD	*Populus*
almendro	ALMOND	*Prunus armeniaca*
arce	MAPLE	*Acer*
cedro	CEDAR	*Cedrus*
cerezo	CHERRY	*Prunus serotina* (the fruit is cereza)
ciprés	CYPRESS	*Cupressus*
ciruelo	PLUM	*Prunus domestica*
cocotero	COCONUT PALM	*Cocos nuciera*
durazno	PEACH	*Prunus persica* (both tree and fruit end in **o**)
flor de la reina	CRAPE MYRTLE	*Lagerstroemia*
fresno	ASH	*Fraxinus*
higuera	FIG	*Ficus carica*
junípero	JUNIPER	*Juniperus*
limonero	LEMON TREE	*Citrus*
manzano*	APPLE	*Malus* (the fruit is manzana)
naranjo	ORANGE	*Citrus sinensis*
olivo	OLIVE	*Olea europea*
olmo	ELM	*Ulmus*
palma datilera	DATE PALM	*Phoenix dactylifera*
peral	PEAR TREE	*Pyrus*
pino	PINE	*Pinus*
pistachero	PISTACHIO	*Pistacia*
sauce	WILLOW	*Salix*
sicómoro	SYCAMORE	*Platanus*

*In many cases, the fruit may end in an **a** while the tree ends in an **o**. Hence, an AP-PLE is **manzana** while the TREE is **manzano**. In other cases, the change between tree and fruit may be the same, as with **durazno** PEACH. With OLIVES, the fruit is **aceituna** but the tree is **olivo**.

Alce
MAPLE
Acer

Álamo
POPLAR, ASPEN,
COTTONWOOD
Populus

Roble
OAK
Quercus

Nogal
WALNUT
Juglans

Olmo
ELM
Ulmus

Fresno
ASH
Fraxinus

Sicómoro
SYCAMORE
Platanus

Mora
MULBERRY
Morus

Amigos y enemigos en el jardín

Friends and enemies in the garden

The general term for weeds is **malezas** or **hierbas malas**. Sometimes the latter is shortened to **hierbas** (also spelled **yerbas**), but **hierbas** can also refer to the herbs used in cooking. The difficulty with defining weeds is that a pretty flower for Gardener A is a weed for Gardener B. In addition, a plant that is a weed where vegetataion is lush can be a pretty flower in a garden were its cultivation is more of a challenge.

Gardeners also face various creatures that feed on desirable plants. However, nature also provides us with other creatures that feed on the ones we don't like.

Malezas
Weeds

These are a few common weeds:

chicoria	DANDELION
yedra (hiedra)	POISON IVY
llantén, yantén	PLANTAIN
esparganio, cárice	SEDGE
cardo	THISTLE

Los que secomen las plantas
The plant eaters

These eat or damage your good plants.

hormigas	ANTS
áfidos	APHIDS
orugas	CATERPILLARS
gusanos	LARVA
saltamontes	GRASSHOPPER
polillas	MOTHS
caracoles	SNAILS

Los que se comen los insectos
The insect eaters

crisopa	LACEWINGS
mariquitas	LADYBUGS
mantis religiosa	PRAYING MANTIDS
arañas	SPIDERS

Herramientas del jardín
Garden tools

Here we introduce the garden tools and other items needed for yard work. Use this to work with others or simply to enjoy your own garden and flowers.

Las tijeras de podar
LOPPERS
para cortar ramas grandes
HEDGE SHEARS

Las tijeras para setos
FOR CUTTING LARGE BRANCHES

La podadora de contrahoja
BYPASS CLIPPERS
para cortar ramas pequeñas
FOR CUTTING SMALL STEMS

Horquilla y palita de mano
HAND FORK AND HAND TROWEL

Boquillas y rociadores para uso con manguera
NOZZLES AND SPRINKLERS FOR USE WITH HOSES

Los serruchos para podar
PRUNING SAWS

Las rastras
RAKES
muchos usos en el jardín
MANY USES IN THE GARDEN

la horquilla
SPADING FORK

Las palas
SHOVELS
**hay varios tipos,
cada uno con su propio uso**
THERE ARE SEVERAL TYPES,
EACH ONE WITH ITS OWN USE

Las azadas, los azadones
THE HOES
tienen muchos usos
THEY HAVE MANY USES

La carretilla
THE WHEELBARROW

para regar las plantas
FOR WATERING PLANTS

La manguera
HOSE

Abono N-P-K en bolsa
Abono de animal en bolsa
FERTILIZER N-P-K IN A BAG
MANURE IN A BAG

Abono u otro químico para el jardín.
FERTILIZER OR OTHER GARDEN CHEMICAL.
Listo para usarse o para mezclar.
READY TO USE OR FOR MIXING.

Abono vegetal
COMPOST
fácil de hacer
EASY TO MAKE

Listo para usar
READY TO USE (RTU)
para matar malezas o
para matar insectos
FOR KILLING WEEDS OR FOR KILLING INSECTS

Cuídese al usar los químicos.
BE SAFE WHEN USING CHEMICALS.

Cómo guardar los químicos
HOW TO STORE CHEMICALS

Siempre guarde los químicos y otros productos peligrosos bien alto en un lugar seguro donde los niños no los puedan alcanzar.
ALWAYS KEEP CHEMICALS AND OTHER DANGEROUS PRODUCTS VERY HIGH IN A SAFE PLACE WHERE CHILDREN CAN'T REACH THEM

Otros productos que se usan en el jardín
Other products to use in the garden

el balde	BUCKET
la bolsa	BAG
la caja	BOX
la cerca	FENCE
la escoba	BROOM
los guantes	GLOVES
el grifo	FAUCET
el insecticida	INSECTICIDE
la jaula	CAGE
la lata	CAN
la llave	VALVE, FAUCET
la maceta	FLOWER POT
el pico	PICK
la recortadora, la podadora	EDGER
las tijeras para césped	LAWN TRIMMERS

Tareas del jardín
Garden tasks

We continue the gardening chapter with some simple gardening chores you do yourself or hire someone to do for you. If you have a yard man (or yard lady) who is not terribly fluent in English, copy the appropriate chores and post them in the tool shed or garage. Better yet, learn to say them yourself. And there's nothing wrong with just reciting some of these as you (and your children) go about your garden.

Esta es la agenda de las tareas del jardín.
THIS IS THE SCHEDULE OF GARDEN CHORES.

Sin agua, las plantas se mueren.
WITHOUT WATER, PLANTS DIE.

Cada día regamos las flores de las macetas porque necesitan agua todos los días.
EVERY DAY WE WATER FLOWERS IN POTS BECAUSE THESE NEED WATER EVERY DAY.

El lunes cortamos la grama.
ON MONDAYS* WE MOW THE LAWN.

El martes se cortan las flores marchitas.
ON TUESDAY THE SPENT FLOWERS ARE CUT.
*For days of the week and related terms, see Chapter 18, Lists

Los miércoles nos aseguramos que todas las plantas tengan suficiente agua. Si es necesario, las regamos con manguera.

ON WEDNESDAYS WE MAKE SURE THAT ALL THE PLANTS HAVE ENOUGH WATER. IF NECESSARY, WE WATER BY HOSE.

Los jueves recogemos las hojas y las flores caídas en el jardín y arrancamos la maleza del césped.

ON THURSDAYS WE GATHER THE FALLEN LEAVES AND FALLEN FLOWERS IN THE GARDEN AND PULL UP WEEDS IN THE LAWN.

Los viernes cortamos flores bonitas para ponerlas en la mesa del comedor. Es importante cortar las flores porque así las plantas dan más.

ON FRIDAYS WE CUT PRETTY FLOWERS TO PUT THEM ON THE DINING TABLE. IT IS IMPORTANT TO CUT FLOWERS BECAUSE THAT WAY THE PLANTS GIVE MORE FLOWERS.

Los sábados vamos a los viveros para comprar semillas o plantas jóvenes para reemplazar las que murieron o ya no van a florecer.

ON SATURDAYS WE GO TO THE NURSERIES TO BUY SEEDS OR YOUNG PLANTS TO REPLACE THOSE THAT HAVE DIED OR HAVE FINISHED BLOOMING.

En la primavera sembramos semillas de lechuga, perejil, espinaca y las verduras que nos gusta comer.

IN SPRING WE PLANT SEEDS OF LETTUCE, PARSLEY, SPINACH AND OTHER GREENS THAT WE LIKE TO EAT.

Durante el verano arrancamos las yerbas malas (la maleza).

IN SUMMER WE PULL WEEDS (THE BAD PLANTS).

Cuidado al arrancar plantas pequeñas. A veces parecen malezas.

CAREFUL PULLIING UP SMALL PLANTS. AT TIMES THEY LOOK LIKE WEEDS.

No arranque las plantas buenas.

DON'T PULL UP THE GOOD PLANTS.

Deje las buenas plantas y quite las malas.

LEAVE THE GOOD PLANTS AND PULL THE WEEDS.

Más tarde cosechamos y comemos de nuestro huertecito.

LATER WE HARVEST AND EAT FROM OUR LITTLE FARM.

`Huerto` is farm, and `-cito` diminishes the size to make it a small farm.

En el otoño sembramos bulbos de tulipán, narciso, azafrán y otros para tener flores lindas en la primavera.

IN AUTUMN WE PLANT BULBS OF TULIP, DAFFODIL, CROCUS AND OTHERS TO HAVE PRETTY FLOWERS IN SPRING.

En las semanas de primavera podamos las rosas.

IN THE WEEKS OF SPRING WE PRUNE ROSES.

Muchos temen podar rosas, pero es mejor hacerlo que dejarlas con todas las ramas y tallos viejos o quebrados.
MANY FEAR PRUNING ROSES, BUT IT IS BETTER TO PRUNE THAN LEAVE OLD OR BROKEN BRANCHES AND SHOOTS FROM PREVIOUS YEARS.

Cuando podamos las rosas, quitamos la tercera parte de las ramas. Empezamos con las más viejas. También quitamos las muertas.
WHEN WE PRUNE ROSES WE TAKE OUT ONE THIRD OF THE OLD STEMS. WE START WITH THE OLDEST. ALSO WE REMOVE THE DEAD ONES.

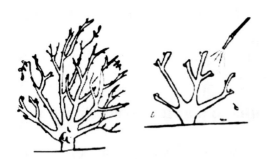

Si la rosa tiene seis ramas en el fondo, quitamos las dos más viejas o más débiles. Si tiene 8 o 9 ramas viejas, quitamos 3 o más si la rosa es muy vieja y tiene muchas ramas casi muertas.
IF THE ROSE HAS 6 STEMS AT THE BASE, WE REMOVE THE OLDEST OR WEAKEST TWO. IF IT HAS 8 OR 9 OLD CANES, WE TAKE OUT 3 OR MORE IF THE ROSE BUSH IS VERY OLD AND HAS MANY ALMOST-DEAD STEMS.

Entonces cortamos las ramas que quedan, quitando una cuarta parte hacia abajo. Cortamos ¼ de pulgada hacia encima de la yema. Escogemos la yema que apunta hacia afuera de la planta.
THEN WE CUT THE REMAINING STEMS, REMOVING ONE FOURTH FROM THE TOP. WE CUT ¼ INCH OVER THE BUD. WE CHOSE A BUD THAT POINTS AWAY FROM THE PLANT.

A fines de mayo o principios de junio las rosas empiezan a florecer.
NEAR THE END OF MAY OR THE START OF JUNE THE ROSES START TO BLOOM.

Los miércoles de verano cortamos las flores marchitas.
ON WEDNESDAYS OF SUMMER WE REMOVE SPENT FLOWERS.

Si se cortan las flores marchitas, la planta vuelve a florecer.
IF THE SPENT BLOOMS ARE CUT, THE PLANT BLOOMS AGAIN.

Cuando se cortan las flores marchitas, siempre se cortan como se ven en este dibujo.
WHEN CUTTING SPENT FLOWERS, ALWAYS CUT THEM AS ILLUSTRATED IN THE SKETCH.

En la primavera florecen muchos arbustos, como las lilas.
Estos arbustos se podan, si es necesario, después de florecer.
IN SPRING MANY SHRUBS, SUCH AS LILACS, BLOOM. THESE SHRUBS ARE PRUNED, IF NECESSARY, AFTER THEY BLOOM.

En lugares de poca lluvia hay que regar dos o tres veces por semana en la primavera, y cada dos o tres días o más en el verano. A veces hay que aumentar la cantidad de agua con una manguera.

IN AREAS OF LITTLE RAIN IT IS NECESSARY TO WATER TWO OR THREE TIMES A WEEK IN SPRING AND EVERY TWO OR THREE DAYS OR MORE IN SUMMER AT TIMES IT MAY BE NECESSARY TO ADD MORE WATER WITH THE HOSE.

Si el suelo es arenoso, hay que regar más a menudo que si el suelo es de arcilla.

IF THE SOIL IS SANDY, IT IS NECESSARY TO WATER MORE OFTEN THAN IF THE SOIL IS CLAY.

Un árbol en el césped necesita más agua que la grama. Hay que regar por donde están todas las raíces del árbol, es decir de un lado al otro de todo el césped y más si se puede.

A TREE IN A LAWN NEEDS MORE WATER THAN THE GRASS. IT IS NECESSARY TO WATER WHERE THE TREE ROOTS ARE, WHICH IS TO SAY FROM ONE SIDE TO THE OTHER OF THE ENTIRE LAWN OR MORE IF THAT CAN BE DONE.

En el invierno regamos una o dos veces por semana si no hay lluvia o nieve.

IN WINTER WE WATER ONE OR TWO TIMES A WEEK IF THERE IS NO RAIN OR SNOW.

En invierno es sumamente importante echarle agua a los árboles, especialmente a los pinos y a los abetos.

IN WINTER IT IS VERY IMPORTANT TO GIVE WATER TO TREES, ESPECIALLY THE PINES AND SPRUCES.

En las semanas del otoño se rastrilla la grama para recoger las hojas y embolsarlas.

DURING THE WEEKS OF AUTUMN THE LAWN IS RAKED TO COLLECT THE LEAVES AND BAG THEM.

En algunas ciudades se prohíbe quemar las hojas. En estos lugares es necesario meterlas en la basura.

IN SOME CITIES IT IS PROHIBITED TO BURN LEAVES. IN THESE AREAS ONE MUST TOSS THEM IN THE GARBAGE.

Cómo regar
How to water

Hay varios modos de regar. Los sistemas automáticos se pueden programar para cada jardín. Los sistemas manuales se prenden y se apagan con una llave. ¡No hay que olvidar apagarlos!

THERE ARE SEVERAL WATERING SYSTEMS. THE AUTOMATIC SYSTEMS CAN BE PROGRAMMED FOR ONE'S OWN GARDEN. THE MANUAL SYSTEMS ARE TURNED ON AND OFF WITH A VALVE. DON'T FORGET TO TURN IT OFF!

Algunas flores y algunas verduras necesitan más agua que otras. Hay que tomar esto en cuenta cuando se añaden plantas al jardín.

SOME FLOWERS AND SOME VEGETABLES NEED MORE WATER THAN OTHERS. WE CONSIDER THIS WHEN WE ADD PLANTS TO THE GARDEN.

131

La manguera es útil para regar esos lugares que los otros sistemas no alcanzan.
THE HOSE IS HANDY FOR GETTING WATER TO AREAS THAT THE OTHER SYSTEMS DON'T REACH.

Cuidando los árboles
Caring for trees

Un árbol es importante para el jardín.
A TREE IS IMPORTANT IN THE GARDEN.

Un árbol da sombra.
A TREE GIVES SHADE.

Los árboles bajan la temperatura durante los días calurosos del verano.
TREES LOWER THE TEMPERATURE DURING THE HOT DAYS OF SUMMER.

Algunos árboles dan flores que alegran en la primavera.
SOME TREES GIVE US FLOWERS THAT ARE A JOY IN SPRING.

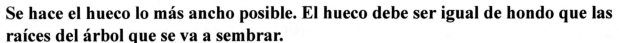

Otros dan frutos en el otoño.
OTHERS GIVE US FRUIT IN AUTUMN.

Al principio es necesario plantar el árbol como es correcto.
AT FIRST IT IS NECESSARY TO PLANT A TREE THE CORRECT WAY.

Se hace el hueco lo más ancho posible. El hueco debe ser igual de hondo que las raíces del árbol que se va a sembrar.
THE HOLE IS MADE AS WIDE AS POSSIBLE. THE HOLE SHOULD BE EQUAL IN DEPTH AS THE ROOTS OF THE TREE TO BE PLANTED.

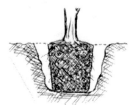

Después se rellena el hueco con la misma tierra.
THEN THE HOLE IS FILLED WITH SAME SOIL.

Es importante echarle agua inmediatamente.
IT IS IMPORTANT TO GIVE THE PLANT WATER IMMEDIATELY.

Las raíces necesitan agua diariamente durante las primeras semanas hasta que el árbol esté creciendo por su cuenta.
THE ROOTS NEED WATER DAILY DURING THE FIRST WEEKS UNTIL THE TREE IS GROWING ON ITS OWN.

No se pone abono de ningún tipo hasta el segundo año.
NO FERTILIZER OF ANY KIND IS APPLIED UNTIL THE SECOND YEAR.

No se le olvide regar durante el invierno.
DON'T FORGET TO WATER DURING WINTER.

No se le olvide
Don't forget

Al usar químicos en el jardín, nunca mezcle productos para matar hierbas con abonos o con insecticidas o fungicidas.

WHEN USING GARDEN CHEMICALS, NEVER MIX WEED-KILLERS WITH FERTILIZERS OR INSECTICIDES OR FUNGICIDES.

Solo se usan los químicos cuando no hay viento.

USE CHEMICALS ONLY WHEN THERE IS NO WIND.

Siempre guarde los químicos del jardín o de limpiar donde ni los niños ni las mascotas los puedan alcanzar.

ALWAYS KEEP CLEANING OR GARDEN CHEMICALS WHERE CHILDREN OR PETS CAN'T REACH THEM.

Guarde los productos en sus envases originales. Algunos de estos productos necesitan envases que no dejen entrar la luz; otros pueden requerir vidrio en vez de plástico.

KEEP PRODUCTS IN THEIR ORIGINAL CONTAINERS. SOME OF THESE NEED LIGHT-PROOF CONTAINERS; OTHERS MAY REQUIRE GLASS INSTEAD OF PLASTIC.

Al usar los químicos lleve ropa que proteja: mangas largas, pantalones largos, guantes, zapatos seguros y máscara para no inhalar productos tóxicos.

WEAR PROTECTIVE CLOTHING WHEN USING GARDEN CHEMICALS: LONG SLEEVES, LONG PANTS, GLOVES , STURDY SHOES AND A MASK SO AS NOT TO INHALE TOXIC PRODUCTS.

Si usa bomba de presión, use una para matar hierbas y nada más. Use otra para fungicidas, abonos o insecticidas. Usar la bomba de mata-hierbas para aplicar abono o insecticidas puede dañar las plantas buenas.

IF YOU USE A PRESSURE PUMP, USE ONE FOR WEED KILLERS AND NOTHING ELSE. USE ANOTHER FOR FUNGICIDES, FERTILIZERS OR INSECTICIDES. USING THE WEED-KILLER PUMP FOR FERTILIZERS OR INSECTICIDES COULD DAMAGE GOOD PLANTS.

Cuando se mezclan químicos, prepare sólo lo que se necesita y úselo todo. Después, lave la bomba tres veces y guárdela donde los niños no la puedan alcanzar.

WHEN MIXING CHEMICAS, PREPARE ONLY WHAT YOU NEED AND USE IT UP. THEN WASH THE PUMP THREE TIMES AND STORE IT WHERE CHILDREN CAN'T REACH IT.

Garden products and their uses

Se usan estos productors para ____
WE USE THESE PRODUCTS TO   ____
PRODUCT NAME
Nombre de producto

_____	**abonar el césped** FERTILIZE THE LAWN
_____	**abonar las flores** FERTILIZE THE FLOWERS
_____	**matar las malezas** KILL WEEDS
_____	**matar los áfidos** KILL APHIDS
_____	**matar los gusanos** KILL GRUBS
_____	**matar las orugas** KILL CATERPILLARS
_____	**matar las polillas** KILL MOTHS
_____	**matar las hormigas** KILL ANTS
_____	**matar los caracoles** KILL SNAILS

13
DO IT YOURSELF
or pay to have it done
Hágalo usted
o pague para que lo hagan

Read through the lists of household items in the other chapters, then try playing with the mix-and-match phrases of this chapter. Use these to tell yourself to do something or to ask a family member or guest to do something else. For those of you fortunate enough to have a cleaning lady or yard man*, there are suggestions for giving orders. When giving orders to employees or family members, it's nice to say "please" and "thank you". Here, we scatter these around, but it doesn't hurt to use them even when the text doesn't have them. For verb conjugations, check your *Spanish Verbs Conjugated* or other reference.

Another suggestion: Write the names of the objects on note cards or sticky notes and paste them or paperclip them on the appropriate item. This way, when you approach the item, seeing the name in Spanish will re-enforce your vocabulary. Then think of the Spanish words for what you need to do at that moment.

If you have trouble with pronunciation, refer (or print for yourself) the chart from Chapter One. Remember, the accent mark is there to tell you when to stress a syllable.

```
*Let's not get sexist about "cleaning lady" or "yard man". These are
merely examples, and in any event they are statistically ok.
```

You need an appliance turned on
Por favor, prende la luz (la estufa, el horno, la lámpara).
PLEASE, TURN ON THE LIGHT (THE STOVE, THE OVEN, THE LAMP).
```
The verb for TO TURN ON is prender; the formal command form is prenda; the fa-
miliar is prende.
```

An appliance needs to be turned off
Necesito apagar el abanico (la radio, el televisor).
I NEED TO TURN OFF THE FAN (THE RADIO, THE TV SET).
```
The verb for TO NEED is necesitar; TO TURN OFF is apagar.
```

There are lights on in unoccupied rooms

Por favor, apaga todas las luces menos las de este cuarto.

PLEASE TURN OFF ALL THE LIGHTS MINUS THOSE IN THIS ROOM.

Something needs to be plugged in or unplugged

Favor, enchufa el tostador (el teléfono celular).

PLEASE PLUG IN THE TOASTER (THE CELL PHONE).

Siempre necesitamos desenchufar* la sartén eléctrica (la plancha) después de cada uso.

WE MUST ALWAYS UNPLUG THE ELECTRIC SKILLET (THE IRON) AFTER EACH USE.

***des** reverses the verb **enchufar**, TO PLUG IN.

Se acabó el café. Hay que desenchufar la cafetera y limpiarla.

THE COFFEE IS FINISHED. IT'S NECESSARY TO UNPLUG THE COFFEE MAKER AND CLEAN IT. **Limpiar** is TO CLEAN; **la** refers back to the item (feminine coffee maker).

Mira en el periódico para ver qué dan en la tele* esta noche.

LOOK IN THE PAPER AND SEE WHAT IS ON THE TV TONIGHT.

***tele** is a nickname for **televisión**, equivalent to TV, our nickname for television. **Mirar** is TO LOOK and **mira** is the command. **Dar** is TO GIVE, but in Spanish what's showing on tv is WHAT GIVES ON THE TV. This is similar to "where are classes held" from chapter 5.

Appliance and gadget placement

El lavaplatos (la estufa, la nevera) está al lado del fregador.

THE DISHWASHER (THE STOVE, THE REFRIGERATOR) IS NEXT TO THE SINK.

Al lado translates NEXT TO, ON THE SIDE OF. The stove, frig and dishwasher are pretty much permantly placed; however, **estar** is still used to designate location.

Las ollas (las sartenes*, las tapas) están en el gabinete grande.

THE POTS (THE FRYING PANS, THE LIDS) ARE IN THE LARGE CABINET.

*dictionaries give **sartén** as either masculine or feminine.

Las cucharas (los tenedores, los cuchillos) se guardan en esta (esa) gaveta (este, ese cajón).

THE SPOONS (THE FORKS, THE KNIVES) ARE KEPT IN THIS (THAT) DRAWER.

Guardar translates TO KEEP. **Se guardan** is the impersonal way to say it. Two words for DRAWER are **gaveta** and **cajón**.

Los platos (las tazas) se guardan en el gabinete a la derecha (izquierda).

THE DISHES (THE CUPS) ARE KEPT IN THE CABINET ON THE RIGHT (LEFT).

El jabón (el detergente) para lavar platos está abajo del fregador.
THE SOAP (THE DETERGENT) FOR WASHING DISHES IS UNDER THE SINK.

Las toallas y los trapos para limpiar se guardan en el cajón (la gaveta) de abajo.
THE TOWELS AND CLEANING RAGS ARE KEPT IN THE BOTTOM DRAWER.

You are about to hire a cleaning lady

Tengo trabajo para quien le guste limpiar.
I HAVE WORK FOR SOMEONE WHO LIKES TO CLEAN.

You set a schedule.

Primero limpiamos el baño, después la cocina.
TODAY WE CLEAN THE BATHROOM, LATER THE KITCHEN.

Hoy se limpia la sala (el dormitorio).
TODAY WE CLEAN THE LIVING ROOM (THE BEDROOM).
`Se limpia, se lava`, etc., are impersonal ways to say something is done, should be done, etc.

Mañana (el lunes, el martes, etc.) limpiamos las ventanas.
TOMORROW (MONDAY, TUESDAY, ETC) WE WASH THE WINDOWS.
For days of the week, see Chapter 18.

Los jueves lavamos la ropa (las sábanas, las toallas).
ON THURSDAYS WE WASH THE CLOTHES (THE SHEETS, THE TOWELS).

Nuestra secadora usa el sol.
OUR CLOTHES DRYER USES THE SUN.

¡No dejes la plancha prendida!
DON'T LEAVE THE IRON ON!

La alfombra se limpia con la aspiradora.
THE RUG IS CLEANED WITH THE VACUUM CLEANER.

El piso de linóleo (de cerámica) se limpia con jabón y agua.
THE FLOOR OF LINOLEUM* (CERAMIC TILE) IS CLEANED WITH SOAP AND WATER.
*In Spanish an item's material is described with **de** OF. In English we say "LINOLEUM FLOOR" but in Spanish we say "THE FLOOR (MADE) OF LINOLEUM."

Hay polvo en los estantes. Hay que limpiarlos.
THERE IS DUST ON THE SHELVES. IT IS NECESSARY TO CLEAN THEM.
Here are two uses for **"hay"** from **haber** (TO HAVE). One is "THERE IS," "THERE EXISTS" and the other is our old friend, **hay que,** the impersonal for something that needs to be done.

El camión de la basura viene los miércoles. Hay que sacar la basura antes de las ocho de la mañana.

THE GARBAGE TRUCK COMES ON WEDNESDAYS. IT IS NECESSARY TO TAKE OUT THE GARBAGE BEFORE 8 A.M.

The term for the municipal gargage collection system is **aseo urbano**.

The tub needs to be filled for someone who is old or ill.

Hay que llenar la bañera (la tina) para el baño de la anciana* (del enfermo*).

IT IS NECESSARY TO FILL THE BATHTUB FOR THE BATH OF THE ELDERLY LADY (ILL MAN).

*These are generic terms. In real life, one would use the name of the person involved: Mrs. Montoya, Mr. Smith. **"Llenar"** is "TO FILL." **Tina** can mean BATHTUB along with other types of vats, depending on the country a person is from.

The hired help is cleaning the office

No mueva los papeles en el escritorio.

DON'T MESS WITH THE PAPERS ON THE DESK.

Mover is TO MOVE, in this case it includes TO MOVE AROUND, TO BOTHER, TO MESS WITH.

Mueva is the command form; **no mueva** is a negative command.

Nunca desenchufe ningún cable eléctrico en la oficina sin preguntar de antemano porque eso puede dañar la computadora.

NEVER UNPLUG ANY ELECTRIC CORD IN THE OFFICE WITHOUT ASKING BEFOREHAND BECAUSE THAT COULD DAMAGE THE COMPUTER.

Antemano is BEFOREHAND. **Nunca ... ningún**, NEVER ... NONE, a double negative, stresses the negative command. **Preguntar** is TO ASK.

Aquí está el sacapuntas para sacar punta a los lápices.

HERE IS THE PENCIL SHARPENER FOR SHARPENING PENCILS.

<u>**Sacar**</u> is TO TAKE OUT, TO PULL OUT. In Spanish the point is drawn out of the pencil.

Las gavetas del archivero están cerradas con llave.

THE DRAWERS OF THE FILE CABINET ARE LOCKED.

The term **"con llave"** (WITH A KEY) stresses the importance of the act.

In the bedrooms

Las sábanas* se cambian los sábados.

THE BED SHEETS ARE CHANGED ON SATURDAYS.

*Notice the accent on the first <u>á</u>. A similar word is **sabana** (grassland), with the second <u>a</u> accented without need of an accent mark.

Las cortinas (las sillas acolchonadas) se limpian con la aspiradora.

THE CURTAINS (THE UPHOLSTERED CHAIRS) ARE CLEANED WITH THE VACUUM CLEANER.

138

The baby needs attention

Tengo qué cambiar el pañal (la camisa, las sábanas) del bebé.

I MUST CHANGE THE DIAPER (THE SHIRT, THE SHEETS) OF THE BABY.

In the bathroom

Las toallas se cambian los sábados, o antes si están sucias.

THE TOWELS ARE CHANGED ON SATURDAYS OR EARLIER IF THEY ARE DIRTY.

Nunca deje las medicinas donde los niños las pueden alcanzar.

NEVER LEAVE MEDICINES WHERE CHILDREN CAN REACH THEM.

Around the house

Sometimes children need to hear these more than once.

Nunca tires la pelota dentro de la casa.

NEVER THROW A BALL INSIDE THE HOUSE.

Cuidado con los cables eléctricos (los jugetes).

CAREFUL WITH ELECTRIC CORDS (TOYS).

Nunca dejes un cable eléctrico (un jugete, la ropa, un zapato) tirado por el suelo. Regrésalo a su propio lugar antes de que alguien se tropiece con él.

NEVER LEAVE AN ELECTRIC CORD (A TOY, THE CLOTHES, A SHOE) TOSSED ON THE FLOOR. RETURN IT TO ITS PROPER PLACE BEFORE SOMEONE WILL TRIP ON IT.

Where are these?

La lavadora y la secadora están en el garaje.

THE WASHER AND DRYER ARE IN THE GARAGE.

As in English, **lavadora** is the CLOTHES WASHER, while DISHWASHER is **lavaplatos**. **Secadora** is clothes dryer. Again note that **estar** is used for location.

La bicicleta está en el garaje.

THE BICYCLE IS IN THE GARAGE.

Las mangueras, las palas y las tijeras* de podar están en el garaje.

THE HOSES, THE SHOVELS AND THE LOPPERS ARE IN THE GARAGE.

*Tijeras is SCISSORS. It is sometimes necessary to specify the use: in this case, TO PRUNE **podar**.

Las maletas para viajar están en el garaje.

THE SUITCASES FOR TRAVEL ARE IN THE GARAGE.

Los archiverios con papeles viejos están en el garaje.

THE FILES WITH OLD PAPERS ARE IN THE GARAGE.

Hay tanto en el garaje que el carro no cabe.

THERE IS SO MUCH IN THE GARAGE THAT THE CAR DOESN'T FIT.

Appliances need repair

La lavadora (la secadora, el lavaplatos, la nevera) está descompuesta.
THE WASHER (DRYER, DISHWASHER, REFRIGERATOR) BROKE DOWN.

El desagüe está tapado y el agua sale por todas partes.
THE DRAIN IS STOPPED UP AND WATER IS COMING OUT ALL OVER.

Necesitamos un plomero para componer el lavamanos (el fregador).
WE NEED A PLUMBER TO FIX THE WASH BASIN (THE KITCHEN SINK).

El televisor no tiene sonido. THE TV SET HAS NO SOUND.

El microondas está descompuesto. No vale la pena componerlo.
THE MICRODWAVE BROKE DOWN. IT'S NOT WORTH THE TROUBLE TO FIX IT.
"No vale la pena" is the idiomatic way to say "it's not worth it,"
"it's not worth while."

La cafetera está descompuesta. Quiero comprar una nueva.
THE COFFEE MAKER BROKE DOWN. I WANT TO BUY A NEW ONE.

Hay un apagón en el vecindario. No hay luz ni aquí ni en las casas de enfrente.
THERE'S BEEN A POWER FAILURE IN THE NEIGHBORHOOD. THERE ARE NO LIGHTS NEITHER HERE
NOR IN THE HOUSES ACROSS THE STREET.
The construction **ni...ni** is equal to the English NEITHER . ..NOR. **Apagón**
(POWER FAILURE, POWER OUTAGE)is from **apagar,** to TURN OFF. The **ón** enlarges the
word, making it a big turn-off.

¡Cortaron el agua!
THE WATER HAS BEEN CUT OFF!

La máquina de coser necesita agujas nuevas.
THE SEWING MACHINE NEEDS NEW NEEDLES.
     Máquina de is a useful term for a number of mechanical devices.
Among these are **"máquina de escribir"** (TYPEWRITER, MACHINE FOR WRITING),
"máquina de forografía" (CAMERA, MACHINE FOR PHOTOGRAPHY) and **"máquina de___."** Keep this term in mind when you can't remember the name of
some other item. For instance if you can't think of the word for DRILL,
try **máquina de hacer huecos** (MACHINE TO MAKE HOLES)and you will be understood. The construction is similar to **tijeras de,** with the use being specified, such as for sewing, for pruning, etc.

Household repairs

La puerta del gabinete (escaparate, clóset) se descompuso. Hay que componerla.
THE DOOR OF THE CABINET (WARDROBE, CLOSET) BROKE. WE NEED TO FIX IT.

Hay que pintar la casa (un cuarto).
THE HOUSE (A ROOM) NEEDS PAINTING.

El niño quiere un color nuevo para las paredes de su cuarto.
THE CHILD WANTS A NEW COLOR FOR THE WALLS OF HIS ROOM.

Tenemos que poner un enchufe (interruptor, bombillo) nuevo.
WE NEED TO PUT IN A NEW PLUG (SWITCH, LIGHT BULB).

El clima está cambiando. Es tiempo de activar el aire acondicionado (el calefactor).
THE WEATHER IS CHANGING. IT'S TIME TO ACTIVATE THE AIR CONDITIONER (THE HEATER).

En la primavera instalamos ventanas de tela metálica para que entre aire fresco en la casa. En el otoño las quitamos y las cambiamos por las de vidrio.
IN THE SPRING WE INSTALL SCREENS ON THE WINDOWS SO WE CAN HAVE FRESH AIR IN THE HOUSE. IN THE FALL, WE TAKE THEM OFF AND PUT IN STORM WINDOWS.

Family hobbies

El sábado quiero terminar un cuadro al óleo que empecé la semana pasada.
ON SATURDAY I WANT TO FINISH AN OIL PAINTING I STARTED LAST WEEK.

A mí me encanta coser para mis nietos.
I LOVE TO SEW FOR MY GRANDCHILDREN.
"Me encanta" is an idiomatic way to refer to something you really like. It can include activities, food, books, etc.

Me gusta jugar al tenis y también me gusta el ajedrez.
I LIKE TO PLAY TENNIS AND ALSO I LIKE CHESS.
Jugar is the term for TO PLAY when it relates to athletics and other games.

Mi hija (hijo) está aprendiendo a tocar el piano (el violín).
MY DAUGHTER (SON) IS LEARNING TO PLAY* PIANO (VIOLIN).
*For TO PLAY musical instruments, the term is **tocar**. Playing sports is **jugar**.

Para el cumpleaños de mis nietos los llevo al zoológico. Allí vemos muchos animales.
FOR THE BIRTHDAYS OF MY GRANDCHILDREN, I TAKE THEM TO THE ZOO. THERE WE SEE MANY ANIMALS.

Nuestro zoológico tiene un elefante, un par de jirafas, algunas mangostas, unos perozosos, una llama, unas culebras, unos monos aulladores y unos monos capuchinos. También hay pájaros y peces.

OUR ZOO HAS AN ELEPHANT, A PAIR OF GIRAFFES, SOME MONGOOSES. SOME SLOTHS, A LLAMA, SOME SNAKES, SOME HOWLER AND CAPUCHINE MONKEYS. ALSO THERE ARE BIRDS AND FISH.

cobra, culebra venenosa

COBRA, POISONOUS SNAKE

llama, animal de Los Andes.

LLAMA, ANIMAL OF THE ANDES.

Some useful command phrases

These commands can come in handy when working at home with your children, spouse, volunteers in the church kitchen, hired help or others.

acomodar TO PLACE ITEMS (OR PEOPLE) IN A GOOD FIT

arreglar TO FIX, TO REPAIR, TO SET IN ORDER

botar TO DUMP, AS GARBAGE

colocar TO PUT, TO PLACE IN ORDER

echar TO TOSS, TO TOSS OUT, TO TOSS IN

jalar TO PULL, TO PULL OUT

meter TO PUT IN, TO INSERT

poner TO PUT, TO SET DOWN

quitar TO TAKE OUT, TO REMOVE

sacar TO TAKE OUT, PULL OUT

tirar TO THROW, TO TOSS

These include standard (stand alone) verbs as well as reflexives. When used as reflexive, they take the pronoun "**lo**" to mean "IT." Notice that masculine, feminine, singulars and plurals take effect, as usual. When dealing with more than one person, use the plural form.

As in English, a pronoun needs a noun as a reference. In casual conversation the noun could be named or indicated through some other means, such as pointing or in a previous sentence.

The conjugations here are somewhat abbreviated. We use the completed past and omit the on-going past because it is the completed past that is most useful when refering to household chores (although we all know that household chores are never completed!).

Acomodar is TO ARRANGE, TO PLACE ITEMS WHERE THEY FIT. **Acomodar** is a regular **–ar** verb.

Acomodemos estos cubiertos en la gaveta.
LET US ARRANGE THESE UTENSILS IN THE DRAWER.

Todo cabe en una taza sabiéndolo acomodar.
EVERYTHING CAN FIT INTO A CUP KNOWING HOW TO ARRANGE IT.

A modern corollary:
Todos los platos caben en el lavaplatos sabiéndolos acomodar.
ALL THE DISHES FIT IN THE DISHWASHER (BECAUSE) YOU KNOW HOW TO ARRANGE THEM.

Arreglar is TO FIX, TO REPAIR, TO ARRANGE. **Arreglar** is a regular **–ar** verb.

Ayer mi esposo arregló la lámpara descompuesta.
YESTERDAY MY HUSBAND REPAIRED THE DISABLED LAMP.

Arregla los libros en orden alfabético.
(YOU) ARRANGE THOSE BOOKS IN ALPHABETICAL ORDER.

Mañana arreglaré este asunto de los impuestos.
TOMORROW I WILL FIX THIS TAX BUSINESS.

Botar is generally TO DUMP, as garbage. It is a regular **–ar** verb. (Similar to **tirar** below)

Ese tomate está podrido. Bótalo (Tíralo).
THAT TOMATO IS ROTTEN. DUMP IT.

Bote ese tomate podrido.
DUMP THAT ROTTEN TOMATO.

Es hora de limpiar el refrigerador y botar todo lo viejo o pasado de uso.
IT IS TIME (THE HOUR) TO CLEAN THE REFRIGERATOR AND DUMP ALL THAT IS OLD OR PAST TIME TO USE IT.

Colocar is TO SET IN PLACE, TO PUT IN SOME ORDER.
Colocar is one of those that changes spellings, otherwise it is a regular **–ar** verb.
Present: **coloco, colocas, coloca, colocamos, colocan**
Past complete: **coloqué, colocaste, colocó, colocamos, colocaron**
Future: **colocará, colocarás, colocará, colocaremos, colocarán**
Command: **coloca** (PUT), **no coloques** (DON'T PUT), **coloquemos, coloquen**

La niña fastidiosa colocó sus muñecas en su lugar.
THE FUSSY GIRL PLACED HER DOLLS IN THEIR PLACE.

Coloquemos estos cuadros en esta pared.
LE US PLACE THESE PAINTINGS ON THIS WALL.

Echar is TO TOSS, TO TOSS OUT, and can include trash or even things of value, including gasoline for the car. It is a regular **–ar** verb. It can have uses similar to **poner** as well as **botar**.

143

Esa botella está quebrada. Échela en la basura.
THAT BOTTLE IS BROKEN. TOSS IT IN THE GARBAGE.

Echa (pon) las camisas para los pobres en esa bolsa y los zapatos en la otra.
TOSS (PUT) THE SHIRTS FOR THE POOR IN THAT BAG AND THE SHOES IN THE OTHER BAG.

Jalar is TO PULL OUT, TO YANK OUT. It is a regular **–ar** verb.

Jala esa cuerda.
PULL THAT STRING.

Hay yerbas en el jardín. Hay que jalarlas.
THERE ARE WEEDS IN THE GARDEN. THEY NEED TO BE PULLED OUT.

Jale las malezas del jardín.
PULL OUT THE WEEDS IN THE GARDEN.

Garden WEEDS are **malezas** or **yerbas**. **Yerbas** can also include HERBS, as grown for cooking. **Maleza** is from **mal**, BAD. This is the word that shows on herbecide labels. WEEDS can also be called **hierbas malas**. **Hierbas** and **yerbas** are alternate spellings. Dictionaries will show either or both.

Meter indicates the item is being PUT inside something, such as a drawer, box, jar, garage, suitcase, purse or other enclosure.

Metan los libros en esas cajas.
(YOU PLURAL) PUT THE BOOKS IN THOSE BOXES .

Mete la bicicleta en el garaje.
PUT THE BICYCLE IN THE GARAGE.

Las sábanas están limpias; mételas en la gaveta (el cajón).
THE SHEETS ARE CLEAN; PUT THEM IN THE DRAWER.

Poner is TO PUT, TO SET IN PLACE.
Poner is irregular, so here are some useful conjugations.
Present: **Pongo, pones, pone, ponemos, ponen**
Past complete: **puse, pusiste, puso, pusimos, pusieron**
Future: **pondré, pondrás, pondrá, pondremos, pondrán**
Command: **pon** (YOU PUT) **no pongas** (DON'T PUT), **pongamos, pongan**

Pon los libros en el estante.
PUT THE BOOKS ON THE SHELF.

No pongas la licuadora en el gabinete; ponla aquí.
DON'T PUT THE BLENDER IN THE CABINET; PUT IT HERE.

Pongamos la mesa para la cena.
LET US SET THE TABLE FOR SUPPER. This is an idiomatic way to say "SET THE TABLE."

Quitar is TO TAKE OFF, TO REMOVE.

Quítate esos zapatos. Están sucios y pueden manchar el piso.
TAKE OFF THOSE SHOES. THEY ARE DIRTY AND CAN SOIL THE FLOOR.

Cuando hace calor me quito el abrigo.
WHEN IT IS HOT I TAKE OFF MY COAT.

144

Sacar is *to* PULL OUT, to take out of some enclosure. Note the spelling change from **sacar** to the command, **saque.** This change keeps the "**k**" sound for the "**c**".

Present: **saco, sacas, saca, sacamos, sacan**

Past complete: **saqué, sacaste, sacó, sacamos, sacaron**

Future: **sacaré, sacarás, sacará, sacaremos, sacarán**

Command: **saca, no saques, saque, saquemos, saquen**

Saca el carro del garaje.
TAKE THE CAR OUT OF THE GARAGE.

Saquen los interiores de las gavetas (los cajones).
(YOU PLURAL) TAKE THE UNDERWEAR OUT OF THE THE DRAWERS.

¡Sáquenme* de aquí!
GET ME OUT OF HERE!

Tirar is TO THROW, TO TOSS.

Tirar is fairly regular. It can also be reflexive, as when you ask someone to throw something to you. Here are some useful conjugations.

Present: **tiro, tiras, tira, tiramos, tiran**

Past complete: **tiré, tiraste, tiró, tiramos, tiraron**

Future: **tiraré, tirarás, tirará, tiraremos, tirarán**

Command: **tira** (THROW), **no tires** (DON'T THROW), **tire, tiremos, tiren**

Esos niños tiraron piedras al lago.
THOSE CHILDREN THREW ROCKS IN THE LAKE.

No tires la muñeca de tu hermanita.
DON'T THROW YOUR LITTLE SISTER'S DOLL.

Tírame* la pelota.
THROW ME THE BALL.

*These are the reflexive forms, in which the action doubles back on the speaker.

14
DOGS, CATS & OTHER PETS
Perros, gatos y otras mascotas

Many of us have pets of some kind. Some people have dogs and/or cats, and others add what the veterinarians list as "exotics." These include cute little mice, gerbils and hamsters; intelligent rats; furry guinea pigs or ferrets; singing or chattering birds; colorful lizards; snakes and even tarantulas or frogs. Fish in tanks are popular in offices as well as homes.

Some gardeners have turtles to control garden insects and others have toads or frogs in outdoor ponds.

Dogs and cats are the most popular pets.

Many breeds keep names from the language of origin and are easy to learn: **labrador, bóxer** and **cocker**. Others make minor changes: DALMATIAN is **dálmata**, and GREAT DANE is **gran danés**. Other names are quite different, such as **galgo** for GREYHOUND.

The term for mixed breed dog in Spanish is **callejero**, from **calle**, STREET, so it translates to STREET DOG, somewhat equivalent to MUTT in English, a not too complimentary term.

In addition, little pets are popular, as they can live in smaller areas and even in apartments. Here are some of those.

Hay trece razas de conejillos de india, algunos de pelo largo y otros de pelo corto.
THERE ARE 13 BREEDS OF GUINEA PIGS, SOME WITH LONG HAIR AND OTHERS WITH SHORT HAIR.

Otro nombre para los conejillos de india es cobayo, cobaya o curiel.
ANOTHER NAME FOR GUINEA PIGS IS COBAYO, COBAYA OR CURIEL.

Ellos comen comida que se vende en tiendas de mascotas. También comen lechuga, perejil, zanahoria, pepino, manzanas, grama y muchas otras verduras y frutas.
THEY EAT FEED THAT IS SOLD AT PET STORES. THEY ALSO EAT LETTUCE, PARSLEY, CARROTS, CUCUMBERS, APPLES, GRASS AND MANY OTHER GREENS AND FRUITS.

La comida para el conejillo de india se guarda en un jarro. Sus verduras están en la nevera.
THE GUINEA PIG'S FOOD IS KEPT IN A JAR. HIS GREENS ARE KEPT IN THE REFRIGERATOR.

Los hurones son muy juguetones. Es importante tener dos porque uno solo se pone triste.

FERRETS ARE VERY PLAYFUL. IT IS IMPORTANT TO HAVE TWO BECAUSE ONE ALONE BECOMES SAD.

Son carnívoros y por eso comen comida parecida a la comida para gatos. Cuando están despiertos les gusta jugar. Se venden castrados.

THEY ARE CARNIVORES, SO THEY EAT FOOD SIMILAR TO CAT FOOD. WHEN THEY ARE AWAKE, THEY LIKE TO PLAY. THEY ARE SOLD NEUTERED.

Algunos conejos tienen orejas paradas y otros tienen orejas flojas.

SOME RABBITS HAVE EARS THAT STAND UP AND OTHERS HAVE FLOPPY EARS.

Los conejos comen comida parecida a la comida para cobayos. También comen verduras.

RABBITS EAT FOOD SIMILAR TO GUINEA PIG FOOD. THEY ALSO EAT GREENS.

Hay que tener las ratas, los ratones, los hamsters y los gerbos en jaulas. Comen una mezcla de semillas que incluye maní y semillas de girasol.

RATS, MICE, HAMSTERS AND GERBILS ARE KEPT IN CAGES. THEY EAT A MIX OF SEEDS, INCLUDING PEANUTS AND SUNFLOWER SEEDS.

Los hámsters duermen de día y juegan de noche. No tienen rabo.

HAMSTERS SLEEP BY DAY AND PLAY AT NIGHT. THEY DON'T HAVE A TAIL

Los gerbos juegan de día y de noche. Estos sí tienen rabo.

GERBILS PLAY BY DAY AND NIGHT. THESE DO HAVE TAILS.

A los niños a veces les gusta tener una cría de estos animalitos. Esto es divertido y les enseña mucho, pero hay que encontrar hogares para las crías.

CHILDREN SOMETIMES LIKE TO RAISE A LITTER OF THESE LITTLE ANIMALS. THIS CAN BE FUN AND EDUCATUONAL, BUT HOMES NEED TO BE FOUND FOR THE LITTERS.

Las lagartijas como mascotas viven en jaulas o tanques. Los camaleones tienen lengua larga para agarrar insectos vivos. Hay otras lagartijas que comen grillos también.

LIZARDS ARE KEPT IN CAGES OR TANKS. CHAMELEONS HAVE LONG TONGUES TO CAPTURE LIVE INSECTS. THERE ARE OTHER KINDS OF LIZARDS THAT ALSO EAT CRICKETS.

Una tarántula es una mascota interesante. Las que se venden en las tiendas de mascotas son hembras. Se pueden mantener en jaulas o tanques. Comen grillos.

A TARANTULA IS AN INTERESTING PET. WHAT PET STORES SELL ARE FEMALES. THEY CAN BE KEPT IN CAGES OR TANKS. THEY EAT CRICKETS.

Las tiendas de mascotas venden pájaros de muchos tipos y tamaños. Deben vivir en jaulas y comen mezclas de semillas que también se venden en las mismas tiendas.
PET STORES SELL BIRDS OF MANY KINDS AND SIZES. THEY ARE KEPT IN CAGES AND EAT SEED MIXES, WHICH ARE ALSO SOLD AT THE SAME STORES.

Los pájaros grandes, como los loros y las cacatúas, necesitan jaulas grandes. Pueden aprender a sentarse sobre el hombro del amo.
LARGE BIRDS, SUCH AS PARROTS AND COCKATOOS NEED LARGE CAGES. THEY CAN LEARN TO SIT ON THE SHOULDER OF THEIR OWNER.

Algunos pájaros pueden aprender palabras. Los canarios cantan todo el día.
SOME BIRDS CAN LEARN WORDS. CANARIES SING ALL DAY.

Algunas personas tienen culebras sin veneno como mascotas. Las culebras comen ratones o ratas.
SOME PEOPLE HAVE NON-POISONOUS SNAKES AS PETS. SNAKES EAT MICE OR RATS.

Here are some conversations to have with or about your pets or instructions to give a pet sitter or to give your child with his first very own pet.

El perro se llama Pancho.
THE DOG IS NAMED PANCHO.
La gata se llama Penny.
THE CAT IS NAMED PENNY.

El perro come dos veces al día.
THE DOG IS FED TWICE A DAY.

La gata come cuando quiere.
THE CAT EATS WHEN SHE WANTS.

El perro pasa el día en el jardín. El jardín tiene rejas para que no se escape. Duerme en su cama en el dormitorio del niño.
THE DOG SPENDS THE DAY IN THE BACK YARD. THE YARD HAS A FENCE SO HE CAN'T ESCAPE. HE SLEEPS IN HIS BED IN THE CHILD'S BEDROOM.

La gata se queda adentro y nunca sale de la casa.
THE CAT STAYS INDOORS AND NEVER GOES OUT.

Mira, hijo. Las jaulas y los tanques para las mascotas pequeñas se limpian cada cuatro días. No se te olvide limpiarlas.
LOOK, SON. THE CAGES AND TANKS FOR THE SMALL PETS ARE CLEANED EVERY FOUR DAYS. DON'T FORGET TO KEEP THEIR CAGES CLEAN.

El tanque de peces tiene varios tipos de peces tropicales.
THE FISH TANK HAS SEVERAL KINDS OF TROPICAL FISH.

El canario canta de día. El canario come semillas. También le gusta un poco de lechuga de vez en cuando.
THE CANARY SINGS DURING THE DAY. THE CANARY EATS SEEDS. IT ALSO LIKES A LITTLE BIT OF LETTUCE ONCE IN A WHILE.

En el jardín, gozamos con los pájaros silvestres.
IN THE GARDEN, WE ENJOY THE WILD BIRDS.

Algunos pájaros del jardín
A few garden birds

gallina, pollo CHICKEN

cuervo CROW , RAVEN

paloma DOVE, PIGEON

pato DUCK

ganzo GOOSE

gaviota GULL

gavilán HAWK

colibrí, chupaflor HUMMINGBIRD

lechuza, búho, curucucú OWL

alcatraz PELICAN

correcaminos, paisano ROADRUNNER

petirrojo ROBIN

gorrión SPARROW

pavo TURKEY

pavo real PEACOCK

carpintero WOODPECKER

cucarachero WREN

El colibrí chupa jugo de las flores rojas.
THE HUMMINGBIRD SUCKS NECTAR FROM RED FLOWERS.

El correcaminos puede volar, pero prefiere correr.
THE ROADRUNNER CAN FLY BUT PREFERS TO RUN.

El cuervo busca nueces en los basureros de las ciudades.
THE CROW LOOKS FOR NUTS IN THE GARBAGE CANS OF CITIES.

El macho del pavo real tiene una cola muy hemosa.
THE MALE PEACOCK HAS A VERY BEAUTIFUL TAIL

15
OUR TOWN
Nuestra ciudad

Here are some miscellaneous uses of Spanish away from home.

The mall
El centro comercial

Vamos al centro comercial.
LET'S GO TO THE MALL.

Vamos a comprar _____
LET'S BUY _____ (use items from lists in other chapters)

El centro comercial se encuentra en la Avenida Central y la calle Cuarta.
THE MALL IS AT CENTRAL AVENUE AND FOURTH STREET. (Use an address in your area.)
In Spanish the phrase **se encuentra** (IT IS FOUND) is used where in English the simple IS
ON carries the message of location.

El centro comercial tiene algunas tiendas donde se vende ropa, otras donde se venden zapatos, otras donde venden velas y algunas más donde se venden cuchillos.
THE MALL HAS SOME STORES THAT SELL CLOTHES, SOME THAT SELL SHOES, SOME THAT SELL CANDLES AND SOME THAT SELL KNIVES.

El centro comercial también tiene un conjunto de restaurantes de comida rápida y un cine.
THE MALL ALSO HAS A GROUP OF FAST-FOOD RESTAURANTS AND A THEATER.

También hay una farmacia, pero me gusta más la que está en la calle Ocho.
THERE IS ALSO A PHARMACY, BUT I LIKE THE ONE ON EIGHTH STREET BETTER.

Muchos van de compras al centro comercial. Vemos bastantes estilos de vestir.
MANY PEOPLE SHOP AT THE MALL. WE SEE MANY STYLES OF CLOTHING.

Hay una señora que lleva un traje de falda y saco blanco. También tiene sombrero y guantes negros.
WE SEE A WOMAN WEARING A WHITE SUIT WITH A SKIRT AND JACKET. SHE ALSO HAS A BLACK HAT AND GLOVES.

Ese hombre lleva camisa de algodón y pantalones negros.
THAT MAN WEARS A COTTON SHIRT AND BLACK PANTS.

Nuestros niños necesitan piyamas nuevas.
OUR CHILDREN NEED NEW PAJAMAS.

No me gustan los trajes de poliéster.
I DON'T LIKE POLYESTER SUITS.

Hay que planchar la ropa de algodón, pero no hay que planchar la de poliéster o la de nailon.
IT IS NECESSARY TO IRON COTTON CLOTHES, BUT IT IS NOT NECESSARY TO IRON CLOTHES OF POLYESTER OR NYLON.

Esta camisa de hombre es blanca y luce bien con la corbata de color.
THIS MAN'S SHIRT IS WHITE AND GOES WELL WITH THE COLORED TIE.

Los zapatos de tacón alto son incómodos.
HIGH HEEL SHOES ARE UNCOMFORTABLE.

Las flores de la florería se cultivan bajo luces especiales en los invernaderos.
THE FLOWERS OF THE FLOWER SHOP ARE GROWN UNDER LIGHTS IN GREENHOUSES.

Compré un ramo de flores para un vecino que falleció.
I BOUGHT A BOUQUET FOR A NEIGHBOR WHO DIED.

En agosto hay muchas ofertas de mochilas, de papeles y cuadernos, de lápices y plumas y otras necesidades de la escuela.
IN AUGUST THERE ARE MANY SALES OF BACKPACKS, OF PAPER AND NOTEBOOKS, OF PENCILS AND PENS AND OTHER NECESSARY ITEMS FOR SCHOOL.

La librería
The bookstore

Mi amigo tiene una librería en el centro donde se venden libros usados.
MY FRIEND HAS A BOOK STORE DOWNTOWN THAT SELLS USED BOOKS.
Don't confuse the English LIBRARY (a public entity that houses books to check out and return) for the Spanish **librería**, where books are sold. The Spanish for LIBRARY is **biblioteca**.

La tienda tiene una puerta que da a la calle y dos ventanas que también dan a la calle.
THE STORE HAS A DOOR TO THE STREET AND ALSO TWO WINDOWS TO THE STREET.

151

Todas las paredes tienen estantes para libros, del piso al techo.
ALL THE WALLS HAVE SHELVES, FROM FLOOR TO CEILING, FOR BOOKS.

El cajero está encima del mostrador.
THE CASH REGISTER IS ON TOP OF THE COUNTER.

Los libros caros se guardan detrás del vidrio del mostrador.
EXPENSIVE BOOKS ARE KEPT BEHIND THE GLASS OF THE COUNTER.

La tienda tiene libros de todas clases: de crimen, de romance y de amor, de poesía, de construcción, para componer el carro, de plomería y de cómo hacerse millonario.
THE STORE HAS BOOKS OF ALL KINDS: OF CRIME, OF ROMANCE AND LOVE, OF POETRY, OF CONSTRUCTION, FOR REPAIRING THE CAR, OF PLUMBING AND OF HOW TO BECOME A MILLIONAIRE.

Se puede pagar con efectivo o con tarjeta de crédito.
IT IS POSSIBLE TO PAY WITH CASH OR WITH CREDIT CARD.

La tienda a menudo tiene libros de gramática y de verbos en español. ¡Compre uno ahora!
THE STORE OFTEN HAS SPANISH GRAMMAR AND VERB BOOKS. BUY ONE NOW!

Nuestro tiempo libre
Our free time

Los sábados llevamos a los niños (los nietos) al parque o al cine.

ON SATURDAYS, WE TAKE THE THE CHILDREN (THE GRANDCHILDREN) TO THE PLAYGROUND OR TO THE MOVIES.

El parque se encuentra a cinco cuadras de casa.
THE PARK IS FIVE BLOCKS FROM HOME.

Nos aseguramos que la película esté clasificada "g" cuando llevamos los niños al cine.
WE MAKE SURE THAT THE MOVIE IS RATED "G" WHEN WE TAKE CHILDREN TO THE MOVIES.

A los varones les gustan las películas de acción.
BOYS LIKE ACTION MOVIES.

A las chicas les gustan las películas de animales.
GIRLS LIKE MOVIES ABOUT ANIMALS.

Los abuelos prefieren películas con mucha risa.
GRANDPARENTS PREFER MOVIES WITH LOTS OF LAUGHS.

A nosotros nos gusta jugar *bridge* con el matrimonio de al lado.
WE LIKE TO PLAY BRIDGE WITH THE COUPLE NEXT DOOR.

152

Un viaje fuera de la ciudad
A trip away from home

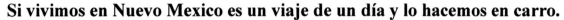

Un viaje a Santa Fe es interesante.
A TRIP TO SANTA FE IS INTERESTING.

Santa Fe es la capital del estado de Nuevo Mexico.
SANTA FE IS THE CAPITAL OF THE STATE OF NEW MEXICO.

Si vivimos en Nuevo Mexico es un viaje de un día y lo hacemos en carro.
IF WE LIVE IN NEW MEXICO IT IS A TRIP OF ONE DAY AND WE MAKE IT BY CAR.

Si vivimos más lejos, es un viaje en avión o en auto.
IF WE LIVE FARTHER AWAY, IT IS A TRIP BY PLANE OR AUTOMOBILE.

Santa Fe tiene muchos museos de historia y de arte.
SANTA FE HAS MANY MUSEUMS OF HISTORY AND ART.

Santa Fe es la capital más antigua de los Estados Unidos. Fue fundada en 1610.
SANTA FE IS THE OLDEST CAPITAL OF THE UNITED STATES. IT WAS FOUNDED IN 1610.

Los museos nos enseñan mucho de la historia del estado.
IN THE MUSEUMS WE LEARN ABOUT THE HISTORY OF THE STATE.

En las tiendas compramos artesanías de muchos artistas de la región.
IN THE STORES WE BUY CRAFTS FROM THE MANY ARTISANS OF THE REGION.

Compramos alfombras hechas por los indios Navajo, cerámica de los pueblos y joyas de plata y turquesa.
WE BUY NAVAJO RUGS, PUEBLO POTTERY AND JEWELRY MADE WITH SILVER AND TURQUOISE.

Al mediodía comemos comida deliciosa.
AT NOON WE EAT DELICIOUS FOOD.

Comemos tamales, enchiladas, chiles rellenos y tacos.
WE EAT TAMALES, ENCHILADAS, STUFFED CHILES AND TACOS.

Cuando viajamos en coche compramos gasolina en la gasolinera (la bomba*).
WHEN WE TRAVEL BY CAR WE BUY GASOLINE AT THE GAS STATION.
*Literally **la bomba** is "THE PUMP."

Si seguimos al norte de Santa Fe podemos llegar al pueblo de Taos.
IF WE CONTINUE NORTH OF SANTA FE WE CAN ARRIVE AT TAOS.

Aquí hay una iglesia muy conocida por todo el mundo porque se ve en pinturas y fotografías de artistas famosos.
HERE THERE IS A CHURCH KNOWN AROUND THE WORLD BECAUSE IT IS FOUND IN PAINTINGS AND PHOTOGRAPHS BY FAMOUS ARTISTS.

Cuando viajamos en avión, vamos en carro al aeropuerto y cuando llegamos a nuestro destino, alquilamos un automóvil para ir por los lugares que queremos ver.
WHEN WE TRAVEL BY AIR, WE DRIVE TO THE AIRPORT AND WHEN WE ARRIVE AT OUR DESTINATION WE RENT A CAR TO GO TO THE PLACES WE WANT TO SEE.

Si el viaje es de más de un día, tenemos que pasar la noche en un hotel o una pensión.
IF THE TRIP IS OF MORE THAN ONE DAY, WE MUST SPEND THE NIGHTS IN A HOTEL OR A BOARDING HOUSE (BED-AND-BREAKFAST).

Si viajamos fuera del país, tenemos que usar nuestros pasaportes.
IF WE TRAVEL OUTSIDE THE COUNTRY, WE MUST USE OUR PASSPORTS.

¡Siempre es agradable regresar a nuestra propia ciudad, nuestra propia casa y nuestra propia cama!
IT IS ALWAYS PLEASING TO RETURN TO OUR OWN CITY, OUR OWN HOME AND OUR OWN BED!

A few useful phrases
Fill in with the appropriate words from what you've learned.

Me gusta
I LIKE TO *(refering to an activity)*

WORK IN THE GARDEN	**trabajar en el jardín**
COOK	**cocinar**
SEW	**coser**
WASH THE CAR	**lavar el carro**
SURF THE INTERNET	**navegar en el internet**
_____	_____ (your favorites)

Me gusta
I LIKE *a specific item*

ICE CREAM	**el helado**
MY DOG	**mi perro**
YOUR HAIRSTYLE	**su peinado**
THAT HORSE	**ese caballo**
_____	_____ (your favorites)

(for more than one item, it's **gustan**)

Me gustan
I LIKE

THOSE CATS	**esos gatos (esas gatas)***
THOSE BIRDS	**esos pájaros**
THOSE FRUITS	**esas frutas**
THOSE SHIRTS	**esas camisas**

_____   _____ (your favorites)

*Remember that masculine can include feminine, but feminine doesn't include masculine.

Me gusta ir
I LIKE TO GO

TO THE BEACH	**a la playa**
TO THE MOUNTAINS	**a las montañas**
TO THE THEATER, TO THE MOVIES	**al teatro, al cine**
SHOPPING	**de compras**
TRAVELING	**de viaje**

_____   _____ (your favorites)

Yo quiero
I WANT

A NEW CAR	**un carro nuevo**
A MOTORCYCLE	**una moto (motocicleta)**
A CELL PHONE	**un teléfono celular**
SOME COMFORTABLE SHOES	**unos zapatos cómodos**

_____   _____ (your favorites)

(Algo) necesita
(AN ITEM) NEEDS

THE BICYCLE TIRE NEEDS AIR.
La llanta de la bicicleta necesita aire.

THE CAR NEEDS GASOLINE.
El carro necesita gasolina.

THE SOUP NEEDS SALT.
La sopa necesita sal.

_____   _____ (your needs)

Porque
BECAUSE

I SAID SO	**así lo digo**
YES	**sí**
THE BOSS ORDERED IT	**el jefe lo exigió**
THE DOG NEEDS IT	**el perro lo necesita**
_____	_____ (your ideas)

Negatives are also handy to know.

No me gusta (for more than one item, it's **gustan**)

I DON'T LIKE

POLITICS	**la política**
THAT TV SHOW	**ese programa de televisión**
THAT MOVIE	**esa película**
THOSE OUTFITS	**esos trajes**
THAT RESTAURANT	**ese resaturante**
_____	_____ (your dislikes)

No quiero

I DON'T WANT

TO GO TO THAT RESTAURANT	**ir a ese restaurante**
TO BUY THOSE DISHES	**comprar esos platos**
TO READ THAT BOOK	**leer ese libro**
TO PLAY SOCCER	**jugar fútbol**
_____	_____ (your dislikes)

16

CONSTRUCTION
Terms and uses
CONSTRCCIÓN
Términos y usos

Palabras y frases
de construcción

Nearly everyone needs a handyman (or woman) to do a job that you can't do yourself. These items are used around the house or in construction and includes terms in the carpentry and masonry fields. They are listed here for anyone involved in work being done at home or on a construction site. The list is long, and not everything in it is for everyone.

As usual, look it over and make note of those terms you may need in some future emergency or some present or future project.

la abrazadera, la tenaza · CLAMP · holds items together

la abrazadera en C · C-CLAMP · holds items together

el aceite · OIL · any kind of oil; includes industrial, cooking, etc.

la aceitera · OIL CAN ·can for oil

el acero · STEEL · strong metal

el alambre · WIRE · bare or coated; can carry electric current

la alfombra · RUG · installed carpet or area rug

los alicates, las pinzas, las tenazas · PLIERS · pulls what needs pulling

el almacén, la bodega · STORAGE PLACE · place for storing goods

el aluminio · ALUMINUM · light weight metal

la arandela · WASHER · used with bolts, screws

la armella · HOOK, EYE; EYEHOOK · a screw with a closed circle

las aserraduras, el aserrín · SAWDUST · what's left from cutting lumber

el asfalto · ASPHALT ·a petrochemical product for paving streets

el balde, la cubeta · BUCKET, PAIL · smaller than barrel

el barril · BARREL · holds liquids or solids

la barrena para tubería · PLUMBER'S SNAKE· unstops drain

la bisagra, el gonze · HINGE· for doors, windows, lids, etc.

el bombillo · LIGHT BULB · incandescent or other

el cable eléctrico, la extensión eléctrica · EXTENSION CORD · many uses

la cadena · CHAIN · links of metal or other product

la calamina, la hojalata, el hierro ondulado, la chapa ondulada · CORRUGATED IRON

el candado · PADLOCK · moveable device

la cañería, el drenaje · PLUMBING · pipes brings water to a building or takes it away

la carretilla · WHEELBARROW · for moving things

el cemento · CEMENT · dry powder for making concrete or mortar

el cepillo para pintar · PAINT BRUSH · for painting large and small items

la cera · WAX · from bees or other substance

la cerradura · LOCK · padlock, dead bolt, etc.

el cincel · CHISEL · used for chipping or shaping wood

la cinta de medir · MEASURING TAPE ·metal or fabric

el clavo · NAIL · many sizes, designs & uses

el concreto · CONCRETE · mix of cement, water & gravel

el conductor de corriente · ELECTRIC CORD · carries current

el contador · METER ·reads gas, electric, water usage

la corriente · ELECTRICITY, CURRENT · powering your tools

la corriente alterna · CURRENT, ALTERNATING · common household current

la corriente continua · CURRENT, DIRECT · current from batteries

el cuatro-por- · 4x- · standard wood size

la cuerda, el cordón · ROPE · natural or artificial fibers

los dardos para matraca · SOCKETS FOR SOCKET WRENCH · special uses

el destapador de plomería, el amigo · PLUNGER · for minor drain stoppages

el destornillador · SCREWDRIVER · many uses

el dos-por- · 2x- · standard wood size

el enchufe · ELECTRIC PLUG · plug or socket

la espátula · PUTTY KNIFE · for applying putty or similar product (see Chapter 7)

el estuco · STUCCO · finishing system on buildings

el fósforo, el cerillo · MATCH · lights fires, candles, etc.

el gancho · HOOK · almost any kind of hook

el gancho con anillo · HOOK AND EYE · hook with a separate eye

la garlopa · PLANE · for smoothing wood

el hierro · IRON · strong metal; basis of steel

el hueco, el agujero · HOLE · **hueco** is larger than **agujero**

el interruptor · SWITCH, ELECTRIC · turns current on or off; wall, in-line or on appliance

el ladrillo · BRICK · of various materials

el lijado · SANDED ITEM · wood or metal that has been sanded

la lijadora · SANDER, ELECTRIC · for smoothing wood

la lima · FILE · for filing or smoothing metal items

la llave · KEY · device for opening & closing

la llave · WRENCH · any wrench in general

la llave allen · WRENCH, ALLEN · special uses

la llave inglesa · WRENCH CRESCENT (MONKEY) · adjustable, for general use

la llave plana · WRENCH, FLAT · comes in several sizes

la lupa · MAGNIFYING GLASS · for studying tiny items

la madera · LUMBER · cut wood

el mango para rodillo · PAINT ROLLER HANDLE · holds disposable roller

la mano de pintura · COAT OF PAINT · applied with brush or roller

el martillo · HAMMER · for installing nails

la moldura · MOLDING · usually strips of wood

el mortero · MORTAR · mix of cement and water; joins bricks

la navaja · KNIFE · pocket, blade, razor, whatever cuts

el nivel · LEVELER · tells if installation is level

el nudo · KNOT · tied on cord

la pala · SHOVEL · for digging

el palo · STICK · usually unfinished piece off a woody plant

el palustre · TROWEL · for installing mortar, concrete, etc.

el papel de lija · SANDPAPER · manual uses

> **el pegamento, la goma, el pega-pega** · GLUE, CEMENT · many kinds
>
> **el perno de ojo** · BOLT WITH EYE, EYEBOLT · special uses
>
> **el perno** · BOLT · many sizes, designs, uses
>
> **la pintura** · PAINT · enamel, acrylic, etc

las pinzas · TWEEZERS · smaller than pliers

el piso, el suelo · FLOOR · floor, soil, etc

la regla · RULER · strip for measuring short distances

las rodajas · CASTERS · wheels for making furniture moveable

el rodillo de pintar · PAINT ROLLER · for painting walls, boards, etc

el rollo · COIL · usually of wire; can be of other material

las ruedas · WHEELS · many kinds

la tabla · BOARD · usually wood or of a synthetic product

el tanque · TANK · holds liquids

la teja, la cerámica · TILE · for roof, floor, ornaments, etc.

el sargento, el sujetador · CLAMP, LARGE · used for larger items

el sellador · CALKING, SEALER · seals cracks or seams

el serrucho, la sierra · SAW · hand or electric

la sierra de mesa · SAW, TABLE · installed on table

la soldadura · WELDED OR SOLDERED · joined metal pieces

la taladradora*, el taladro · DRILL · for drilling or making holes

el taladro*, las brocas · DRILL BITS · used with drill

> *some reference books list· **taladro** as the manual drill and **taladradora** as the electric drill and **taladros** as the drill bits.

> **el tanque** · TANK · holds liquids
>
> **la tapa, el tapón** · PLUG, LID, COVER · covers jars, pails, etc
>
> **la teja, la cerámica** · TILE · for roof, floor, ornaments, etc.

la tela metálica · SCREEN · many kinds, many uses

el tornillo · SCREW · many sizes, many uses

los trapos · RAGS · for cleaning up at end of job

el tubo · PIPE, TUBE · metal or plastic

la tuerca · NUT (FOR BOLT) · used with bolt

la tuerca con orejas · WING NUT · easy to use

el vidrio · GLASS · for windows, table tops, etc.

la viga · BEAM · usually horizontal to hold up roof

Some verbs relating to construction:

agujerear	TO MAKE A SMALL HOLE
atornillar	TO SCREW (A SCREW OR BOLT)
clavar	TO NAIL
cortar	TO CUT, TO SAW
destapar	TO UNPLUG, TO UNCORK, TO REMOVE A LID
destornillar	TO UNSCREW
martillar	TO HAMMER
sacar	TO TAKE OUT, TO PULL OUT
serruchar	TO SAW WITH A HAND OR POWER SAW
sujetar	TO ADJUST
taladrar	TO DRILL WITH AN ELECTRIC OR HAND DRILL

Hablando con sus empleados
Talking to your employees

Here are some phrases relating to construction.

El martillo se usa para clavar o sacar clavos.
THE HAMMER IS USED FOR NAILING OR PULLING OUT NAILS.

There is an old Spanish "dicho" that declares: **"Un clavo saca otro clavo".** Loosely translated it means "IT TAKES ONE TO KNOW ONE" or "IT TAKES ONE TO FIND ANOTHER OF THE SAME ILK."

El destapador de baño (el amigo) ayuda durante una emergencia en el excusado.

THE PLUNGER (THE FRIEND) IS A BIG HELP IN AN EMERGENCY IN THE BATHROOM. As in English, the plunger is also called "THE FRIEND". Another Spanish term is **destapador de plomería**. This is the name that is found in hardware stores.

El destornillador atornilla y desatornilla el perno y también el tornillo.
THE SCREWDRIVER SCREWS AND UNSCREWS BOLTS AS WELL AS SCREWS.

Se usa el serrucho (la sierra) para cortar madera.
THE SAW IS USED TO CUT WOOD.

También hay serruchos especiales para cortar piezas de metal.
ALSO THERE ARE SPECIAL SAWS FOR CUTTING METAL PIECES.

La arandela se pone cuando se mete un tornillo o un perno y una tuerca en la madera.
THE WASHER IS USED WHEN PUTTING A SCREW OR NUT AND BOLT ON WOOD.

Los carpinteros usan clavos en construcciones de madera.
CARPENTERS USE NAILS IN CONSTRUCTION WITH LUMBER.

La taladradora se usa para hacer agujeros en madera o en piezas de metal.
THE DRILL IS USED FOR MAKING SMALL HOLES IN WOOD OR PIECES OF METAL.

Es importante usar las brocas correctas para hacer los agujeros.
IT IS IMPORTANT TO USE THE CORRECT BITS WHEN MAKING THESE HOLES.

Siempre se considera que un cable tiene corriente.
ALWAYS CONSIDER THAT WIRE HAS ELECTRICITY(IS CHARGED).

Puedes estar seguro que no tiene corriente si se ven las dos puntas.
YOU CAN BE SURE THAT IT HAS NO ELECTRICITY IF THE TWO ENDS ARE VISIBLE.

El palustre se usa para trabajar con el mortero.
THE TROWEL IS USED WHEN WORKING WITH MORTAR.

Para hacer mortero se mezcla cemento con agua.
TO MAKE MORTAR, CEMENT IS MIXED WITH WATER.

Para hacer concreto se mezcla cemento con agua y grava (piedritas).
TO MAKE CONCRETE, CEMENT IS MIXED WITH WATER AND GRAVEL (STONES)

La madera de 2 por 4 y de 2 por 6 se usa en construcción y en carpintería.
LUMBER OF 2 BY 4 AND 2 BY 6 ARE USED IN CONSTRUCTION AND CARPENTRY.

Tengo que ir a la ferretería para comprar unas herramientas.
I NEED TO GO TO THE HARDWARE STORE TO BUY SOME TOOLS.

Necesito brocas nuevas porque las viejas ya no agujeran la madera con que estoy trabajando.
I NEED NEW DRILL BITS BECAUSE THE OLD ONES NO LONGER MAKE HOLES IN THE LUMBER WITH WHICH I AM WORKING.

También necesito una garlopa nueva porque mi vecino me pidió la mía prestada y no la ha devuelto.
I ALSO NEED A NEW PLANE BECAUSE MY NEIGHBOR BORROWED MINE AND HAS NOT RETURNED IT.

Y yo necesito papel de lija para terminar el trabajo.
AND I NEED SANDPAPER TO FINISH THE JOB.

Cómo usar tornillos y pernos: Atornillar a la derecha y desatornillar a la izquierda.
HOW TO USE SCREWS AND BOLTS: SCREW TO THE RIGHT AND UNSCREW TO THE LEFT.

Necesito una tabla de dos por cuatro, de tres pies de largo.
I NEED A TWO-BY-FOUR BOARD THAT IS THREE FEET LONG.

Mañana ayudaré a mi vecino que quiere pintar las paredes del garaje.
TOMORROW I WILL HELP MY NEIGHBOR WHO WANTS TO PAINT THE WALLS OF HIS GARAGE.

Cuando serrucho madera el aserrín cae al suelo. Eso me recuerda esta canción: "Aserrín, aserrán, los maderos de San Juan; piden queso y les dan un hueso, piden pan y no les dan. Aserrín, aserrán".
WHEN I SAW LUMBER THE SAWDUST FALLS ON THE FLOOR. IT REMINDS ME OF THIS SONG: "SAW-DUST, SAWDUST, THE CARPENTERS OF SAN JUAN; THEY ASK FOR CHEESE GET A BONE; THEY ASK BREAD AND DON'T GET ANY."

Este balde se llenó de agua y ahora los clavos y los tornillos que quedaron allí están oxidados.
THIS BUCKET GOT FILLED WITH WATER AND THE NAILS AND SCREWS THAT WERE LEFT THERE ARE RUSTED.

What's the key?

Wrenches are often a **llave** of some sort, including CRESCENT **(llave inglesa)**, FLAT **(llave plana)**, FRENCH, IMPACT, TORQUE, ALLEN, several PIPE WRENCHES **(llaves para tubos)** and other specialized wrenches.

Other **llaves** can include several types of VALVES or TAPS used in plumbing and in chemistry laboratories to control the flow of a liquid. Fire hydrants have **llaves** to open and close the water. The SAFETY LATCH on a rifle is a **llave de cierre**. Even music has a **llave** on a FLUTE and PIANO TUNERS use a **llave de afinar**.

One often sees or hears the word **llave**, so keep in mind the variety of devices that use this term. At home a common **llave** is the FAUCET in the kitchen, the bathroom and outdoors for the garden hose. And let's not forget **la llave** (THE KEY) for **la cerradura** (THE LOCK) on **la puerta** (THE DOOR) or **el carro** (THE CAR).

However, SOCKET WRENCHES are **matracas**. And the key to solve a mystery is **la clave.**

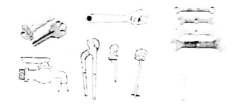

The list in English

ALUMINUM **el aluminio**

ASPHALT **el asfalto**

BARREL **el barril**

BEAM **la viga**

BOARD **la tabla**

BOLT WITH EYE, EYEBOLT **el perno de ojo**

BOLT **el perno**

BRICK **el ladrillo**

BUCKET, PAIL **el balde, la cubeta**

CALKING, SEALER **el sellador**

CASTERS **las rodajas**

CEMENT **el cemento**

CHAIN **la cadena**

CHISEL **el cincel**

CLAMP **la abrazadera, la tenaza**

CLAMP, C (C-CLAMP) **la abrazadera en C**

CLAMP, LARGE **el sargento, el sujetador**

COAT OF PAINT **la mano de pintura**

COIL **el rollo**

CONCRETE **el concreto**

CURRENT, ALTERNATING **la corriente alterna**

CURRENT, DIRECT **la corriente continua**

CORRUGATED IRON **la calamina, hojalata, hierro ondulado, chapa ondulada**

DRILL **la taladradora*, el taladro**

DRILL BITS **el taladro*, las brocas**

*Some reference books list **taladro** as the manual drill, **taladradora** as the electric drill and **taladros** as the drill bits.

ELECTRICITY, CURRENT **la corriente**

ELECTRIC CORD **el conductor de corriente**

ELECTRIC PLUG **el enchufe**

ELECTRIC SOCKET **el enchufe**

EXTENSION CORD **el cable eléctrico, la extensión eléctrica**

FILE **la lima**

FLOOR **el piso, el suelo**

GLASS **el vidrio**

GLUE, CEMENT **el pegamento, la goma, el pega-pega**

HAMMER **el martillo**

HINGE **la bisagra, el gonze**

HOL E **el hueco, el agujero; hueco** is larger than **agujero**

HOOK **el gancho**

HOOK, EYE; EYEHOOK **la armella**

HOOK AND EYE **el gancho y el anillo**

IRON **el hierro**

KEY **la llave**

KNIFE **la navaja**

KNOT **el nudo**

LEVELER **el nivel**

LIGHT BULB **el bombillo**

LOCK **la cerradura**

LUMBER **la madera**

MAGNIFYING GLASS **la lupa**

MATCH **el fósforo, el cerillo**

MEASURING TAPE **la cinta de medir**

METER **el contador**

MOLDING **la moldura**

MORTAR **el mortero**

NAIL **el clavo**

NUT (FOR BOLT) **la tuerca**

NUT, WING **la tuerca con orejas**

OIL **el aceite**

OIL CAN **la aceitera**

PADLOCK **el candado**

PAINT **la pintura**

PAINT BRUSH **el cepillo para pintar**

PAINT ROLLER **el rodillo de pintar**

PAINT ROLLER HANDLE **el mango para rodillo**

PIPE, TUBE **el tubo**

PLANE **la garlopa**

PLIERS **los alicates, las pinzas, las tenazas**

PLUG, LID, COVER **la tapa, el tapón**

PLUMBER'S SNAKE **la barrena para tubería**

PLUMBING, PIPES **la cañería, el drenaje**

PLUNGER **el destapador de plomería, el amigo**

PUTTY KNIFE **la espátula**

RAGS **los trapos**

ROPE **la cuerda, el cordón**

RUG **la alfombra**

RULER **la regla**

SANDED ITEM **el lijado**

SANDER, ELECTRIC **la lijadora**

SANDPAPER **el papel de lija**

SAW **el serrucho, la sierra**

SAW, TABLE **la sierra de mesa**

SAWDUST **las aserraduras, el aserrín**

SCREEN **la tela metálica**

SCREW **el tornillo**

SCREWDRIVER **el destornillador**

SHOVEL **la pala**

SOCKETS FOR SOCKET WRENCH **los dardos para matraca**

STEEL **el acero**

STICK **el palo**

2x- **el dos-por-**

4x- **el cuatro-por-**

STORAGE PLACE **el almacén, la bodega**

STUCCO **el estuco**

SWITCH, ELECTRIC **el interruptor**

TANK **el tanque**

TILE **la teja, la cerámica**

TROWEL **el palustre**

TWEEZERS **las pinzas**

WASHER **la arandela**

WAX **la cera**

WELDED OR SOLDERED **la soldadura**

WHEELBARROW **la carretilla**

WHEELS **las ruedas**

WIRE **el alambre**

WRENCH **la llave**

WRENCH CRESCENT (MONKEY) **la llave inglesa**

WRENCH, ALLEN **la llave allen**

WRENCH, FLAT **la llave plana**

17
HOW TO SAY IT
Cómo se dice

Here are some expressions from daily life. These are listed by topic, but not in any special order. These are not terms you will find in a dictionary. They are idiomatic expressions and/or word combinations that convey certain ideas.

Some show how to say the same thing in different ways. Some illustrate differences of similar words.

Look them over so as to remember where to find them when you need them. These expressions are then sumarized and alphabetized in English and Spanish.

When necessary change THE WORD HERE or the blank spaces to the word you have in mind or a term you learned earlier.

*Here are some phrases dealing with **commerce**, **buying**, **selling**, **renting**, etc.*

A la orden AT YOUR SERVICE

Se alquila FOR RENT

Se vende FOR SALE

¿Se vende? IS IT FOR SALE?

¿Cuánto vale? HOW MUCH IS IT WORTH?

¿Cuánto pide por el (la) ___? WHAT ARE YOU ASKING FOR ___?

Tenemos ___ en venta WE HAVE ___ TO SELL

Sin enganche NO DOWN PAYMENT

Se habla español SPANISH SPOKEN HERE

Hacer cola, hacer línea TO STAND IN LINE (as at a checkout counter)

Tomar turno TO TAKE YOUR TURN

*Here are some dealing with human **feelings & functions***
(For verb conjugations, consult your *Spanish Verbs Conjugated* or similar reference book.)

Mil gracias A THOUSAND THANKS

Oler a ___ TO SMELL OF ___

Por favor PLEASE

Reírse con ___ TO LAUGH WITH ___

Reírse de ___ TO LAUGH AT ___

Soñar con ___ TO DREAM WITH ___

Soñar con ___ TO DREAM OF ___

Tener cita con ___ TO HAVE AN APPOINTMENT WITH, A DATE WITH, ETC.

Tener éxito TO BE SUCCESSFUL

Tener ganas de ___ TO WANT TO DO (SOMETHING)

Perder las ganas de ___ TO LOSE INTEREST IN DOING (SOMETHING)

Tener hambre TO BE HUNGRY

Tener que ___ TO MUST (DO SOMETHING)

More than one way to say it

Tengo prisa I'M IN A HURRY

Tengo que apurarme I MUST HURRY

Tengo dolor de cabeza (de muela) I HAVE A HEADACHE (TOOTH ACHE)

Me duele la cabeza (el pie, el dedo pulgar) MY HEAD (FOOT, THUMB) HURTS

Me da lo mismo IT'S ALL THE SAME TO ME

No me importa IT DOESN'T MATTER TO ME

Así es, es cierto, es verdad IT'S TRUE

Por casualidad BY COINCIDENCE, BY CHANCE

Tengo miedo I AM AFRAID, I AM SCARED

Estoy asustado I AM AFRAID, I AM SCARED

¡Qué susto! WHAT A FRIGHT! WHAT A SCARE!

Tome asiento HAVE A SEAT

Siéntese SIT (formal)

Siéntate SIT (familiar)

*Here are some dealing with **education**, reading, writing, etc.*

Se escribe con mayúscula IT'S WRITTEN WITH A CAPITAL LETTER

Se escribe con minúscula IT'S WRITTEN WITH A LOWER CASE LETTER

Hacer caso TO PAY ATTENTION

Léelo en voz alta READ IT ALOUD

Léelo en voz baja READ IT IN A WHISPER (TO YOURSELF)

*Here are some dealing with household **chores***

Hacer las maletas TO PACK THE SUITCASES

Se usa para (limpiar, sumar, etc.) IT'S USED FOR (CLEANING, ADDING, ETC.)

*Here are some dealing with **time** and **place***

A lo lejos AT A DISTANCE, FAR AWAY

A la misma vez AT THE SAME TIME

Al mismo tiempo AT THE SAME TIME

A la vez AT THE SAME TIME

Va y viene COMES AND GOES

Al pie de la letra EXACTLY RIGHT (usually said when giving instructions)

A fines de la semana NEAR THE END OF THE WEEK

A fines del mes NEAR THE END OF THE MONTH

A fines del año NEAR THE END OF THE YEAR

A menudo OFTEN, FREQUENTLY

De repente SUDDENLY, ALL AT ONCE

Con cuidado CAREFULLY

De todos modos ANYWAY, ANYHOW

Lo dan de alta HE'S BEING RELEASED (FROM THE HOSPITAL)

Sírvase HELP YOURSELF

No cabe IT DOESN'T FIT

No cabe duda NO DOUBT ABOUT IT

Faltar, por falta de LACKING, FOR LACK OF

No te importa IT'S NONE OF YOUR BUSINESS

No vale nada IT'S NOT WORTH ANYTHING

No sirve para nada IT'S WORTHLESS

Más o menos SO-SO, MEDIOCRE

Vale la pena IT'S WORTH (DOING)

No vale la pena IT'S NOT WORTH (DOING)

No es así THAT'S NOT RIGHT, IT'S NOT SO

¿Para qué sirve? WHAT'S IT GOOD FOR?

Retírate, por favor. PLEASE LEAVE (the polite way to say it)

Sal, por favor PLEASE LEAVE (a bit stronger)

¡Vete! (very strong) GO AWAY! (a much stronger way to ask someone to leave)

Manos a la obra LET'S GET TO WORK

Tanto mejor SO MUCH THE BETTER

Tanto peor SO MUCH THE WORSE

Meter la pata TO INTERFERE, TO STICK ONE'S FOOT WHERE IT DOESN'T BELONG

Qué sé yo. HOW WOULD I KNOW.

Quién sabe. WHO KNOWS.

Questions and other comments that may or may not need answers

¿Qué? WHAT?

¿Cómo? HOW?

¿Dónde? WHERE?

¿Por dónde? WHICH WAY?

¿Cómo? WHY?

¿Por qué? WHY?

¿Diga? SAY IT AGAIN.

¿Qué dice (dices, dijo)? WHAT DID YOU SAY?

¿Qué quiere decir? WHAT DOES THIS MEAN?

¿Qué tal? HOW'S IT GOING?

168

¿Te gusta? HOW DO YOU LIKE IT?

¿Quién, yo? WHO ME?

¿A mí, qué? I DON'T CARE

¿Qué importa? WHO CARES?!

¿Y qué? SO WHAT?

Comments and exclamations that express thoughts, feelings, even requests. Be sure to use the proper gender when using these in conversation.

¡Hola! HELLO!

¡Voy! COMING!

¡Cómo no! OF COURSE! WHY NOT!

¡Hasta luego! SO LONG!

¡Qué! ¡En serio! NO KIDDING

¡Cómo! ¡En serio! REALLY! NO KIDDING!

¡Qué chiste! WHAT A JOKE!

¡Qué palo de agua! WHAT A RAINSTORM!

¡Basta! ENOUGH!

¡Cállense! QUIET! (to several people)

¡No me diga! DON'T TELL ME!

¡No puede ser! IT CAN'T BE SO!

¡No quiero! I DON'T WANT TO!

¡No lo quiero! I DON'T WANT IT!

¡Qué va! NO WAY!

¡Qué hediondo! HOW STINKY! WHAT A SMELL!

¡Qué asco! UGH! DISGUSTING!

¡Estoy harto! I'M TIRED (SICK) OF IT!

¡No lo soporto! CAN'T STAND HIM (fairly strong)

¡No lo soporto ni en pintura! I CAN'T STAND HIM, EVEN IN A PAINTING! (even stronger)

¡Cuidado! CAREFUL!

¡Alto! HALT! STOP!

¡Peligro! DANGER!

¡Socorro! ¡Auxilio! HELP!

¡Fuego! FIRE!

Notice the difference in meaning when a question mark is changed to an exclamation point. **¿Cómo?** (HOW?) becomes **¡Cómo!** (NO KIDDING!) and **¿Qué?** (WHAT?) becomes **¡Qué!** (REALLY!)

As you advance in Spanish

Here we do a little advanced work in Spanish. These lists are not in any special order. Read them over and then check on them again when the need arises.

Placement is important

When the adjective comes before a noun instead of the customary after, it can change the meaning of the phrase. As usual agreement of gender and number apply. Here are some examples.

Referring to people

Un vestido nuevo   A BRAND NEW DRESS

Un nuevo vestido   A NEW (DIFFERENT) DRESS, (change of clothes)

Un amigo viejo   AN OLD (ELDERLY) FRIEND

Un viejo amigo   AN FRIEND OF LONG STANDING

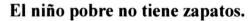

El niño pobre no tiene zapatos.

THE POOR CHILD HAS NO SHOES. (he lives in poverty)

El pobre niño tiene examen mañana. THE POOR CHILD HAS A TEST TOMORROW. (he is pitied, probably because he hasn't studied).

Una viuda rica   A RICH WIDOW

Un hombre rico   A RICH MAN

La viuda alegre   THE MERRY WIDOW (Capitalize when referring to musical composition.)

El jardinero mismo   THE GARDENER HIMSELF

El mismo jardinero   THE SAME GARDENER

referring to size or shape

Un gran hombre   A GREAT MAN

Un hombre grande   A LARGE MAN

Un gran hombre que también es grande   A GREAT MAN WHO IS ALSO LARGE

Un río grande   A LARGE RIVER

El Río Grande   THE BIG RIVER (a specific waterway)

Notice that **gran** is great, but **grande** is large. Generally speaking, the two are not interchangeable. The **e** of **grande** is always pronounced.

Bien *and* ***bueno*** *can cause confusion. These may help clarify:*

Ella está bien.

SHE IS WELL.

Las naranjas son buenas para la salud.

ORANGES ARE GOOD FOR (ONE'S) HEALTH.

Mi perro es bueno porque se porta bien.
MY DOG IS GOOD BECAUSE HE BEHAVES WELL.

*Use **el** or **la** for a specific person or thing, use **un** or **una** for an unidentified individual.*

El hombre alto   THE TALL MAN
Una mujer bonita   A PRETTY WOMAN

On occasion the descriptive term comes first, as in English

La primera vez   HE FIRST TIME
Hace mal tiempo   WE'RE HAVING BAD WEATHER

Sometimes it doesn't matter

El primer capítulo   THE FIRST CHAPTER
El capítulo primero   THE FIRST CHAPTER
El capítulo uno   CHAPTER ONE

El capital   MONEY, CAPITAL
La capital   THE CAPITAL CITY

    Se necesita capital para empezar un negocio.
    ONE NEEDS CAPITAL TO START A BUSINESS.
    Caracas es la capital de Venezuela.
    CARACAS IS THE CAPITAL OF VENEZUELA.

El corte   THE CUT — A HAIRCUT, THE CUT OF A SUIT, ETC.
La corte   THE ROYAL COURT, A COURT OF LAW

    Me gusta <u>el</u> corte de este traje (este peinado).
    I LIKE THE CUT OF THIS SUIT (THIS HAIRCUT).
    <u>La</u> corte de la reina Isabela era lujosa.
    THE COURT OF QUEEN ISABELA WAS LUXURIOUS.
    El ladrón fue juzgado en <u>la</u> corte del juez Gonzales.
    THE THIEF WAS JUDGED IN THE COURT OF JUDGE GONZALES.

El cura   THE PRIEST
La cura   THE CURE, as in healing
    Ese hombre está tan enfermo que se parece a una iglesia vacía: no tiene cura.
    THAT MAN IS SO ILL HE RESEMBLES AN EMPTY CHURCH: HE DOESN'T HAVE A CURE.
    Some puns work well in Spanish, but don't translate into English. This is one
of them.

El papá   THE DAD, THE FATHER
El Papa   THE POPE (sometimes not capitalized)
La papa   THE POTATO

    El papá del Papa comía papas fritas.
    THE FATHER OF THE POPE USED TO EAT FRIED POTATOES.

El radio THE RADIUS, THE COMPAS

La radio THE RECEIVER OF RADIO TRANSMISSIONS.

However, in ordinary conversation, is common to hear **el radio** for the radio.

watch for the differences with **n** *and* **ñ**

El año THE YEAR, 365 DAYS

El ano THE ANUS (a body part. Save this word for medical uses. Don't e-mail a friend to have a "feliz ano nuevo" if the e-mail doesn't let you do an **ñ**. For one thing, it can't be done and your friend might be insulted.)

El pino THE PINE TREE

La piña THE PINEAPPLE (fruit)

La pena THE PITY

La peña THE BOULDER

El puño THE FIST

El paño THE RAG

¡Qué pena! se le quebró el puño cuando le pegó a la piña.
WHAT A PITY! HE BROKE HIS FIST WHEN HE HIT THE PINEAPPLE.

Esos son los paños para limpiar el piso.
THOSE ARE THE RAGS FOR CLEANING THE FLOOR.

La campana THE BELL

La campaña THE CAMPAIGN, POLITICAL, MILITARY, ETC.

El candidato (el ejército) perdió (ganó) la campaña.
THE CANDIDATE (ARMY) LOST (WON) THE CAMPAIGN.

El cura toca la campana cada hora.
THE PRIEST RINGS THE BELL EVERY HOUR.

Ordenar TO PUT IN ORDER, TO ORDER SOMEONE TO DO SOMETHING

Ordeñar TO MILK THE COW, GOAT, ETC

No es necesario poner las vacas en orden alfabético para ordeñarlas.
IT IS NOT NECESSARY TO PUT THE COWS IN ALPHABETICAL ORDER IN ORDER TO MILK THEM.

r and **rr**

Caro EXPENSIVE

El carro AUTOMOBILE, CAR

¡Ese carro sí resultó caro!
THAT CAR SURE TURNED OUT TO BE EXPENSIVE!

Pero BUT

Perro DOG, CANINE

El perro ladra, pero nadie le hace caso.
THE DOG BARKS BUT NO ONE PAYS ATTENTION TO HIM.

172

Abrasar   TO BURN, TO BARBECUE

Abrazar   TO HUG, TO EMBRACE

El señor abrasó el bistec y ahora no lo puede comer.

THE MAN BURNED THE STEAK AND NOW HE CAN'T EAT IT.

La señora abraza a los niños.

THE WOMAN HUGS THE CHILDREN.

Casar   TO MARRY

Cazar   TO HUNT

(to hunt game, not to hunt for a lost item)

Me casé con una mujer que no me deja cazar.

I MARRIED A WOMAN WHO WON'T LET ME HUNT.

Cocinar   TO COOK (what the chef does)

Cocer   TO COOK THE ITEM, TO BOIL FOOD

Coser TO SEW BY HAND OR MACHINE

Mi madre coce la comida mientras mi abuela cose a mano.

MY MOTHER COOKS FOOD WHILE MY GRANDMOTHER SEWS BY HAND.

Liza   A JOUSTING FIELD, as in Medieval events

Lisa, liso   SMOOTH, AS GLASS OR A WATER SPILL ON TILE

Los caballeros entrenaban en la liza.

THE KNIGHTS TRAINED ON THE JOUSTING FIELD.

Esta madera es lisa.

THIS WOOD IS SMOOTH.

*check those **c**'s and **ch**'s*

La cocina   THE KITCHEN, THE STOVE

La cochina   THE FEMALE PIG (ANIMAL);

As an adjective, a sloppy housekeeper, unkept woman; the masculine version is **el cochino.**

Spanish is not Italian. A **c** is a **c** (not a **ch**) and a **ch** is a **ch**. A **ch** is not an **sh**, and neither is **ch** a **k**.

La cocina de mi amiga es grande.

MY FRIEND'S KITCHEN IS LARGE.

El señor de la casa es un cochino.

THE MAN OF THE HOUSE IS A PIG.

a few more look-alikes

Las acciones   THE STOCKS (investments)

La acción   THE ACTION, HAPPENING, EVENT

Perdí mucho dinero cuando vendí mis acciones de la compañía.

I LOST LOTS OF MONEY WHEN I SOLD MY STOCKS IN THE COMPANY.

A los niños les gustan las películas de acción.

CHILDREN LIKE ACTION MOVIES.

Actual, actualidad   AT PRESENT, NOW
Verdadero   ACTUAL, REAL

El actual alcalde es el Sr. Fulano.

THE CURRENT MAYOR IS MR. DOE.

La señorita Carmen es la verdadera reina del concurso de belleza. La que lleva la corona ahora es una impostora.

MISS CARMEN IS THE REAL QUEEN OF THE BEAUTY CONTEST. THE ONE THAT IS WEARING A CROWN NOW IS AN IMPOSTOR.

Atender   TO WAIT ON, TO SERVE
Asistir   TO ATTEND, AS A CLASS OR LECTURE

La enfermera atiende a los enfermos.

THE NURSE ATTENDS TO THE PATIENTS.

Los alumnos asisten a las clases.

THE STUDENTS ATTEND CLASSES.

Aprovechar   TO TAKE ADVANTAGE OF
Anticipar   TO ACT IN ADVANCE, TO ANTICIPATE
Esperar   TO EXPECT, TO WAIT

Tenemos un día fresco. Hay que aproverlo para cortar flores en el jardín.

WE HAVE A COOL DAY. LET'S TAKE ADVANTAGE OF IT TO CUT FLOWERS IN THE GARDEN.

El perro salió corriendo hacia su amo porque anticipó que él estaba a punto de llamarlo.

THE DOG BROKE INTO A RUN TOWARD HIS OWNER BECAUSE HE ANTICIPATED THAT HIS OWNER WAS ON THE VERGE OF CALLING HIM. **"a punto de"** is a way to express "ON THE VERGE OF," "ABOUT TO," and similar expressions.

Espero que tengas buenas notas en tu examen.

I EXPECT THAT YOU WILL HAVE GOOD GRADES ON YOUR TEST.

Lo espero aquí.

I WILL WAIT FOR YOU HERE.

La bolsa   THE BAG, THE SACK, THE PURSE
La Bolsa   THE STOCK EXCHANGE

Se acabó la bolsa de arroz.

THE BAG OF RICE IS FINISHED.

La Bolsa bajó ayer.

THE STOCK MARKET FELL YESTERDAY.

El cuarto   THE ROOM IN A HOUSE OR BUILDING

Un cuarto   ONE FOURTH, ONE QUARTER (25%)

El reloj del cuarto marca un cuarto para las cinco.

THE CLOCK IN THE ROOM SHOWS A QUARTER TO FIVE.

Cambiar   TO CHANGE (CHANGE SHIRTS, SHOES, ETC)

El cambio   THE CHANGE, AS AT THE CASH REGISTER; INCLUDES COINS

Cambia el canal de la tele, por favor.

CHANGE THE CHANNEL ON THE TV, PLEASE.

¿Tiene cambio para un billete de 20 dólares?

DO YOU HAVE CHANGE FOR A $20 BILL?

La cobra   A TYPE OF SNAKE

El cobre   COPPER (THE METAL)

Cobrar   TO CHARGE, TO PRESENT A BILL, TO SET A PRICE

La cobra es una culebra venenosa.

THE COBRA IS A POISONOUS SNAKE.

Chile se conoce por sus minas de cobre.

CHILE IS KNOWN FOR ITS COPPER MINES.

¿Cuánto cobra por este trabajo?

WHAT DO YOU CHARGE FOR THIS JOB?

El cuello THE NECK (links head and body)

El collar THE NECKLACE

El cuello de Nefertiti era muy largo y por eso podía llevar muchos collares.

THE NECK OF NEFERTITI WAS VERY LONG AND FOR THAT REASON SHE COULD WEAR MANY NECKLACES.

Cargar   TO CARRY, TO TOTE

Cargar   TO CHARGE (as in charging a battery), TO UPLOAD

Descargar   TO UNLOAD, as with cargo, TO DOWNLOAD ELECTRONICALLY (a modern extension of the existing word)

Los burros de los campesinos cargan leña.

THE DONKEYS OF THE PEASANTS CARRY FIREWOOD.

Hay que cargar la pila del teléfono celular.

IT IS NECESSARY TO CHARGE THE BATTERY OF THE CELL PHONE.

El equipo descargó los muebles del camión.

THE CREW UNLOADED THE FURNITURE FROM THE TRUCK.

Mi amigo descargó el documento que le mandé por correo electrónico.

MY FRIEND DOWNLOADED THE DOCUMENT I SENT HIM BY E-MAIL

La lengua, el idioma   THE LANGUAGE

La lengua THE TONGUE, THE MOUTH PART

Una persona puede comer lengua de res, pero no puede comer idioma.
A PERSON CAN EAT TONGUE, BUT CAN'T EAT LANGUAGE.

Dirección ADDRESS,
Dirección THE OFFICE OF THE DIRECTOR (OR OTHER HIGH OFFICIAL)
Dirección DIRECTION, ORIENTATION

¿Cuál es su dirección?
WHAT IS YOUR ADDRESS?

Me mandaron a la Dirección para firmar los papeles.
I WAS SENT TO THE OFFICE OF THE DIRECTOR TO SIGN THE PAPERS.

El avión va en dirección a Miami.
THE PLANE WAS HEADED FOR MIAMI.

Efectivo REAL, EFFECTIVE, THE TIME SOMETHING TAKES EFFECT
Efectivo CASH, AS OPPOSED TO CHECKS OR PLASTIC

El contrato será efectivo el año entrante.
THE CONTRACT TAKES EFFECT NEXT YEAR.

Aquí se paga sólo en efectivo.
HERE YOU PAY IN CASH ONLY.

Ensalada SALAD, GREENS, FRUIT ETC
Enchilada FOOD CONTAINING CHILE

La ensalada tiene lechuga, tomate y cebolla, pero no tiene chile.
THE SALAD HAS LETTUCE, TOMATOES AND ONIONS BUT DOESN'T HAVE CHILE.

La enchilada se llama así porque tiene chile.
ENCHILADAS ARE THUS NAMED BECAUSE THEY CONTAIN CHILE.

Las esposas THE WIVES
Las esposas THE HANDCUFFS

El policía le puso las esposas a los ladrones mientras sus esposas miraban.
THE POLICEMAN PUT HANDCUFFS ON THE THIEVES WHILE THEIR WIVES WATCHED.

Listo, lista READY FOR ACTION
Listo, lista SHARP, QUICK WITTED

La abuela está lista para salir
THE GRANDMOTHER IS READY TO LEAVE (TO GO OUT, GO SHOPPING, ETC)

La abuela tiene ochenta y cinco años pero es muy lista.
THE GRANDMOTHER IS 85 YEARS OLD BUT IS VERY SHARP.

El mueble A SPECIFIC PIECE OF FURNITURE
Los muebles THE FURNITURE AS A WHOLE

Este mueble no va con los otros muebles.
THIS PIECE OF FURNITURE DOESN'T GO WITH THE OTHER FURNISHINGS.

La muñeca   THE DOLL
La muñeca   THE WRIST

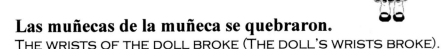

Las muñecas de la muñeca se quebraron.
THE WRISTS OF THE DOLL BROKE (THE DOLL'S WRISTS BROKE).

El negocio   THE BUSINESS DEAL
Los negocios   BUSINESS AS A WHOLE

El negocio del Sr. Mendoza está en quiebra.
THE BUSINESS OF MR. MENDOZA IS BANKRUPT.

Los negocios andan mal por los altos impuestos.
BUSINESSES ARE DOING POORLY BECAUSE OF THE HIGH TAXES.

La noticia   A PIECE OF NEWS
Las noticias   NEWS OF THE DAY FROM NEWSPAPERS, RADIO, TV, INTERNET, ETC.

¿Qué noticias tiene de su primo?
WHAT NEWS DO YOU HAVE OF YOUR COUSIN?

¿Vio las noticias anoche en la tele?
DID YOU WATCH THE NEWS LAST NIGHT ON THE TV?

Pequeño   SMALL IN SIZE
Poco   FEW, SMALL IN NUMBER

Ese tomate es muy pequeño. Hay que usar dos para esta receta.
THAT TOMATO IS TOO SMALL. WE NEED TO USE TWO FOR THIS RECIPE.

Póngale muy poca sal a la enchilada.
PUT A VERY SMALL AMOUNT OF SALT ON THE ENCHILADA.

La escuela es pequeña y tiene pocos alumnos.
THE SCHOOL IS SMALL AND HAS FEW STUDENTS.

Quebrar
TO BREAK SOMETHING SOLID, LIKE GLASS

Romper
TO TEAR, AS FABRIC, PAPER, ALSO AN ENGAGEMENT

El muchacho tiró una pelota y quebró el vidrio de la ventana.
THE BOY THREW A BALL AND BROKE THE GLASS OF THE WINDOW.

El gato rompió el mantel y ahora no se puede usar.
THE CAT TORE THE TABLECLOTH AND NOW IT CAN'T BE USED.

La novia* rompió su compromiso.
THE GIRLFRIEND* BROKE HER ENGAGEMENT.

*novia can be more serious than girlfriend, as with an engagement with a ring.

***Romper** can be a synonym for **quebrar**, but **quebrar** is rarely a synonym for **romper**.*

Sábana
SHEETS, FOR THE BED

Sabana
A LARGE GRASSY AREA, A GEOGRAPHIC DESCRIPTION (NOT A LAWN)

Las sábanas se cambian cada lunes.

THE SHEETS ARE CHANGED EVERY MONDAY.

La Gran Sabana es una región grande en Venezuela.

THE GRAN SABANA IS A LARGE REGION IN VENEZUELA.

Menudo
OFTEN, FREQUENTLY, TINY

Menudo
MEAT DERIVED FROM THE ANIMAL'S STOMACH AND PREPARED WITH CERTAIN SPICES AND FLAVORINGS.

A menudo comemos menudo.

WE OFTEN EAT MENUDO.

Suelo
FLOOR, SOIL

Piso
FLOOR (INDOORS), A BUILDING STORY

El pobre hombre se cayó al suelo.

THE POOR MAN FELL TO THE FLOOR.

Esa casa tiene tres pisos.

THAT HOUSE HAS THREE FLOORS.

Algunas plantas necesitan suelos ácidos.

SOME PLANTS NEED ACID SOIL.

These are somewhat similar:

El colegio and **la escuela** refer to SCHOOL (K-12 IN THE U.S.). The terms are synonymous. **La preparatoria** is HIGH SCHOOL (Sometimes shortened to **la prepa**). **La universidad** is UNIVERSITY, COLLEGE, HIGHER EDUCATION.

Carro, coche, auto, automóvil all refer to CARS, AUTOS, ETC. **Coche** is more common for car in México, while **carro** is in general use in South America. In some areas, **coche** may refer to TRAIN COACHES or even HORSE-DRAWN CARRIAGES. Also, **carro** could refer to CARTS or other modes of wheeled transportation. Different countries may have their own preferences. **Automóvil** and **auto** are always a safe way to refer to sedans, station wagons, hatchbacks, SUVs, etc.

Camión and **camioneta** are TRUCKS. An 18-WHEELER can be **camión de 18 ruedas**, just as in English. **Camioneta** is a smaller TRUCK, A PICKUP. **Camión** can also refer to a BUS in some countries, though BUS is generally **autobús**.

Apartamento is an APARTMENT, usually a rental unit. **Departamento** can also refer to an APARTMENT unit, although **departamento** is more generally used as DEPARTMENT in English, a division of a larger whole (a store, a government, etc.)

Some English and Spanish words look like Spanish words but are quite different in meaning.

Two sets of words to be aware of are **embarazada** and **preservativo**. They may look like "embarrassed" or "preserved", but are far from that. Be careful using  them. **Embarazada** is PREGNANT. **Preservativo** is CONDOM. **Preservar** in Spanish is more related to PROTECTING. PRESERVING can be more closely expressed with **guardar** (TO KEEP). TO BE EMBARRASSED is **tener vergüenza**. Don't be embarrassed with **ducha**. It's a simple SHOWER BATH.

Looking it up another way

Here is the same list, without explanations, in alphabetical order in English.

A THOUSAND THANKS **mil gracias**

ACTION, HAPPENING, EVENT **acción**

ACTUAL, REAL **verdadero(a)**

SOMETHING NEEDS TO BE DONE **algo necesita hacerse**

ANYWAY, ANYHOW **de todos modos**

ANUS **el ano**

AT A DISTANCE, FAR AWAY **a lo lejos**

AT PRESENT, NOW **actual**

AT THE SAME TIME **a la misma vez**

AT THE SAME TIME **a la vez**

AT THE SAME TIME **al mismo tiempo**

AT YOUR SERVICE **a la orden**

AUTOMOBILE, CAR, EVEN A CART **carro**

BAG, THE SACK **la bolsa**

BECAUSE **porque**

BELL **la campana**

BIG RIVER **el Río Grande** (a specific waterway)

BRAND NEW DRESS **un vestido nuevo**

BUSINESS AS A WHOLE **los negocios**

BUSINESS DEAL **el negocio**

BUT **pero**

BY COINCIDENCE, BY CHANCE **por casualidad**

CAMPAIGN, POLITICAL, MILITARY, ETC. **la campaña**

CAPITAL CITY **la capital**

CAREFUL! **¡Cuidado!**

CAREFULLY **con cuidado**

CASH, as opposed to checks or plastic **efectivo**

CHANGE, at the cash register; includes coins **el cambio**

CHAPTER ONE **Capítulo uno**

COBRA, (a type of snake) **la cobra**

COMING! **¡Voy!**

COPPER (the metal) **cobre**

CURE, AS IN HEALING **la cura**

CUT — OF A SUIT, A HAIRCUT, ETC **el corte**

DAD, FATHER **el papá**

DISH CONTAINING CHILE **la enchilada**

DOG, CANINE **el perro**

DOLL **la muñeca**

DON'T DO IT **no lo hagas**

DON'T TELL ME! **¡No me lo diga!**

EMBARRASSED **tener vergüenza**

ENOUGH! **¡Basta!**

EXACTLY RIGHT **al pie de la letra**

EXPENSIVE **caro**

FIRST CHAPTER **el capítulo primero**

FIRST CHAPTER **el primer capítulo**

FIRST TIME **la primera vez**

FIST **el puño**

FLOOR (INDOORS), A BUILDING STORY **el piso**

FLOOR, SOIL **el suelo**

FOR RENT **se alquila**

FOR SALE **se vende**

FRIEND OF LONG STANDING **un viejo amigo**

FURNITURE AS A WHOLE **los muebles**

GARDENER HIMSELF **el jardinero mismo**

GO AWAY! (much stronger) **¡váyase!**

GRASSY AREA, a geographic description **sabana**

GREAT MAN **un gran hombre**

GREAT MAN WHO IS ALSO LARGE **un gran hombre que también es grande**

HALT! STOP! **¡Alto!**

HANDCUFFS **las esposas**

HAVE A SEAT **tome asiento**

HE'S BEING RELEASED (FROM THE HOSPITAL) **lo dan de alta**

HELLO! **¡Hola!**

HELP YOURSELF **sírvase**

HELP! **¡Socorro!**

HIGH SCHOOL **la preparatoria, (la prepa)**

HOW MUCH ARE YOU ASKING FOR ___? **¿Cuánto pide por el (la) ___?**

HOW MUCH IS IT WORTH? **¿Cuánto vale?**

HOW STINKY! WHAT A SMELL! **¡Qué hediondo!**

HOW WOULD I KNOW? **¿Qué sé yo?**

HOW'S IT GOING? **¿Qué tal?**

I CAN'T STAND HIM! **¡No lo soporto!**

I AM AFRAID, I AM SCARED **Tengo miedo, Estoy asustado**

I CAN'T STAND HIM, EVEN IN A PAINTING! **¡No lo soporto ni en pintura!**

I DON'T CARE **¿A mí qué?**

I DON'T LIKE **no me gusta**

I DON'T WANT **no quiero**

I DON'T WANT IT! **¡No lo quiero!**

I DON'T WANT TO! **¡No quiero!**

I HAVE A HEADACHE **tengo dolor de cabeza**

I HAVE A TOOTH ACHE **tengo dolor de muela**

I LIKE **me gusta**

I MUST HURRY **tengo que apurarme**

I'M IN A HURRY **tengo prisa**

I'M SCARED **estoy asustado(a)**

I'M SCARED **tengo miedo**

I'M TIRED (SICK) OF IT! **¡Estoy harto!**

IS IT FOR SALE? **¿Se vende?**

IT CAN'T BE SO! **¡No puede ser!**

IT DOESN'T FIT **no cabe**

IT'S ALL THE SAME TO ME **me da lo mismo**

IT'S COLD. IT'S HOT **hace frío. hace calor**

IT'S NONE OF YOUR BUSINESS **eso no le incumbe**

IT'S NOT WORTH ANYTHING **no vale nada**

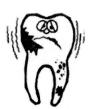

IT'S NOT WORTH DOING **no vale la pena**

IT'S SO; THAT'S RIGHT **así es**

IT'S TRUE **es cierto, es verdad, así es**

IT'S USED FOR ___ **se usa para ___**

IT'S WORTH DOING **vale la pena**

IT'S WORTHLESS **no sirve para nada**

IT'S WRITTEN WITH A CAPITAL LETTER **se escribe con mayúscula**

IT'S WRITTEN WITH A LOWER CASE LETTER **se escribe con minúscula**

JOUSTING FIELD **liza**

LACK, FOR LACK OF **faltar, por falta de**

LANGUAGE **la lengua, el idioma**

LARGE MAN **un hombre grande**

LARGE RIVER **un río grande**

LET'S GET TO WORK **manos a la obra**

MERRY WIDOW **la viuda alegre**

MONEY, CAPITAL **el capital**

MY HEAD HURTS **me duele la cabeza**

NEAR THE END OF THE MONTH **a fines del mes**

NEAR THE END OF THE WEEK **a fines de la semana**

NEAR THE END OF THE YEAR **a fines del año**

NECK **el cuello**

NECKLACE **el collar**

NEW (DIFFERENT) DRESS, CHANGE OF CLOTHES **un nuevo vestido**

NO DOUBT ABOUT IT **no cabe duda**

NO DOWNPAYMENT **sin enganche**

NO KIDDING! **¡Qué!**

NO WAY! **¡Qué va!**

OF COURSE! WHY NOT! **¡Cómo no!**

OFTEN, FREQUENTLY **a menudo**

OLD (IN YEARS) FRIEND **un amigo viejo**

PLEASE LEAVE (stronger) **salga, por favor**

NEWS OF THE DAY (newspapers, radio, tv) **las noticias**

ONE FOURTH, ONE QUARTER (25%) **un cuarto**

PIECE OF NEWS **la noticia**

PINE TREE **el pino**

PINEAPPLE, THE FRUIT **la piña**

PITY **la pena**

PLEASE LEAVE (the polite way to say it) **retírese, por favor**

POOR CHILD **El niño pobre no tiene zapatos.**

POOR CHILD **El pobre niño tiene examen mañana.**

QUIET! (PL) **¡Cállense!**

POPE (sometimes capitalized) **el Papa**

POTATO **la papa**

PRETTY WOMAN **mujer bonita**

PRIEST **el cura**

RADIO: RECEIVER OF TRANSMISSIONS **la radio**

RADIUS, THE COMPAS **el radio**

REAL, EFFECTIVE, THE TIME SOMETHING TAKES EFFECT **efectivo**

REALLY! NO KIDDING! **¡Cómo!**

RICH MAN **un hombre rico**

RICH WIDOW **una viuda rica**

ROOM IN A HOUSE OR BUILDING (ONE) **un cuarto**

ROOM IN A HOUSE OR BUILDING (THE) **el cuarto**

ROYAL COURT, A COURT OF LAW **la corte**

SALAD (greens, fruit etc) **ensalada**

SAME GARDENER **el mismo jardinero**

SAY IT AGAIN **¿Diga?**

SCHOOL, ELEMENTARY TO HIGH SCHOOL **colegio**

SCHOOL, ELEMENTARY TO HIGH SCHOOL **escuela**

SHEETS, for the bed **sábana**

SIT **siéntese** (formal) **siéntate** (informal)

SMALL IN NUMBER **poco**

SMALL IN SIZE **pequeño**

SMOOTH **lisa**

SO LONG! **¡Hasta luego!**

SO MUCH THE BETTER **tanto mejor**

SO MUCH THE WORSE **tanto peor**

SO WHAT? **¿Y qué?**

SO-SO **más o menos**

SPANISH SPOKEN HERE **se habla español**

SPECIFIC PIECE OF FURNITURE **el mueble**

STOCK EXCHANGE **la Bolsa**

STOCKS (INVESTMENTS) **las acciones**

SUDDENLY, ALL AT ONCE **de repente**

TALL MAN **el hombre alto**

THAT'S NOT RIGHT, IT'S NOT SO **no es así**

THAT'S RIGHT **así es**

THERE'S A FULL MOON **hay luna llena**

TO BE HUNGRY **tener hambre**

TO BE SUCCESSFUL **tener éxito**

TO BREAK SOMETHING SOLID, LIKE GLASS **quebrar**

TO BURN **abrasar**

TO CHANGE (CHANGE SHIRTS, SHOES, ETC) **cambiar**

TO CHARGE, TO PRESENT A BILL, TO SET A PRICE **cobrar**

TO COOK THE ITEM, BOILING IT **cocer**

TO COOK, WHAT THE CHEF DOES **cocinar**

TO DOWNLOAD ELECTRONICALLY **descargar**

TO DREAM OF (WITH) **soñar con**

TO DREAM WITH **soñar con**

TO HAVE AN APPOINTMENT WITH __ **tener cita con___**

TO HUG, EMBRACE **abrazar**

TO HUNT (game) **cazar**

TO INTERFERE **meter la pata**

TO LAUGH AT **reírse con**

TO LAUGH WITH **reírse con**

TO LOSE INTEREST IN ___ **perder las ganas de ____**

TO MARRY **casar ___**

TO MILK THE COW, GOAT, ETC **ordeñar**

TO MUST (DO SOMETHING) **tener que___**

TO PACK THE SUITCASES **hacer las maletas**

TO PAY ATTENTION **hacer caso**

TO PUT IN ORDER, TO ORDER SOMEONE TO DO SOMETHING **ordenar**

TO SEW BY HAND OR MACHINE **coser**

TO SMELL OF **oler a**

TO STAND IN LINE, AS AT A CHECKOUT LINE **hacer cola, línea**

TO TEAR, AS FABRIC, PAPER, AN ENGAGEMENT **romper**

TO UNLOAD, (AS WITH CARGO) **descargar**

TO WANT TO DO (SOMETHING) **tener ganas de. . .**

TONGUE (MOUTH PART) **la lengua**

UGH! DISGUSTING! **¡Qué asco!**

UNIVERSITY, COLLEGE **universidad, la**

WE HAVE ____ (FOR SALE) **tenemos ____**

WE'RE HAVING BAD WEATHER **hace mal tiempo**

WHAT A JOKE! **¡Qué chiste!**

WHAT A RAINSTORM! **¡Qué palo de agua!**

WHAT A SCARE! **¡que susto!**

WHAT ARE YOU ASKING FOR ___? **¡Cuánto pide por el (la) ___?**

WHAT DID YOU SAY? **¿Qué dice (dices)?**

WHAT DOES THIS MEAN? **¿Qué quiere decir?**

WHAT? **¿Qué?**

WHAT'S IT GOOD FOR? **¿Para qué sirve?**

WHERE? **¿Dónde?**

WHICH WAY? **¿Por dónde?**

WHO CARES?! **¿Qué importa?**

WHO KNOWS? **¿Quién sabe?**

WHY? **¿Cómo?**

WHY? **¿Por qué?**

WIVES **las esposas**

WRIST **la muñeca**

YEAR, 365 DAYS **el año**

18
THE LISTS
Las listas

This chapter provides lists and other items not covered in the topical chapters. Review the lists quickly and then use them for reference as necessary. In summary, this section includes days of the calendar (months, days of the week.) numbers and math; telling time; seasons; holidays; family members, fun and games, travel, cars and traffic, weather, occupations and even insults and praises.

Los meses
The months

el (un) mes, los (unos) meses THE (A) MONTH, THE (SOME) MONTHS

enero JANUARY

febrero FEBRUARY

marzo MARCH

abril APRIL

mayo MAY

junio JUNE

julio JULY

agosto AUGUST

septiembre SEPTEMBER

octubre OCTOBER

noviembre NOVEMBER

diciembre DECEMBER

¿Cuál es tu día de cumpleaños?
WHAT IS YOUR BIRTHDAY?

Yo nací el doce de abril, ¿y tú?
I WAS BORN APRIL 12, AND YOU?

¿En qué año nació su esposa?
IN WHAT YEAR WAS YOUR WIFE BORN?

¡Uno nunca le hace esa pregunta a una señora!
ONE NEVER ASKS THAT QUESTION OF A LADY!

Los días de la semana
Days of the week

día, días DAY, DAYS

domingo SUNDAY

lunes MONDAY

martes TUESDAY

miércoles WEDNESDAY

jueves THURSDAY

viernes FRIDAY

sábado SATURDAY

Unlike English, names of months and days of the week are capitalized only at the start of a sentence or the start of a book title.

hoy TODAY

mañana TOMORROW

pasado mañana DAY AFTER TOMORROW

ayer YESTERDAY

anteayer DAY BEFORE YESTERDAY

semana WEEK

la semana (el mes) que viene NEXT WEEK (MONTH)

la semana pasada (el mes pasado) LAST WEEK (MONTH)

There two ways to say the days of the month. In English we say JANUARY ONE, JULY FOUR. In Spanish this is rendered **enero uno, julio cuatro, etc.**

Another way is **el primero de ___** (THE FIRST OF ___): **el primero de enero, de marzo**, but after the first day it's **el dos de febrero, el cinco de mayo, el seis de octubre** (Literally THE TWO OF, THE FIVE OF, ETC).

Weeks of the month are: **la primera semana, la segunda semana**, etc. THE FIRST WEEK, THE SECOND WEEK

For certain days of the week, it's **el segundo jueves, el tercer lunes**. THE SECOND THURSDAY, THE THIRD MONDAY

¿A qué hora empieza el trabajo?
WHAT TIME DO WE START WORK?

Empezamos a las ocho de la mañana.
WE START AT 8 A.M.

¿A qué hora salimos del trabajo?
WHAT TIME DO WE LEAVE WORK?

La tienda se cierra a las seis y media de lunes a viernes y a las cinco los sábados.
THE STORE CLOSES AT 6:30 P.M. MONDAY THROUGH FRIDAY AND 5 P.M. SATURDAYS.

Números cardinales
Cardinal numbers

número NUMBER
cero ZERO
uno ONE
dos TWO
tres THREE
cuatro FOUR
cinco FIVE
seis SIX
siete SEVEN
ocho EIGHT
nueve NINE
diez 10
once 11
doce 12
trece 13
catorce 14
quince 15
dieciséis 16
diecisiete 17
dieciocho 18
diecinueve 19
veinte 20
veintiuno 21
veintidós 22
veintitrés 23
veinticuatro 24
trienta 30

now add **y** *with the correct number*
treinta y uno 31
cuarenta 40
cuarenta y uno 41
cincuenta 50
sesenta 60
setenta 70
ochenta 80
noventa 90
cien 100
ciento uno 101

Numbers in the 100s are:

doscientos 200

trescientos 300, to **ochocientos** 800, but **novecientos** 900.

Ciento goes ahead of smaller numbers: **ciento diez** 110; **ochocientos diez y siete** 817, etc. In the thousands, it's **mil, dos mil, tres mil,** etc.

Números ordinales
Ordinal numbers

primer, primero, primera FIRST

segundo(a) SECOND

tercer, tercero, tercera THIRD

cuarto(a) FOURTH

quinto(a) FIFTH

sexto(a) SIXTH

séptimo(a) SEVENTH

octavo(a) EIGHTH

noveno(a) NINTH

décimo(a) TENTH

Notice that **primer** and **tercer** don't have the **o** masculine ending except in certain cases, but they do take the **a** ending for feminine.

Examples: **el primer día** THE FIRST DAY; **la primera vez** THE FIRST TIME; **el tercer helado** THE THIRD ICE CREAM; **la tercera taza,** THE THIRD CUP; **la segunda semana** THE SECOND WEEK, etc. BUT **el primero del mes** THE FIRST OF THE MONTH.

En nuestra ciudad algunas calles tienen nombres, pero en otras ciudades tienen números.

IN OUR CITY SOME STREETS HAVE NAMES, BUT OTHER CITIES HAVE NUMBERS.

Mi dirección es novecientos cincuenta y nueve en la cal- le
Central.

MY ADDRESS IS 959 CENTRAL STREET.

Mis suegros viven en un apartamento en la Calle Cuarta.

MY INLAWS LIVE IN AN APARTMENT ON FOURTH STREET.

¿Cuál es su dirección? ¿Dónde vive usted?

WHAT IS YOUR ADDRESS? WHERE DO YOU LIVE?

Asking the same in the familiar:

¿Cuál es tu dirección? ¿Dónde vives?

WHAT IS YOUR ADDRESS? WHERE DO YOU LIVE?

En muchas ciudades de América Latina las casas tienen nombres en vez de números.

IN MANY CITIES OF LATIN AMERICA THE HOUSES HAVE NAMES INSTEAD OF NUMBERS.

Uno se imagina cómo un cartero se puede confundir con este sistema.
ONE IMAGINES HOW A MAIL CARRIER CAN BE CONFUSED BY THIS SYSTEM.

Las horas
Telling time

In spoken Spanish, it's **de la madrugada, de la mañana, de la tarde** or **de la noche** to designate morning, afternoon or night. **Madrugada** is roughly 1-4 a.m., before dawn. The others are more flexible. **Mañana** goes to noon; tarde goes from noon through 7 or 8 p.m. and **noche** is 7 or 8 p.m. to about midnight. However, with daylight saving time or your location, these descriptions may change.

When telling time, **de la mañana** and **de la tarde** are used where in English we use A.M. and P.M. or IN THE MORNING or IN THE AFTERNOON.

In English, O'CLOCK is used when a.m. and p.m. are understood or undetermined. In Spanish **de la ___** is skipped when the part of the day is not needed.

So, when you are asked: **¿Qué hora es?** WHAT TIME IS IT? the answer could be:

Es la una. IT'S ONE O'CLOCK. **De la tarde** is not needed in general daytime conversations. **De la tarde** would be used when speaking of the future or even the past to clarify any ambiguity. **De la noche** would make it clear that the hour is at night and not in the afternoon.

Other answers for WHAT TIME IS IT?

Es casi la una. IT'S ALMOST ONE. **Casi** is ALMOST and has other uses, such as for distance: **"casi una milla"** ALMOST ONE MILE.

Son las tres en punto. IT IS 3 O'CLOCK SHARP. **en punto** means ON THE DOT, so that with time it translates SHARP. This works for other uses, too.

Son las cuatro y pico. IT IS A LITTLE AFTER FOUR. **"Pico"** is an idiomatic way to add a little to something, time in this case. It could show up in measurements: **una taza y pico** meaning ONE CUP AND A SMIDGE MORE, **una milla y pico** A LITTLE MORE THAN A MILE.

Notice that one (1) is singular. The rest are plural.

Son las diez de la mañana. IT'S 10 A.M.

Son las tres y quince. IT'S 3:15 (THREE AND FIFTEEN) Likely p.m. If it were early morning, **de la madrugada** would be added.

Son las cuatro y media. IT'S 4:30 (FOUR AND A HALF). Again, **de la madrugada** is used if the reference is a.m.

Son las cinco menos quince. IT'S 4:45 (FIVE LESS FIFTEEN) also

Faltan quince para las cinco. (FIVE LACKING 15)

Son las ocho y (con) ocho de la noche. IT'S 8:08 P.M. (EIGHT AND EIGHT, EIGHT WITH EIGHT) or

Son ocho minutos después de las ocho. EIGHT MINUTES AFTER EIGHT.

Es mediodía. IT'S NOON

Es medianoche. IT'S MIDNIGHT

Technically, noon and midnight are instants in time. Any fraction of a second before or after are a.m. or p.m. Therefore a.m. and p.m. are not used with midnight or noon.

In a question from the past **¿Qué hora era?** WHAT TIME WAS IT? the answers are given in the past.

Eran las once de la noche. IT WAS 11 AT NIGHT.

Similarly, the future should specify if there could be a doubt.

¿A qué hora nos vemos? AT WHAT TIME DO WE MEET?

Nos vemos a las nueve de la mañana. WE'LL MEET AT 9 IN THE MORNING.

In schedules and similar texts, a.m. and p.m. are used. Some countries use "military" time, the 24-hour clock, on schedules and time tables.

Las matemáticas
Doing math

Math tables

Addition uses **más** or **y** where English uses PLUS or AND. Your choice.

Subtraction uses **menos** where English uses MINUS or LESS.

Multiplication uses **por** where English uses TIMES or MULTIPLIED BY.

Division uses **divido por** where English uses DIVIDED BY.

The results are given with **son,** except **uno por uno <u>es</u> uno**, again keeping singulars with singulars. **Cero (0)** also takes <u>es</u>: **siete por cero es cero.**

Uno más uno son dos. $1 + 1 = 2$

Dos más dos son cuatro. $2 + 2 = 4$

Tres y tres son seis. $3 + 3 = 6$

Cuatro y cuatro son ocho. $4 + 4 = 8$

Nueve menos cuatro son cinco. $9 - 4 = 5$

Tres por tres son nueve. $3 \times 3 = 9$

Diez dividido por cinco son dos. $10 \div 5 = 2$

Cien dividido por cuatro son veinticinco. $100 \div 4 = 25$

Contestando el teléfono
Answering the phone

How you answer the phone in Spanish depends on where you are or where you are from. So don't be surprised if your Spanish speaking house guest or hired help uses different words to answer a call. Among common words are **Alo** or **Aló**, **Bueno**, **Diga** or others.

¿De parte de quién? translates to MAY I ASK WHO IS CALLING? It is a standard way that office or store employees direct calls to the boss or another employee.

Número equivocado is how you tell a caller that he dialed the WRONG NUMBER.

A few other phrases for telephone use:

Dime tu número de teléfono, por favor.
TELL ME YOUR TELEPHONE NUMBER, PLEASE.

Mi número de teléfono es 123-4567. Apúntalo.
MY TELEPHONE NUMBER IS 123-4567. MAKE A NOTE OF IT.

¿Quién termina una conversación por teléfono?
WHO ENDS A TELEPHONE CONVERSATION?

El que hizo la llamada es el que termina la conversación.
THE ONE WHO MADE THE CALL IS THE ONE WHO ENDS THE CONVERSATION

El cuerpo
The body

los anteojos EYEGLASSES

el brazo, los brazos THE ARM, THE ARMS

la barba BEARD

la barbilla CHIN

la barriga, la panza BELLY, TUMMY

el bigote MUSTACHE

la boca MOUTH

la cabeza HEAD

el cadáver CADAVER

el cabello, el pelo HAIR

las caderas THE HIPS

las cejas EYEBROWS

la cintura WAIST

el codo ELBOW

el corazón HEART

el cuerpo BODY

los dedos THE FINGERS

el dedo pulgar THUMB

los dedos del pie TOES

el diente TOOTH

el esqueleto SKELETON

el estómago STOMAC

la garganta THROAT

las huellas digitales FINGERPRINTS

la frente FOREHEAD

los huesos BONES

los labios LIPS

la lengua TONGUE

la mano HAND

la mejilla, el cachete CHEEK
la muela MOLAR
la muñeca WRIST
los músculos MUSCLES
la nariz NOSE
los ojos EYES
las orejas, los oídos EARS
el pecho CHEST
la piel SKIN
la pierna LEG
las pestañas EYELASHES
las nalgas THE SEAT, THE BEHIND, THE REAR
la presión arterial BLOOD PRESSURE
los pulmones LUNGS
el puño FIST
la rodilla KNEE
la sangre BLOOD
el seno, la mama BREAST
el talón HEEL
el tobillo ANKLE
las uñas FINGERNAILS
las uñas de los pies TOENAILS

Reír
TO LAUGH

Dormir
TO SLEEP

Cantar
TO SING

Lo que hace el cuerpo
Body actions

andar TO WALK, TO MOVE ON
buscar TO LOOK FOR
caminar TO WALK
cantar TO SING
correr TO RUN
dar a luz TO GIVE BIRTH

decir TO SAY, TO TALK
dormir TO SLEEP
escupir TO SPIT
estornudar TO SNEEZE
hablar, decir TO SPEAK, TO TALK
oír TO HEAR
oler TO SMELL
reír TO LAUGH
respirar TO BREATHE
sentir TO FEEL
tocar TO TOUCH also TO PLAY a musical instrument
toser TO COUGH
tragar TO SWALLOW
ver, mirar TO SEE, TO LOOK
una tos A COUGH
un dolor de cabeza A HEADACHE
un dolor de diente A TOOTH ACHE
un estornudo A SNEEZE

Me duele la cabeza cuando oigo a los políticos mintiendo.
I GET A HEADACHE WHEN I HEAR POLITICIANS TELL LIES.

El bebé llora cuando lo llevan en un viaje en avión porque le duelen los oídos.
THE BABY CRIES WHEN HE IS TAKEN ON A TRIP ON AN AIRLINER BECAUSE HIS EAR HURTS.

Me río mucho de los cuentos chistosos de mi suegra.
I LAUGH A LOT OVER THE FUNNY STORIES OF MY MOTHER-IN-LAW.

Padres y parientes
Kith and kin

la familia THE FAMILY
el matrimonio THE MARRIED COUPLE
los padres THE PARENTS
el papá THE DAD
la mamá THE MOM

el padre (more formal, also a clerical title) THE FATHER
la madre (more formal, also a clerical title) THE MOTHER
el esposo, el marido THE HUSBAND
la esposa, la mujer THE WIFE
el hijo THE SON

la hija THE DAUGHTER
los hijos THE SONS

las hijas THE DAUGHTERS

los hijos THE CHILDREN (mixed sexes)

el hermano THE BROTHER

la hermana THE SISTER

los hermanos THE BROTHERS

las hermanas THE SISTERS

los hermanos THE SIBLINGS (mixed sexes)

las gemelas TWIN GIRLS

los gemelos TWIN BOYS

los parientes RELATIVES

la abuela GRANDMOTHER

el abuelo GRANDFATHER

los abuelos GRANDPARENTS

la tía AUNT

el tío UNCLE

las tías AUNTS

los tíos UNCLES (can include aunts)

el primo COUSIN (m)

la prima COUSIN (f)

los primos COUSINS (m&f)

el primo hermano FIRST COUSIN (m)

la prima hermana FIRST COUSIN (f)

la sobrina NIECE

el sobrino NEPHEW

los sobrinos CHILDREN OF AUNT OR UNCLE

la bisabuela GREAT GRANDMOTHER

el bisabuelo GREAT GRANDFATHER

los bisabuelos GREAT GRANDPARENTS

los tatarabuelos GREAT-GREAT GRANDPARENTS

la suegra MOTHER-IN-LAW

el suegro FATHER-IN-LAW

el yerno SON-IN-LAW

la nuera DAUGHTER-IN-LAW

Marriage, divorce and children

A note on married women's names in the Spanish tradition. **Silvia Pérez** marries **Antonio Ramos**. She becomes **Silvia Pérez de Ramos**, the **de** (OF, BELONGING TO) signifying she belongs to Mr. Ramos. Their children take on both parents' names thus: **Juan Ramos Pérez** or **Marta Ramos Pérez**. This keeps the father's last name ahead of the mother's maiden name. In the U.S. these names may be hyphenated or the Pérez may be dropped. Some men may drop the mother's maiden name and use only an initial:

Juan Ramos P.

When **Silvia** and **Antonio** divorce, she reverts back to **Silvia Pérez**. In the U.S., if she wants to keep the Ramos name, she could use **Silvia Ramos** or **Silvia Pérez Ramos**. She removes the **de**, as she no longer belongs to Mr. Ramos.

A few phrases relating to family

Tengo tres primos. ¿Cuántos tiene usted?
I HAVE THREE COUSINS. HOW MANY DO YOU HAVE?

No tengo ni un primo.
I DON'T HAVE ANY COUSINS.
Remember that the double negative is ok in Spanish.

Mi hermana vive en Denver con su esposo y sus hijos.
MY SISTER LIVES IN DENVER WITH HER HUSBAND AND CHILDREN.

Mi suegra es una persona muy chistosa.
MY MOTHER-IN-LAW IS A VERY FUNNY (JOKING) PERSON.

Mi suegro es flojo y pasa todo su tiempo mirando el fútbol en la tele.
MY FATHER-IN-LAW IS LAZY AND SPENDS HIS TIME WATCHING SOCCER ON THE TV.

El niño bueno cumple las órdenes de su mamá.
THE GOOD BOY OBEYS THE ORDERS OF HIS MOTHER.

La niña es desordenada y por eso nunca encuentra lo que busca.
THE GIRL IS SLOPPY AND BECAUSE OF THAT SHE NEVER FINDS WHAT SHE LOOKS FOR.

Encontramos las palabras "damas" y "caballeros" en las puertas de los baños de restaurantes de comida mexicana.
WE FIND THE WORDS "DAMAS" AND "CABALLEROS" ON THE DOORS OF RESTROOMS OF RESTAURANTS THAT SERVE MEXICAN FOOD.

Los abuelos y el nieto
GRANDPARENTS AND GRANDSON

Los trabajos
Occupations, jobs

el abogado, la abogada LAWYER

el actor ACTOR

la actriz ACTRESS

el/la albañil MASON

el/la alcalde MAYOR

el animador, la animadora RADIO (TV) HOST

el/la artista ARTIST

el/la chef CHEF

el/la chofer * de autobús BUS DRIVER

el/la chófer * CHAUFFEUR

     * Some dictionaries place the accent on the **o** and others on the **e**.

el cocinero, la cocinera COOK

el costurero, la costurera SEAMSTRESS

el/la dentista DENTIST

el/la electricista ELECTRICIAN

el escritor, la escritora WRITER

el jardinero, la jardinera GARDENER

el jefe, la jefa BOSS, CHIEF

el maestro, la maestra, el profesor, la profesora TEACHER

el/la médico, el doctor, la doctora DOCTOR

el músico, la música MUSICIAN

el pastor, la pastora PASTOR (OF CHURCH)

el peluquero BARBER

la peluquera BEAUTICIAN

el/la periodista REPORTER (press, radio, tv)

el/la piloto PILOT

el pintor, la pintora PAINTER

el plomero, la plomera PLUMBER

el político, la política POLITICIAN

el sacerdote, el cura, el pastor, la pastora PASTOR, MINISTER, PRIEST

el/la sastre TAILOR

el/la sindicalista UNION MEMBER

la sirvienta, la señora de la limpieza MAID, CLEANING LADY

el/la taxista TAXI DRIVER

el vaquero, la vaquera COWBOY, COWGIRL

el vendedor, la vendedora SALES PERSON

el veterinario, la veterinaria VETERINARIAN

Older friend to child:

¿Qué quieres hacer cuando seas grande?

WHAT DO YOU WANT TO BE WHEN YOU GROW UP?

The child answers:

Quiero ser un piloto (un policía, un galán de televisión).

I WANT TO BE A PILOT (A POLICEMAN, A LEADING MAN ON TELEVISION)

At work

¿Dónde trabaja su vecina?

WHERE DOES YOUR NEIGHBOR WORK?

Ella es peluquera y trabaja en un salón de belleza.

THE HAIRDRESSER WORKS IN A BEAUTY PARLOR.

Mi nieto se graduó de ingeniero, pero trabaja como mesero en un restaurante.

MY NEPHEW GRADUATED AS AN ENGINEER BUT HE WORKS AS A WAITER IN A RESTAURANT.

Not all occupations are admirable.

¿Qué hace su hermano?

WHAT DOES YOUR BROTHER DO (TO EARN A LIVING)?

Mi hermano es un político (un ladrón, un chantajista).

MY BROTHER IS A POLITICIAN (A THIEF, A BLACKMAILER).

Trabajando
Working

La cajera
THE CASHIER

La abogada
THE LAWYER

La enfermera
THE NURSE

El dentista
THE DENTIST

El médico
THE DOCTOR (MD)

La salvavidas
THE LIFEGUARD

El excavador
THE DIGGER

La costurera
THE DRESSMAKER

Religiones y nacionalidades
Religions & nationalities

católico, católica ROMAN CATHOLIC
cristiano, cristiana CHRISTIAN
judío, judía JEWISH
luterano, luterana LUTHERAN
musulmán, musulmana MOSLEM
BUT . . .
metodista (m&f) METHODIST

Nationalities depend on citizen preferences:
argentino(a) ARGENTINE
beliceño(a) BELIZEAN
brasilero (a), brasileño(a) BRAZILIAN
chileno(a) CHILEAN
costarricense COSTA RICAN
ecuatoriano(a), cuatoriano(a) ECUADORIAN
estadounidense US CITIZEN
francés, francesa FRENCH PERSON
inglés, inglesa BRITISH, ENGLISH PERSON
mexicano(a) MEXICAN
nicaragüense NICARAGUAN
uruguayo(a) URUGUAYAN
venezolano(a) VENEZUELAN

Juegos y pasatiempos
Fun and games

Some words relating to sports may translate or not work in unexpected ways. **Jugar** is used for playing in sports, and also for playing the lottery and playing cards.

Where the games are played is also worth checking into. For instance, **cancha** is a FIELD or COURT, such as for basketball or soccer. **Campo** can also refer to a soccer field, though **campo** is also an open area, outside a city or even an open area inside a city. In military terms, **campo de batalla** is a FIELD OF BATTLE.

Some of the games we play:
ajedrez CHESS
baloncesto BASKETBAL
barajas, naipes, cartas CARDS (DECK)
beisbol BASEBALL
bola, balón, pelota BALL (different sizes)
bridge BRIDGE

brincar la cuerda JUMP ROPE

canasta CANASTA

cancha COURT or ARENA where games are played

crucigrama CROSSWORD PUZZLE

damas CHECKERS

equipo TEAM

escondite HIDE-AND-SEEK

fútbol americano FOOTBALL

fútbol SOCCER

gol GOAL

golf GOLF

jonrón HOMERUN

juegos de cartas, de naipes, de barajas CARD GAMES

monopolio MONOPOLY

patinaje SKATING (roller)

póker POKER

rompecabezas JIGSAW PUZZLE

Muchos deportes se juegan en cancha al aire libre y otros se juegan en una cancha dentro de un gimnasio.
MANY SPORTS ARE PLAYED IN A FIELD IN THE FRESH AIR, AND OTHERS ARE PLAYED INDOORS IN A GYM.

Se necesitan cuatro personas para jugar bridge, pero la canasta se puede jugar entre dos y ocho personas.
FOUR PEOPLE ARE NEEDED TO PLAY BRIDGE BUT CANASTA CAN BE PLAYED BY TWO UP TO EIGHT.

Jugar a la pelota es bueno para la salud de los niños, pero puede ser malo para la ventana.
PLAYING WITH A BALL IS GOOD FOR THE HEALTH OF CHILDREN BUT CAN BE BAD FOR A WINDOW.

El automóvil
The automobile

la bolsa de aire, la almohada inflable AIRBAG

el aire acondicionado AIR-CONDITIONER

el anticoagulante ANTIFREEZE

los frenos BRAEKS

la luz del freno BRAKE LIGHT

el parachoques, la defensa BUMPER

el encendedor CIGARETTE LIGHTER

el tablero DASHBOARD

el escape EXHAUST

el guardafango FENDER

la luz antineblina FOG LIGHT

la gasolina GASOLINE

el medidor de gasolina GAS GAUGE

la gasolinera, la bomba GAS STATION

el tanque de gasolina GAS TANK

la guantera GLOVE BOX

la luz delantera HEADLIGHT

el calentador HEATER

el capó, la capota HOOD

la corneta, el claxon, la bocina HORN

el tapacubos HUBCAP

el arranque IGNITION

el gato JACK

la placa lICENSE PLATE

el silenciador, el mofle MUFFLER

el odómetro, el kilometraje ODOMETER

el aceite OIL

el medidor de aceite OIL PRESSURE GAUGE

el radiador RADIATOR

la radio RADIO

la luz trasera REAR LIGHT

el espejo retrovisor REARVIEW MIRROR

el espejo lateral REARVIEW MIRROR OUTSIDE

el asiento SEAT

el cinturón de seguridad SEAT BELT

la palanca de velocidades, el velocímetro, el cuentakilómetros SPEEDOMETER

el volante STEERING WHEEL

el tocacintas, el tocadiscos TAPE (DISK) PLAYER

el medidor de temperatura TEMPERATURE GAUGE

el neumático, la llanta TIRE

el pinchazo THE FLAT TIRE

el repuesto TIRE, SPARE

el maletero TRUNK

la rueda WHEEL

el parabrisas WINDSHIELD

el limpiaparabrisas WINDSHIELD WIPERS

el choque THE WRECK

E de échele E FOR EMPTY is the humorous way to say the tank needs to be filled (**echar**, to put in).

F de ful F FOR FULL The word "ful" has come into Spanish, very informally, via air travel and gas tank gauges.

What people do in their cars

acelerar TO ACCELERATE

frenar TO BREAK

cambiar de carril TO CHANGE LANES

pitar TO HONK

bajar de velocidad TO SLOW DOWN

parar TO STOP

dar vuelta a la izquierda TO TURN LEFT

dar vuelta a la derecha TO TURN RIGHT

Some phrases relating to the car

Su carro chocó y se tuvo que reemplazar el guardafango.
YOUR CAR WAS IN A WRECK AND YOU HAD TO REPLACE THE FENDER.

Mi carrito japonés usa poca gasolina
MY LITTLE JAPANESE CAR USES VERY LITTLE GASOLINE.

Mi amigo tiene un carro eléctrico y por eso sus viajes están limitados a doscientas millas de ida y vuelta.
MY FRIEND HAS AN ELECTRIC CAR SO HIS TRAVEL IS LIMITED TO 200 MILES GOING AND COMING BACK.

Dile a tu esposo que la luz del freno de su auto no funciona.
TELL YOUR HUSBAND THAT THE BRAKE LIGHT ON HIS CAR IS NOT WORKING.

Su mecánico dice que tiene que reemplazar sus limpiaparabrisas.
YOUR MECHANIC SAYS YOU NEED TO REPLACE YOUR WINDSHIELD WIPERS.

Mi hijo me dice que el tocadiscos del carro está descompuesto.
MY SON TELLS ME THAT THE TAPE OR DISK PLAYER IN THE CAR HAS QUIT WORKING.

Cuando se sube a un coche, hay que abrocharse el cinturón de seguridad.
WHEN YOU GET IN THE CAR, BE SURE TO FASTEN YOUR SEAT BELT.

Cuando hace mucho frío, a veces el carro no arranca.
WHEN IT IS VERY COLD, SOMETIMES THE CAR WON'T START.

sedan
SEDAN

convertible
CONVERTIBLE

deportivo
SPORTS CAR

camioneta
PICKUP

autobús
BUS

camión
TRUCK, VAN

camión de 18 ruedas
18-WHEEL TRUCK

El tráfico y las calles
Traffic and Roads

la acera SIDEWALK

el auto, el carro, el coche CAR

el autobús BUS

la autopista FREEWAY

la ambulancia AMBULANCE

la avenida AVENUE

el brazo de la encrucijada RR CROSSING ARM

la calle STREET

la calle de flecha, la calle de un solo sentido ONE WAY STREET

el callejón ALLEY

el camellón STREET MEDIAN

el camión THE TRUCK

el camión de bomberos FIRE TRUCK

la carretera HIGHWAY, ROAD

el carril TRAFFIC LANE

el carril cerrado TRAFFIC LANE CLOSED

el carril reabierto TRAFFIC LANE REOPENED

el choque THE WRECK

la comisaría THE POLICE STATION

el conductor DRIVER

el conductor ebrio, el conductor borracho DRUNK DRIVER

la construcción CONSTRUCTION

la cuneta THE CURB

el embotellamiento TRAFFIC JAM

la encrucijada JUNCTION

el estacionamiento PARKING LOT

la encrucijada de ferrocarril RR CROSSING

el ferrocarril, el tren RAILROAD, THE TRAIN

la flecha ONE WAY ARROW AS A STREET SIGN

la flecha de paso, la flecha verde THE GREEN ARROW (on a traffic light)

heridas leves INJURIES, MINOR

heridas serias INJURIES, SERIOUS

el hospital HOSPITAL

el hueco, **el bache** THE HOLE

el límite de velocidad THE SPEED LIMIT

la luz verde LIGHT, GREEN

la luz roja LIGHT, RED

la luz amarilla LIGHT, YELLOW

las luces descompuestas LIGHTS OFF OR FLASHING

el mirador OVERLOOK

el paso elevado OVERPASS

el paso inferior, el paso a desnivel UNDERPASS

el parquímetro PARKING METER

la patrulla POLICE CAR

el peatón PEDESTRIAN

la pista THE CLUE, THE HINT (as in crime investigation)

el policía POLICE

el puente BRIDGE

la rampa RAMP

el semáforo TRAFFIC LIGHT

la sirena SIREN

el tráfico TRAFFIC

la velocidad THE SPEED

Some phrases relating to trafic

Se comió la luz roja. `Literally "he ate the red light."`
HE RAN THE RED LIGHT.

Another way to say it is **"Se pasó la luz roja"**.

Se comió la flecha. `Literally "he ate the arrow."`
HE WENT THE WRONG WAY ON A ONE-WAY STREET.

Another way to say it is **"Se pasó la flecha"**.

Hay un choque en la Avenida Central y el tráfico está limitado a una vía (un carril).
THERE IS A WRECK ON CENTRAL AVENUE AND TRAFFIC IS LIMITED TO ONE LANE.

Un camión de 18 ruedas se volcó por la nieve y el hielo y la autopista está cerrada.
AN 18-WHEEL TRUCK FLIPPED OVER BECAUSE OF THE SNOW AND ICE AND THE FREEWAY IS CLOSED.

Hay un carro descompuesto en la rampa de la autopista y la policía mandó pedir una grúa.
THERE'S A STALLED CAR ON THE FREEWAY RAMP AND THE POLICE CALLED FOR A WRECKER.

¿Qué se hace cuando la luz cambia de verde a amarillo?
WHAT DOES ONE DO WHEN THE LIGHT CHANGES FROM GREEN TO YELLOW?

 **¿Qué se hace cuando se oye la sirena de una ambulancia (un camión de bomberos, una patrulla)?**
WHAT DO YOU DO WHEN YOU HEAR THE SIREN OF AN AMBULANCE, (A FIRE TRUCK, A POLICE CAR)?

Ten cuidado en la carretera de Tucson porque se cayó el puente y el tráfico no puede seguir.
CAREFUL ON THE ROAD TO TUCSON BECAUSE A BRIDGE FELL AND TRAFFIC CAN'T GET THROUGH.

Hay un bache grande por la lluvia. El tráfico está embotellado.
THERE IS A BIG HOLE AS A RESULT OF THE RAIN. THE TRAFFIC IS BOTTLED UP.

El policía encontró una bolsa de drogas cuando registraba un camión.
THE POLICEMAN FOUND A BAG OF DRUGS WHEN HE SEARCHED A TRUCK.

Las noticias en la tele
News on the TV

If you took our advice and are trying to watch the news on a Spanish language television channel, here are some words you may hear. The news program is usually called **Noticiero**, from **noticias**, NEWS. You will also see the usual commercials, so we include some words from those.

acción ACTION

alerta ALERT

amenaza, amenazar THREAT, TO THREATEN

asegurar TO INSURE

asegurado INSURED

asegurador(a) INSURER (a person or company)

atribuir TO ATRIBUTE, TO BLAME OR CREDIT

beneficiario BENEFICIARY

campaña CAMPAIGN (political, military)

cancelación CANCELLATION

cárcel THE JAIL, PRISON

choque WRECK

departamento DEPARTMENT (in a newscast, usually of government)

deportes SPORTS

dirección DIRECTION, ADDRESS

Dirección (capitalized) THE OFFICE OF A DIRECTOR (of government)

en oferta ON SALE

final FINAL, LAST, (as in the end of the newscast)

fiscalía AN OFFICIAL RELATED TO PROSECUTING A CASE, A DA, ETC

frontera BOUNDARY, as of a country

heridas WOUNDS, INJURIES (on the body)

juez JUDGE

justicia JUSTICE

lesión, lesiones CUTS, BRUISES, WOUNDS

manifestación DEMONSTRATION, (a group of people objecting to something)

matar TO KILL

mejor momento BEST TIME, as BEST TIME to buy or order

morir TO DIE

muerto DEAD

obligado OBLIGATED

propuesta PROPOSAL

protesta OBJECTION, DEMONSTRATION against something

regresar TO RETURN; can be physical or related to weather

reportes REPORTS, as in news reports

rescate RESCUE

saquear TO PILLAGE, TO LOOT, etc

secuestrar TO KIDNAP

secuestro KIDNAP

según ACCORDING TO

seguros INSURANCE

violencia VIOLENCE

violento VIOLENT can be a human action or a weather event

zona ZONE, AREA, NEIGHBORHOOD

El clima, el tiempo y las estaciones
Climate, weather and seasons

caliente HOT

calor HEAT

fresco COOL

frío COLD

nubes CLOUDS

viento WIND

lluvia RAIN

nieve SNOW

granizo HAIL

hielo, helado ICE, ICY

helado FROZEN (also ICE CREAM)

tormenta STORM

huracán HURRICANE

trueno THUNDER

relámpago LIGHTNING

resbaloso SLIPPERY

la primavera SPRING

el verano SUMMER

el otoño FALL, AUTUMN

el invierno WINTER

el sol THE SUN

la luna THE MOON

las estrellas THE STARS

Here are some phrases with these words

En el invierno hace frío.

IN THE WINTER IT IS COLD.

En el verano pasado tuve calor porque se descompuso el aire acondicionado.
LAST SUMMER I WAS HOT BECAUSE THE AIR CONDITIONER BROKE.

Dicen que tendremos granizo hoy.
THEY SAY WE WILL HAVE HAIL TODAY.

Las hojas de los árboles caen en el otoño.
THE LEAVES OF TREES FALL IN THE AUTUMN.

¿Cuándo hace viento donde vive?
WHEN DOES THE WIND BLOW WHERE YOU LIVE?

Casi siempre el viento llega en la primavera.
NEARLY ALWAYS THE WIND BLOWS IN SPRING.

Cuando hay viento, mis hijos quieren volar sus papalotes (sus cometas).
WHEN THE WIND BLOWS, MY CHILDREN WANT TO FLY KITES.

Días de fiesta
Holidays and special events

Año Nuevo NEW YEAR'S DAY

Día* de la Marmota GROUNDHOG DAY (FEB. 2)

Día de los Reyes Magos EPIPHANY (JAN.6)

Día de San Valentín VALENTINE'S DAY

Cuaresma LENT

Viernes Santo GOOD FRIDAY

Semana Santa HOLY WEEK

Pascua Florida EASTER

Día de las Madres, de la Madre MOTHER'S DAY

Día del Padre FATHER'S DAY

Cuatro de Julio FOURTH OF JULY

Día del Trabajo (de los Trabajadores) LABOR DAY (FIRST MONDAY OF SEPTEMBER)

Día de la Raza COLUMBUS DAY

Día de Brujas HALLOWEEN

Día de Muertos ALL-SAINTS DAY (NOV. 1)

Día de Acción de Gracias THANKSGIVING

Hanuka HANUKKAH

Nochebuena CHRISTMAS EVE

Navidad CHRISTMAS

Noche de Fin de Año, la víspera de Año Nuevo. NEW YEAR'S EVE

The EVE OF a holiday is **la víspera de . . .**

* **día** is masculine and takes **el** as its article, but the article may not always be needed with holidays, so the article is omitted on most of these special days.

Me gusta mucho el Día de la Marmota porque pronto tendremos la primavera.
I LIKE GROUNDHOG DAY BECAUSE SOON WE WILL HAVE SPRING.

A los niños les gustan las Navidades porque les dan regalos.
CHILDREN LIKE CHRISTMAS BECAUSE THEY ARE GIVEN GIFTS.

Hay más viajeros para el Día de Acción de Gracias que cualquier otro día de fiesta.
THERE ARE MORE TRAVELERS FOR THANKSGIVING THAN FOR ANY OTHER HOLIDAY.

Tenemos días para las madres y para los padres, pero no hay día especial para los tíos o las tías.
WE HAVE DAYS FOR MOTHERS AND FOR FATHERS BUT THERE IS NO SPECIAL DAY FOR UNCLES OR AUNTS.

Las Navidades siempre caen el 25 de diciembre, pero Hanuka cambia un poco cada año.
CHRISTMAS ALWAYS FALLS ON DEC. 25, BUT CHANUKA CHANGES A LITTLE EACH YEAR.

Muchos cristianos dejan de comer algo que les gusta durante la Cuaresma.
MANY CHRISTIANS STOP EATING SOMETHING THAT THEY LIKE DURING LENT.

Para los niños, esto casi siempre son los dulces o el chicle.
FOR CHILDREN, THIS IS ALMOST ALWAYS CANDY OR CHEWING GUM.

Para los adultos esto puede ser la pizza o la hamburguesa. Casi nunca es la ensalada.
FOR ADULTS THIS COULD BE PIZZA OR HAMBURGER. IT HARDLY EVER IS SALAD.

También puede ser las bebidas alchólicas, como el vino, la cerveza o el aguardiente.
IT COULD ALSO BE ALCOHOLIC DRINKS, SUCH AS WINE, BEER OR SPIRITS.

Insultos y elogios
Insults and praises

We include these so you won't insult someone inadvertedly or be caught being insulted and not knowing it. We also include praises, so you can use those on family members who are doing well in their Spanish lessons.

antipático AN UNPLEASANT PERSON
atrevido DARING in the negative sense
borracho(a) DRUNK, DRUNKARD
brujo(a) WITCH, as in English; a nasty person
burro(a) DONKEY, STUPID
cabeza hueca EMPTY HEADED, STUPID
cabezudo(a) STUBBORN, having a big head, unwilling to change
camaleón CHAMELEON, a person who changes his mind, his politics, his religion to fit cur-

rent opinions, etc

chantajista BLACKMAILER, FROM **chantaje:** BLACKMAIL

chismoso(a) GOSSIPER

cobarde COWARD

cochino(a) PIG, A DIRTY PERSON

desordenado(a) SLOPPY, DISORGANIZED, MESSY. **des** reverses **ordenado**

equivocado(a) WRONG, MISTAKEN

estafador(a) CHEATER, READY TO DEFRAUD

estúpido(a) STUPID

flojo(a) LAZY, LAX

gringo(a) A PERSON FROM THE U.S. At one time an insult but now a person who is of Anglo-Saxon origin

idiota(a) IDIOT, STUPID

infiel UNFAITHFUL, CHEATS ON SPOUSE

injusto(a) UNJUST

insecto INSECT, A VERY LOW PERSON, PERSON OF NO VALUE

ladrón(a) THIEF

malagradecido(a) UNGRATEFUL

malcriado(a) BRATTY, HAVING BAD MANNERS

malo(a), maluco(a) A BAD PERSON

mentiroso(a) LIAR

moscamuerta PLAYING POSSUM, PRETENDING TO DO SOMETHING WHILE DOING SOMETHING TO THE CONTRARY

una cualquiera A LOOSE WOMAN

mujeriego WOMAN CHASER

negocio turbio A DIRTY DEAL, QUESTIONABLE BUSINESS

pecado, pecador(a) SIN, SINNER

pendejo(a) a serious insult in some countries, to merely CLEVER in others

perezoso(a) LAZY

rata RAT, BAD PERSON

ratero(a) CHEATER

sinvergüenza CROOK, CHEATER

soquete STUPID, FOOLISH

sucio(a) DIRTY, PHYSICALLY OR METAPHORICALLY

terco(a) STUBBORN

tonto(a) STUPID

vagabundo(a) BUM

voraz GREEDY

zorra PROSTITUTE

Don't try to translate English insults into Spanish, as they don't always work. Putting someone IN THE DOG HOUSE (**está en la casa del perro**) is unintelligible in Spanish. Same for being BEHIND THE EIGHT BALL. **La pelota ocho** makes no sense in Spanish. In English, YELLOW implies cowardice, but **amarillo** is just a color in Spanish.

Elogios para trabajos buenos
Praises for good works

atrevido DARING in the positive sense

bondadoso(a) KIND, HELPFUL

bueno(a), buenísimo(a) GOOD, VERY GOOD

caballero GENTLEMAN

cumplido(a) DUTIFUL

experto(a) EXPERT

fiel FAITHFUL

honrado(a) HONEST

inteligente INTELLIGENT

obediente OBEDIENT

ordenado(a) SYSTEMATIC, NEAT, KEEPS THINGS IN ORDER

simpático(a) PLEASANT, LIKEABLE

Mild insults occur, especially among the younger set. One old verse has to do with learning the vowels.

a, e, i, o, u más sabe el burro que tú, cabeza de medio almud.
A, E, I, O, U THE BURRO KNOWS MORE THAN YOU, HEAD OF HALF AN ALUMD.

The **almud** was an ancient measure.

Adiós, que le vaya bien is an old phrase of parting. It translates GOODBYE, MAY IT GO WELL WITH YOU. Children then add the rest: **que le pise el tren, que le ponga la cara como un sartén.** MAY YOU BE RUN OVER BY A TRAIN AND THAT YOUR FACE BECOME LIKE A FRYING PAN.

Sometimes one person starts with

Adiós que le vaya bien.

The other answers with

Que le pise el tren

and the first (or another) finishes

Que le ponga la cara como un sartén.

19
THE SAYINGS
Los Dichos

Dichos are saying that reflect some aspect of daily life. In English we have sayings that date back centuries. Some date to Ben Franklin's proverbs. Many of these reflect our Judeo-Christian heritage, coming from the Old and New Testament.

Dichos, too, date to ancient times, from Spain and from the New World.

Dichos are passed from generation to generation, by memory more so than by any written document.

The Dichos here come from several sources, as books of dichos have been compiled by different authors and in different countries. As you read through these you will see similarities to their English counterparts.

Notice, too, the subtlety of some. For instance, **Gato con guantes no caza ratón**. Sure, it can mean you can't do manual work while wearing gloves, but the underlying message is you can't accomplish much with personal or other encumbrances. Likewise, **El que nada no se ahoga** tells us to be prepared.

El que más tiene, más quiere.
HE WHO HAS MUCH, WANTS MUCH.

El que poco tiene, poco teme.
HE WHO HAS LITTLE, WORRIES LITTLE.
El que mucho tiene, mucho inquieta.
HE WHO HAS MUCH, WORRIES MUCH.

Libro cerrado no saca letrado.
CLOSED BOOK DOESN'T SHOW WORDS.
(YOU CAN'T TELL A BOOK BY ITS COVER.)

**No es degracia ser pobre,
pero es muy inconveniente.**
IT IS NO DISGRACE TO BE POOR,
BUT IT IS VERY INCONVENIENT.
El dinero habla.
MONEY TALKS.
Poderoso es Don Dinero.
POWERFUL GENTLEMAN IS MR. MONEY.

Más vale tarde que nunca.
BETTER LATE THAN NEVER.

Flores encantan, pero no alimientan.
FLOWERS ARE ENCHANTING BUT THEY DON'T NOURISH.
Garza volando no es alimiento.
HERON FLYING IS NOT FOOD.
Más vale pájaro en mano que cien volando.
BETTER A BIRD IN THE HAND THANT ONE HUNDRED FLYING.

Cuando la rana eche pelo.
WHEN THE FROG GROWS HAIR.

Al decir las verdades se pierden amistades.
TELLING THE TRUTH CAN CAUSE THE LOSS OF FRIENDS.

Males confiados suelen ser remediados.
SHARING PROBLEMS, THEY WILL SURELY BE SOLVED.

Más flojo que un espárago mojado.
LAZIER THAN A WET ASPARAGUS.

Donde menos se piensa, salta la liebre.
WHEN YOU LEAST EXPECT IT,
THE JACKRABIT (HARE) JUMPS IN.

Lo que no mires no duele.
WHAT YOU DON'T SEE WON'T HURT YOU.

El miedoso de su sombra huye.
THE FEARFUL PERSON FROM HIS SHADLOW FLEES.
Tiene miedo hasta de su sombra.
HE IS AFRAID OF HIS OWN SHADOW.

No des un paso adelante sin ver para atrás.
DON'T GIVE A STEP FORWARD BEFORE LOOKING BACK.

Los trapos sucios se lavan en casa.
DIRTY LAUNDRY IS WASHED AT HOME.

Le falta un tornillo. Le falta la tuerca.
HE LACKS A SCREW. HE LACKS THE NUT (WITH THE BOLT)

Quien siembra espinas no puede andar descalzo.
HE WHO PLANTS THORNS CAN'T WALK BAREFOOT.

Loro viejo no aprende a hablar.
OLD PARROT DOESN'T LEARN TO TALK.
(YOU CAN'T TEACH AN OLD DOG NEW TRICKS.)

Estar con la cola entre las piernas.
HE HAS HIS TAIL BETWEEN HIS LEGS (HE IS EMBARRASSED).

De lo grande se puede hacer chiquito,
pero de lo chiquito no se hace grande.
FROM A LARGE (PIECE) YOU CAN GET A SMALL ONE,
BUT FROM A SMALL ONE YOU CAN'T GET A LARGE ONE.

Quien mucho duerme, poco aprende.
HE WHO SLEEPS MUCH, LEARNS LITTLE.
La pereza es la llave de la pobreza.
LAZYNESS IS KEY TO POVERTY.

Quien ama el peligro en él perece.
HE WHO LOVES DANGER, BY IT (DANGER) HE DIES.

El que nada no se ahoga.
HE WHO SWIMS DOESN'T DROWN (PREPARATION DOESN'T FAIL)

Panza llena, corazón contento.
FULL BELLY, HAPPY HEART.

El cilantro bueno, pero no tanto.
CILANTRO IS GOOD, BUT NOT TOO MUCH (MODERATION IN EVERYTHING)

Tiene grillos en la cabeza.
HE HAS CRICKETS IN HIS HEAD.

El que canta, sus males espanta.
HE WHO SINGS SCARES AWAY HIS WOES.

De la mano a la boca se pierde la sopa.
FROM THE HAND TO THE MOUTH THE SOUP IS LOST.
Del dicho al hecho hay mucho trecho.
FROM WORD TO DEED THERE IS A LONG DISTANCE.

Más vale saber que tener.
BETTER TO KNOW THAN TO HAVE (GOODS).

Mi casa – su casa.
MY HOUSE, YOUR HOUSE.

El trabajo es virtud.
WORK IS VIRTUOUS.

Cuando una puerta se cierra, dos mil se abren.
WHEN ONE DOOR CLOSES, TWO THOUSAND OPEN.

El que da y quita, el diablo lo visita.
HE WHO GIVES AND TAKES AWAY, THE DEVIL WILL PAY A VISIT.

Un clavo saca otro clavo.
ONE NAIL TAKES OUT ANOTHER
IT TAKES ONE TO KNOW (OR FIND) ONE.

Si la envidia fuera tinta, todo el mundo se teñiría.
IF ENVY WERE INK (PAINT) ALL THE WORLD WOULD BE STAINED.

Son ricos aquellos que tienen amigos.
THOSE ARE RICH WHO HAVE FRIENDS.

Cada uno para sí y Dios para todos.
EACH ONE FOR HIMSELF AND GOD FOR ALL.

El que busca, halla.
HE WHO SEEKS, FINDS,
El que a Dios busca, Dios halla.
HE WHOM GOD SEEKS, GOD FINDS.

Gato llorón, no caza ratón.
A CRYING CAT DOESN'T CATCH MICE.
Gato maullador, pobre cazador.
MEOWING CAT DOESN'T CATCH MICE.
Gato con guantes no caza ratón.
CAT WEARING GLOVES CAN'T CATCH MICE.

Al que madruga, Dios lo ayuda.
HE WHO AWAKES EARLY, GOD HELPS HIM.

El traje no hace al hombre, pero le da figura.
THE SUIT DOESN'T MAKE THE MAN BUT IT MAKES HIM LOOK GOOD.

Echando a perder se aprende.
ONE LEARNS BY ONE'S MISTAKES.

A buen entendedor pocas palabra bastan.
FOR A GOOD LISTENER, FEW WORDS ARE NEEDED.

Cada oveja con su pareja.
EACH ONE WITH HIS KIND.
Pájaros de la misma pluma vuelan juntos.
BIRDS OF A FEATHER FLY TOGETHER.

El árbol se conoce por su fruto.
A TREE IS KNOWN BY ITS FRUITS.

Una mano lava la otra y las dos lavan la cara.
ONE HAND WASHES THE OTHER AND BOTH WASH THE FACE.

El león no es como lo pintan.
THE LION IS NOT HOW HE IS PAINTED.
La apariencias engañan.
LOOKS DECEIVE.

Una fruta mala pudre el canasto.
ONE BAD FRUIT ROTS THE BASKETFUL.

Esa leche tiene agua.
THAT MILK HAS WATER.
(A LIE, AN IMPURITY)

Three ways to say he was fired:

Se le quebró el serrucho.
HIS SAW WAS BROKEN.
Se le quemó la arepa (la tortilla, el pan)
HIS AREPA* (TORTILLA, BREAD) WAS BURNED.
Le cortaron el cambur.
THEY (THE BOSS) BROKE (CUT) HIS BANANA.
*arepa is a cornmeal roll of northern South America.

216

Epilogue

Now that you've picked up some useful Spanish, we hope you will want to learn more. This is the time to browse new and used book stores and the internet for new ways to learn more.

Many books are for travelers, many others are geared to high school or college students. You may not be interested in finding a hotel in Madrid or talking to school classmates, but these books contain a lot of useful information that can be adapted to more practical conversations around your home and office. Some recommended books are in the bibliography.

Another excellent source is the **Instituto Cervantes**. This organization is found all over the non-Spanish speaking world. Classes in Spanish are offered in all levels, from beginners to advanced writers. The Instituto originates in Madrid and teachers are all native Spanish speakers. There are chapters in just about any major city in the United States. The Instituto is independent of other colleges or schools.

It may take some work to find informal groups that gather to chat in Spanish. Larger cities may have some that meet in homes or at restaurants. Some may post themselves on internet social sites.

If you have the time and the money, you could enroll in a high school or college class in Spanish. These, though, may not be suitable to the person with the 8-to-5 job.

Judy Nickell
Carmen Julia Holguín Chaparro
2017

Bibliography

This list includes some of the references used for ***EASY, CASUAL EVERYDAY SPANISH***. Not listed are general purpose grammar books. Many of these can be found in general or used book stores. When you see one that looks useful, buy it. It will contain much useful information. It may also have exercises for you to use with yourself or your family.

Some choices will be geared to high school or college students or will include travel phrases and words. Add those to your collection, especially when you find such books used and cheap at thrift stores and yard sales.

Not listed here are the many general grammar books available to the general public. There are so many that the best recommendation is that you prowl stores or the internet and find one or two that are available and buy what you need.

Gerrard, A. Bryson, *Beyond the Dictionary in Spanish*. Cassell, 1972. This book looks at individual words or phrases that may carry a meaning not usually found in standard dictionaries.

Keenan, Joseph J. *Breaking out of Beginner's Spanish*. University of Texas Press, 1994. This book goes into meanings of words and phrases that can cause problems if you don't get them right.

Nash, Rose PhD, *NTC's Dictionary of Spanish Cognates Thematically Organized*. McGraw-Hill, 1997. Does a Spanish word sound like an English one? The two may not have parallel meanings.

Resnick, Seymour and **William Guiliano** *En Breve A Concise Review of Spanish Grammar*. Not an ordinary grammar book, this little book reviews what the Spanish student has already learned (or should have learned) and does a thorough review of the material.

Books of verb conjugations

Verb conjugation books have been recommended throughout this book. This is a list of some of those that can be found in new or used book stores or on your favorite internet source.

Some general grammar books will have sample verb conjugations, but these two have them all (or almost all).

Barron's 501 Spanish Verbs (new version includes a CD-ROM). Barron's 2007
2,000+ Essential Spanish Verbs, (new version includes a CD-ROM). Living Language, 2003

Also dealing with verbs:

Brodsky, David, *Spanish Verbs Made Simple(r)*, University of Texas Press, 2005. Need an explanation for the various forms of Spanish verbs? This book explains a lot more than we did in ***Easy Casual Everyday Spanish***. Brodsky's book covers some of the ground in *750 Spanish Verbs and their Uses* but in different forms, including some of the background of the words.

Zamir, Jan R., Edgardo J. Pantigoso PhD, and Eduardo Estevanovich, *750 Spanish Verbs and their Uses*, John Wiley & Sons. Verbs and phrases are given with their translations.

Specialty books for special needs

The Oxford Business Spanish Dictionary, Oxford University Press 2002. Geared to office work, this book would be handy in any business application.

Harvey, William C. M.S., *Spanish for Health Care Professionals*, Barron's 2008. Listed here are ailments, procedures and equipment involved in the health care industry.

José M. Díaz and **María F. Nadel**, *McGraw-Hills Spanish for Educators*, McGraw-Hill. 2006. This book is geared to teachers of various subjects who want to add Spanish to the current class subject.

Diccionario de sinónimos y antónimos, Santillana, 1996. Once you are fluent in Spanish you can use this book to find synonyms and antonyms for Spanish words. Santillana is a Madrid publisher.

Oxford-Duden Pictorial Spanish and English Dictionary, Oxford-Duden, 1995. This book is a collection of drawings by category with each item numbered for reference on the same page. 384 pages of diagrams plus extensive E-S/S-E index.

David Burke, *Street Spanish Dictionary & Thesaurus*. John Wiley & Sons, 1999. In dictionary form, this small volume explains the slang meanings to ordinary words or phrases - the meanings no one will tell you!

Stavans, Ilam, *Spanglish, The making of a new American Language*. Harper-Collins, 2003. In some states, such as New Mexico, much of the Spanish-speaking population can trace its ancestors to 1610 if not earlier. In other states, more recent arrivals have mixed English and Spanish to create "Spanglish." Here you will find **breca** from BRAKE (on a car), instead of **freno**; or **suap** from SWAP, instead of **cambio**.

Other books used in the writing of *Easy, Casual Everyday Spanish.*

Jean Andrews, *Peppers, the Domesticated Capsicums*, University of Texas Press, 1985

Cornell University's *Hortus Third* for plant names.

Lorus and Margery Milne, *Living Plants of the World,* Random House.

Reay Tannahill, *Food in History*, Stein and Day, 1973, a review of the development of food use and production throughout the world, starting with prehistoric times.

Books to buy:

_____

_____

_____

_____

_____

_____

_____

The Indexes

The first index is in Spanish. The second in English. Index is by chapter. Words are given when first introduced or when explained in some detail. Those words may or may not appear after that in other chapters. Not every word in the book is indexed. We leave that to you to deal with, using a good E-S/S-E dictionary. Words are in masculine singular. Change them as needed. Some common words, such as **hombre, mujer, niño, niña, perro, gato**, etc are found throught and are not indexed.

Indice en español

Index in English

GET YOUR OWN COPY OF EASY CASUAL EVERYDAY SPANISH
OR ORDER ONE FOR A FRIEND

$18.⁹⁵ (PLUS $6.⁰⁵ FOR TAX AND SHIPPING)/$25.⁰⁰ PER COPY
CHECK OR CREDIT CARD ACCEPTED

NAME _____

ADDRESS_____

CITY_____

STATE/ZIP _____

HOME PHONE _____

EMAIL ADDRESS _____

NO. OF COPIES _____ TOTAL $_____

CHECKS SHOULD BE PAYABLE TO JUDY A. NICKELL

CARD NO._____
VISA OR MASTERCARD

EXPIRE DATE_____

3-DIGIT CVS NO. FROM BACK OF CARD _____

SEND YOUR ORDER TO:
JUDY NICKELL, 3817 CALLE DEL MONTE NE, ALBUQUERQUE, NM 87110

GET YOUR OWN COPY OF EASY CASUAL EVERYDAY SPANISH
OR ORDER ONE FOR A FRIEND

$18.⁹⁵ (PLUS $6.⁰⁵ FOR TAX AND SHIPPING)/$25.⁰⁰ PER COPY
CHECK OR CREDIT CARD ACCEPTED

NAME _____

ADDRESS_____

CITY_____

STATE/ZIP _____

HOME PHONE _____

EMAIL ADDRESS _____

NO. OF COPIES _____ TOTAL $_____

CHECKS SHOULD BE PAYABLE TO JUDY A. NICKELL

CARD NO._____
VISA OR MASTERCARD

EXPIRE DATE_____

3-DIGIT CVS NO. FROM BACK OF CARD _____

SEND YOUR ORDER TO:
JUDY NICKELL, 3817 CALLE DEL MONTE NE, ALBUQUERQUE, NM 87110

CPSIA information can be obtained
at www.ICGtesting.com
Printed in the USA
FFOW01n0211270618
47229716-50026FF